Mastering Vector Databases

The Future of Data Retrieval and AI

Robert Johnson

For permissions and other inquiries, write to:
P.O. Box 3132, Framingham, MA 01701, USA

Contents

5

Introduction

In the contemporary digital era, the landscape of data management is undergoing a significant transformation driven by the increasing need for efficient, scalable, and sophisticated data retrieval systems. At the forefront of this evolution are vector databases, a technology that is revolutionizing how we store, query, and manipulate data. The relevance of vector databases has surged with the exponential growth of data, most notably in fields such as artificial intelligence (AI), machine learning, and big data analytics. The essence of vector databases lies in their ability to manage complex, multidimensional datasets that are central to the functioning of AI applications and advanced data retrieval systems.

Vector databases are distinguished by their capability to handle high-dimensional data, enabling powerful semantic search and similarity measures that are crucial for AI-driven data processes. Unlike traditional databases that rely on structured, scalar data fields, vector databases operate with numeric data vectors, allowing for the nuanced representation and processing of real-world phenomena in a manner that is computationally feasible. This capability forms the foundation for various data-intensive applications, including recommendation systems, natural language processing, image retrieval, and more. As such, vector databases are pivotal in harnessing the full potential of AI technologies.

This book, "Mastering Vector Databases: The Future of Data Retrieval and AI", is crafted to provide an in-depth understanding of vector databases, exploring both their theoretical underpinnings and practical applications. Divided into a series of carefully structured chapters, it addresses the core concepts and methodologies that define vector databases. The early chapters explore the foundational aspects, such as understanding vectors and their significance in modern data management, along with the basic principles that govern vector databases. As we progress, the book delves into more advanced topics, including the integration of vector databases with artificial intelligence, performance optimization techniques, and the critical aspects of security and privacy.

One of the principal aims of this book is to demystify vector databases for readers, particularly those new to this field. Through detailed explanations and comprehensive examples, readers will gain insights into how vector databases differ from conventional database models, as well as the unique challenges they present. The book also ventures into future trends, providing valuable foresight into the continuing evolution of vector databases and their ever-expanding role in the realm of AI and data science.

The intended readership encompasses a broad spectrum, from students and professionals in computer science and information technology to data scientists and AI developers seeking to enhance their understanding of advanced data retrieval systems. By focusing on both fundamental theories and real-world applications, this book ensures that readers are well-equipped to apply the concepts of vector databases in various professional contexts.

As you engage with this book, you will not only expand your technical knowledge but also appreciate the significant impact that vector databases have on the future of data management. The ability to efficiently handle and retrieve vast and varied datasets is a critical competency in today's data-driven world, and mastering vector databases is a key step towards achieving excellence in this domain.

Chapter 1

Introduction to Vector Databases

Vector databases represent a cutting-edge approach to data management, specifically designed to handle multidimensional data efficiently. Emerging from the need to process large-scale and complex datasets, they provide a robust framework for tasks that involve similarity search and high-dimensional vector operations, which are integral to various AI and machine learning applications. Unlike traditional databases, vector databases are optimized for handling and retrieving vectorized data, making them essential for modern data retrieval challenges. This chapter explores the foundational aspects and significance of vector databases, elucidating their unique features and applications across industries, with a focus on how they compare to and complement established database systems.

1.1   Definition and Overview

Vector databases represent a pivotal innovation in data management, tailored explicitly for the efficient processing and retrieval of high-dimensional vectorized data. As data structures become increasingly complex, traditional databases often struggle to maintain optimal performance levels, particularly when dealing with multidimensional datasets such as those encountered in AI, machine learning, and data science applications. Vector databases bridge the gap between the burgeoning needs of modern data applications and the limitations of traditional database architectures.

The core concept underlying vector databases is the representation of each data object as a vector, which is an array of numerical values. These vectors can encapsulate various data features, making them suitable for a range of applications, including similarity searches, where the goal is to find data points that are most alike. Given the high dimensionality of vectors, traditional relational database management systems (RDBMS) encounter performance bottlenecks, as they are optimized for tabular data and not for executing complex mathematical operations required for vector comparison and retrieval tasks.

A vector database's primary advantage is its ability to index and search through vast quantities of vector data with high efficiency. This is achieved through specialized algorithms and data structures designed to support operations such as nearest neighbor searches, which are crucial for tasks like image recognition, natural language processing, and recommendation systems. The capability of handling these operations efficiently becomes particularly crucial as the volume and complexity of data grow.

Consider a simple, yet illustrative, example of indexing and retrieving feature vectors in a vector database. Assume we have a dataset consisting of multiple feature vectors derived from image data. Each vector represents an image's features obtained via techniques such as convolutional neural networks (CNNs). When these vectors are input into a vector database, the system must efficiently index each vector to allow rapid retrieval based on similarity queries.

```
from sklearn.neighbors import NearestNeighbors
import numpy as np

# Sample dataset: 1000 images, each represented as a 128-dimensional feature vector
feature_vectors = np.random.rand(1000, 128)

# Initialize the Nearest Neighbors model
nbrs = NearestNeighbors(n_neighbors=5, algorithm='ball_tree').fit(feature_vectors)
```

```
# Query vector, representing a new image
query_vector = np.random.rand(1, 128)

# Find the 5 nearest neighbors
distances, indices = nbrs.kneighbors(query_vector)
```

In the code above, we simulate a vector database using 1000 randomly generated feature vectors, each 128 dimensions in size. The Nearest Neighbors algorithm is employed to find the five nearest feature vectors to an input query vector. This operation embodies a fundamental principle of vector databases—efficient similarity searching—which is essential in practical applications.

Understanding the data structures and algorithms employed by vector databases is fundamental to appreciating their performance and scalability benefits. Primary among these structures is the use of indexes that enable rapid similarity searches. Among the prevalent indexing methods are the KD-tree, VP-tree, and Locality Sensitive Hashing (LSH). Each method has its strengths and trade-offs, tailored to specific types of data distribution and query patterns.

For instance, the KD-tree is applicable for low to moderate-dimensional data and operates by dividing the data space into a series of nested hyperrectangles. However, its performance degrades significantly with very high-dimensional spaces, which is a common scenario in vector databases. Therefore, LSH often serves as a more suitable choice for indexing in high dimensions, allowing for approximate nearest neighbor searches that are highly efficient.

Consider the construction of a KD-tree:

```
from scipy.spatial import KDTree

# Initialize KD-Tree with the feature vectors
kd_tree = KDTree(feature_vectors)

# Query KD-Tree for nearest neighbor of the query_vector
distance, index = kd_tree.query(query_vector)
```

In this example, a KD-tree is constructed with the same dataset of 1000 feature vectors. The query operation retrieves the nearest neighbor efficiently for low to moderate dimensions, illustrating the KD-tree's efficacy in such contexts.

In addition to indexing, vector databases employ various optimization

11

techniques to ensure that computational and storage efficiencies are maximized. These include data compression methods to reduce the storage footprint of high-dimensional vectors, as well as caching mechanisms that leverage recent query patterns to enhance retrieval speed. Such strategies are essential in handling the exponential growth of data without compromising accessibility and processing speed.

The design of a vector database also emphasizes scalability and distributed computing, essential attributes in managing big data workloads prevalent in today's data-driven environments. Systems are built to allow horizontal scaling, where additional nodes can be seamlessly integrated to handle greater data volumes and increased query loads without sacrificing performance.

Let's further examine an example in a distributed setting using approximate nearest neighbors:

```
from annoy import AnnoyIndex

# Dimensionality of feature vector
f = 128

# Create Annoy index for approximate nearest neighbors
annoy_index = AnnoyIndex(f, 'angular')

# Add feature vectors to Annoy index
for i in range(1000):
    annoy_index.add_item(i, feature_vectors[i])

# Build the index with 10 trees
annoy_index.build(10)

# Perform the query for nearest neighbors of the query_vector
# Converts query_vector to 1-dimensional array for Annoy
nearest_neighbors = annoy_index.get_nns_by_vector(query_vector.ravel(), 5)
```

The above script demonstrates the use of the Annoy library, which facilitates approximate nearest neighbor searches across distributed systems. By constructing multiple trees to approximate distances in large datasets, Annoy achieves balance between computational load and accuracy, pivotal for scalable systems.

The adoption of vector databases is driven by their capacity to support applications that require dynamic and flexible data management capabilities, notably in artificial intelligence and machine learning (AI/ML) ecosystems. As AI/ML systems rely heavily on efficient processing of large datasets, especially in operations involving similarity matching, vector databases provide a streamlined infrastructure that supports advanced analytics and decision-making processes.

Given the robustness and versatility of vector databases, they enable various end-to-end machine learning workflows, from data preprocessing and storage to real-time inferencing and feedback loops. They support integration with various machine learning frameworks, allowing practitioners to lodge machine learning artifacts as native vectors and retrieve them using semantic or strict numerical queries.

Therefore, a defining characteristic of vector databases lies in their ability to transcend the conventional boundaries imposed by ordinary data structures, enabling sophisticated analytical functions that are imperative for the next generation of intelligent systems. This capability positions vector databases as indispensable in fields as diverse as genomics, recommendation systems, and autonomous systems, where complex, high-dimensional data interactions are routine.

Vector databases constitute a new paradigm in data management that effectively addresses the challenges presented by high-dimensional datasets prevalent in innovative application fields. With advanced indexing and querying capabilities, coupled with scalability and integration features, these databases form the cornerstone of modern AI and machine learning infrastructure, facilitating the efficient processing and analysis of complex, multidimensional data.

1.2   Historical Context

The evolution of vector databases is intricately linked to the broader history of data management systems and the increasing complexity of data types. Traditional databases primarily focused on structured data stored in rows and columns, suitable for the needs of businesses through the latter half of the 20th century. The predominant model at the time was the relational database model, which emerged in the 1970s, famously introduced by Edgar F. Codd. This model effectively addressed the need for managing structured data with its use of tables, schemas, and SQL for data manipulation and retrieval.

However, as the digital era advanced, there emerged a growing need to handle unstructured and semi-structured data, most notably spurred by the advent of the internet and the proliferation of multimedia. Text, images, audio, and video content presented both an opportunity and a challenge for data management systems, as these data types do not conform readily to traditional tabular structures.

The early 2000s marked a turning point where the limitations of traditional databases became more pronounced. As organizations began aggregating large datasets derived from diverse sources such as sensor feeds, web logs, and multimedia content, it became clear that a new approach was necessitated. Existing database systems struggled particularly with tasks requiring high-dimensional vector operations, such as those stemming from machine learning and AI applications.

This period also witnessed the rise of NoSQL databases, which were designed to handle large-scale datasets much more efficiently than traditional RDBMS by eschewing the strict ACID properties in favor of more flexible data models. NoSQL databases like MongoDB, Cassandra, and Couchbase gained traction for their ability to scale horizontally and their support for various data models, such as key-value, document, columnar, and graph.

Parallel to these developments, machine learning and artificial intelligence began to take center stage as essential components of technological advancement. These fields rely heavily on vectorized data processing, demanding databases that can manage and search through high-dimensional data spaces with efficiency and speed. Recognizing this need, the research community and industry practitioners alike began exploring more ways to index and retrieve vector data effectively.

Consider the evolution of indexing techniques which played a pivotal role in shaping vector databases:

```python
from sklearn.feature_extraction.text import TfidfVectorizer
from sklearn.decomposition import TruncatedSVD

# Text corpus indicating the shift to document-based databases
corpus = [
    'the emergence of big data was a game changer',
    'databases needed evolution to handle unstructured data',
    'vector databases manage high-dimensional feature spaces'
]

# Transform the text data to vectors using TF-IDF
vectorizer = TfidfVectorizer()
X = vectorizer.fit_transform(corpus)

# Reduce dimensionality with SVD
```

```
svd = TruncatedSVD(n_components=2)
X_reduced = svd.fit_transform(X)
```

In the code snippet above, textual data is transformed into vectors using TF-IDF and then reduced using SVD, highlighting the need for managing and processing high-dimensional text data efficiently, a challenge vector databases are designed to tackle.

As data science disciplines matured, they heralded workflows that necessitated not only the ingestion of raw and preprocessed features into vector forms but also the immediate retrieval of relevant vectors upon request, often with strict time constraints. This paradigm promoted the development and implementation of sophisticated data models, such as those relying on feature extraction from complex inputs like neural networks.

The growing ubiquity of machine learning models, particularly deep learning architectures, further solidified the need for vector databases. These models often output or transform data into fixed-length vectors, encoding information about class membership, semantic meaning, or other features that traditional databases could not efficiently handle or search.

For instance, consider the application of neural language models in natural language processing (NLP), where pre-trained word embeddings or contextual representations like those produced by BERT or GPT models are employed. These models demonstrate the type of high-dimensional data that necessitates specialized storage and retrieval mechanisms, such as those offered by vector databases.

```
from transformers import BertModel, BertTokenizer
import torch

# Load pre-trained model and tokenizer
tokenizer = BertTokenizer.from_pretrained('bert-base-uncased')
model = BertModel.from_pretrained('bert-base-uncased')

# Encode the input text
text = "vector databases are crucial in modern AI applications"
inputs = tokenizer(text, return_tensors='pt')

# Create embeddings from text
outputs = model(**inputs)
embeddings = outputs.last_hidden_state
```

In this example, the BERT model creates embeddings from input text, generating high-dimensional vectors encapsulating semantic information, suitable for storage in a vector database that can provide fast similarity retrieval.

Another driving factor in the emergence of vector databases has been the increase in personalized and intelligent applications. As organizations strive to provide more customized user experiences, the need to analyze and act on customer data in real-time has intensified. Applications, such as recommendation systems, fraud detection, and real-time sentiment analysis, require databases that not only store but also retrieve pertinent data vectors seamlessly.

The expansion of vector databases can also be observed in their integration into various platforms that emphasize scalability and distributed computing. Modern vector databases are often designed with cloud-native architectures in mind, facilitating their deployment in distributed environments which manage giga-scale data across numerous data nodes with the assurance of fault-tolerance and consistent performance.

Moreover, the cross-industry adoption of deep analytics techniques has necessitated the handling of multidimensional data that interacts in complex ways beyond simple linear relationships. Vector databases provide the scaffolding necessary to support the computational requirements of these intricate data operations, becoming a staple in sectors as varied as bioinformatics, e-commerce, finance, and automotive industries.

The historical trajectory of vector databases exemplifies a technological response to the evolving complexity and scale of data-driven needs. Engineered for the requirements of the most demanding modern applications, they stand as a testament to the ongoing innovation within the database landscape, grounded in the realities of a world perpetually generating massive quantities of complex, high-dimensional data. Through the refinement of algorithms, improved hardware capabilities, and advanced data structures, vector databases have secured their place as indispensable tools for contemporary data management and analytics.

1.3 Key Features of Vector Databases

Vector databases distinguish themselves from traditional databases through several integral features specifically engineered to handle high-dimensional vector data effectively. These characteristics enable efficient storage, retrieval, and processing of complex datasets, making vector databases indispensable in fields that require rapid and precise analysis of vectorized information. Highlighting the key features of vector databases provides insight into why these systems are critical to modern analytics and data-intensive applications.

One of the defining attributes of vector databases is their capacity for advanced indexing techniques designed for high-dimensional data. Traditional databases typically rely on B-trees or hash indexes, which are not efficient for vector query operations, particularly as dimensions increase. Instead, vector databases leverage sophisticated structures such as KD-trees, R-trees, and metric trees, which facilitate rapid nearest neighbor searches and related operations. However, given the curse of dimensionality associated with KD-trees and similar structures, vector databases frequently utilize approximate methods, such as Locality Sensitive Hashing (LSH) and quantization techniques, to balance between accuracy and performance.

Consider the implementation of LSH for high-dimensional vectors:

```
from sklearn.neighbors import LSHForest

# Sample high-dimensional data
n_samples, n_features = 1000, 512
data = np.random.rand(n_samples, n_features)

# Create an LSH Forest to index the data
lshf = LSHForest(random_state=42)
lshf.fit(data)

# Query with new high-dimensional data
query = np.random.rand(1, n_features)
distances, indices = lshf.kneighbors(query, n_neighbors=5)
```

In this example, an LSHForest is employed to efficiently manage and query a dataset of 512-dimensional vectors, illustrating the advantages of LSH in handling high-dimensional indexing with scalability in mind.

Another feature of note in vector databases is their support for complex query types beyond simple retrieval functions. These databases

17

are designed to perform similarity searches, nearest neighbor lookups, and even sophisticated geometric transformations directly within their querying capabilities. This is facilitated through embedding distance-based metrics into query functions, allowing users to specify range searches, k-nearest neighbors, or custom similarity metrics tailored to their specific application domains.

For instance, in applications where semantic similarity is paramount, vector databases can integrate with natural language processing models to encode documents or queries as vectors, enabling semantic search capabilities. These mechanisms often include the use of cosine similarity, Euclidean distance, or Manhattan distance metrics, chosen based on the nature of the data and the specific requirements of the application.

Here is an illustration of cosine similarity used for semantic search:

```
from sklearn.metrics.pairwise import cosine_similarity

# Example vectors representing semantic contents
vector_a = np.array([[0.1, 0.3, 0.7, 0.5]])
vector_b = np.array([[0.2, 0.6, 0.5, 0.4]])

# Calculate cosine similarity
similarity = cosine_similarity(vector_a, vector_b)
```

This reflects how cosine similarity is used to quantify the angle between vectors, providing a measure of semantic similarity which is frequently utilized in vector databases to enhance search functionalities.

The flexible data schema is another standout feature of vector databases. Unlike traditional SQL databases with fixed schema requirements, vector databases operate with adaptable schemas, making them conducive to evolving datasets that may require different dimensions or data types over time. This feature enhances the ability of organizations to scale their data models as new features or dimensions become pertinent, without the need for major overhauls in data architecture.

Moreover, vector databases are built to seamlessly integrate with machine learning and AI workflows. Many vector databases provide out-of-the-box support for data formats and interfaces conducive to popular machine learning frameworks, like TensorFlow, PyTorch, and scikit-learn. This facilitates the direct inclusion of model outputs as

18

vectorised data into a database, enabling streamlined processes from feature extraction to model assertions, all supported by efficient data retrieval.

An example of integration with a PyTorch model to produce embeddings might look as follows:

```
import torch
import torch.nn as nn

# Simple feedforward network to generate embeddings
class SimpleNet(nn.Module):
    def __init__(self, input_dim, output_dim):
        super(SimpleNet, self).__init__()
        self.fc = nn.Linear(input_dim, output_dim)

    def forward(self, x):
        return self.fc(x)

# Initialize model
input_dim, output_dim = 1024, 128
model = SimpleNet(input_dim, output_dim)

# Sample input vector
sample_input = torch.rand(1, input_dim)

# Generate an embedding
embedding = model(sample_input)
```

This snippet demonstrates a neural network transformation of an input vector into an embedding, indicative of the kind of processing vector databases are tailored to manage efficiently.

Scalability and performance optimizations present in vector databases cater to the significant increase in data volume, velocity, and variety that modern applications demand. Distributed architectures, such as those based on sharding, replication, and load balancing, are commonly integrated into vector database systems to manage data at scale, enabling horizontal scaling without sacrificing performance or reliability.

Furthermore, enhanced data import and export capabilities ensure that vector databases fit seamlessly into the broader ecosystem of data processes. These systems often provide APIs and connectors suited for real-time data ingestion from diverse sources such as streaming platforms, ETL pipelines, and batch processes, allowing vector data to be ingested, processed, and queried in a uniform and efficient manner.

Finally, vector databases are equipped with robust security and compliance features appropriate for managing sensitive data, crucial in sectors with stringent data privacy requirements. Features such as encryption-at-rest, access control, and audit logs ensure comprehensive data protection practices are adhered to, while allowing systems to conform to regulations such as GDPR or HIPAA as necessary.

The culmination of these features underscores the transformative role vector databases play in modern data management. They provide a robust architecture for handling increasingly complex data queries necessitated by cutting-edge applications, distinctively positioning themselves as critical components within AI-driven data ecosystems. By embracing innovative indexing, flexible data models, seamless integration, and detailed security protocols, vector databases address the intricate needs of today's data-intensive environments.

1.4 The Importance of Vector Databases

Vector databases have emerged as a critical component in the architectures of modern data-driven applications, offering unique advantages for managing and analyzing high-dimensional data characteristic of artificial intelligence (AI) and machine learning (ML) workflows. Their importance is primarily attributed to their ability to efficiently handle complex object representations and to perform similarity searches, which are integral to numerous contemporary computational tasks. Understanding the importance of vector databases requires exploring their roles in various application contexts, their ability to enhance performance, and their contributions to advancing AI and ML capabilities.

A major factor that underscores the significance of vector databases is their proficiency in managing high-dimensional vectors, which serve as the backbone of many AI and ML solutions. In these domains, data is often transformed into vectors representing either features of a model, intermediate computations, or final outputs. For instance, neural networks commonly convert images, text, or audio data into embedding vectors. These representations encapsulate complex patterns and relationships that would be difficult to store and retrieve using traditional databases due to the high dimensionality and non-linearities involved.

To understand the impact of vector databases, consider a modern search engine whose performance and user experience are significantly enhanced by their capability to offer semantic search. Semantic search uses query understanding and generates search results more aligned with the user's intent rather than just matching keyword occurrences. Vector databases are fundamental in powering such search engines by encoding words, phrases, and entire documents into vector embeddings, allowing for precise and meaningful similarity comparisons. Semantic matching with vector representations is crucial for improving search relevance, thus contributing to richer user interactions and satisfaction.

Consider a basic implementation of a semantic search using word embeddings and cosine similarity:

```
from sklearn.metrics.pairwise import cosine_similarity
from gensim.models import Word2Vec

# A small sample corpus
corpus = ["Vector databases provide fast similarity search.",
          "Semantic search enhances search engine performance."]

# Generate word vectors using Word2Vec
model = Word2Vec(sentences=[sentence.split() for sentence in corpus], vector_size
      =100, window=5, min_count=1, workers=4)

# Create embedding for sentences by averaging word embeddings
embedding_1 = sum([model.wv[word] for word in corpus[0].split()]) / len(corpus[0].
      split())
embedding_2 = sum([model.wv[word] for word in corpus[1].split()]) / len(corpus[1].
      split())

# Calculate cosine similarity between sentence embeddings
similarity = cosine_similarity([embedding_1], [embedding_2])
```

This example highlights the practical utility of vector databases in maintaining, querying, and contextualizing embedding vectors to perform semantic analysis effectively.

Beyond search engines, vector databases play a critical role in recommendation systems. These systems leverage user interaction data to predict and suggest items that a user might be interested in, such as movies, music, products, or news articles. Representing users and items as vectors allows for the computation of distances or similarities, facilitating the identification of relevant experiences across vast item catalogs. With the ever-growing volume of interaction data and the expansion of potential recommendations, the use of efficient vector databases ensures that recommendation algorithms operate within

21

manageable time frames, providing near real-time suggestions as users interact with the platform.

The integration of vector databases in real-time analytics and decision-making pipelines is another area where their importance is evident. Modern enterprises are tasked with analyzing massive datasets to derive actionable insights. Vector databases contribute to quick feature retrieval, enabling real-time model predictions and decision-making. For example, fraud detection in financial systems utilizes vector databases to instantly compare transactions against historical data, flagging suspicious patterns that deviate from norms in vector spaces.

Image recognition is another domain significantly benefiting from vector databases. Traditional databases are not well-suited for storing the complex high-dimensional features extracted from images through convolutional neural networks (CNNs). Vector databases efficiently handle and facilitate retrieval of these image embeddings for tasks such as object detection, image classification, and similarity-based image retrieval. The ability of vector databases to manage embeddings ensures that systems can perform recognitions and comparisons at scale, a feat imperative for applications ranging from autonomous vehicles to medical diagnostic tools.

Consider a scenario with image retrieval using precomputed deep learning model embeddings:

```
from sklearn.neighbors import NearestNeighbors
import numpy as np

# Assume we have image embeddings extracted from a deep neural network
image_embeddings = np.random.rand(10000, 2048) # 10,000 images with 2048-
    dimensional embeddings

# Create nearest neighbors index
nn_model = NearestNeighbors(n_neighbors=5, algorithm='auto').fit(
    image_embeddings)

# Query with a new image's embedding
query_embedding = np.random.rand(1, 2048)
distances, indices = nn_model.kneighbors(query_embedding)
```

This snippet simulates the use of a k-nearest neighbors algorithm on deep learning embeddings to find similar images in a dataset, showcasing the scalability benefits of vector databases for high-dimensional look-ups.

Furthermore, vector databases are crucial in natural language processing (NLP) tasks where they handle language models and embeddings
for documents and tokens. Sentiment analysis, summarization, and
translation are examples of applications where vector databases support rapid and accurate processing of text in its vectorized form. Vector databases enable companies to store and retrieve these embeddings
efficiently, underpinning scalability and robustness in NLP pipelines.

The advancements in vector databases also tie into improvements in
hardware capabilities which allow for parallel computation, significantly decreasing the time taken for complex query operations. In combination with optimized algorithms, this convergence has been pivotal
in transitioning vector databases from research prototypes into widely
adopted enterprise solutions. Such databases facilitate multi-modal
interactions, enhancing user experience through optimized and integrated data representation and retrieval capabilities.

Vector databases, inherently designed to offer fine-grained control
over similarity measures, permit customization of distance functions
which is of utmost importance in diverse domains. Whether utilizing Euclidean distance, cosine similarity, or learned metrics, the flexibility available in crafting bespoke similarity measures is fundamental in ensuring that data retrieval aligns with domain-specific requirements. This adaptability ensures that vector databases remain applicable across a spectrum of use cases from genomics where genetic
proximity calculations are critical to e-commerce where personalization customizes user interactions.

Overall, the importance of vector databases lies not only in their core
ability to manage high-dimensional data but also in their role as enablers of innovative applications that touch everyday life. Their contribution to AI progression, capacity to handle complex data efficiently,
and facilitation of real-time analytics epitomize their strategic value in
modern computational ecosystems. Through continued advancements
in indexing, querying, and scalability, vector databases address the
nuanced demands of today's data-centric world, unlocking potentials
within both emerging and established industries. As organizations continue to prioritize speed, accuracy, and scalability in how they process
and extract value from data, vector databases will indubitably remain
at the forefront of facilitating these endeavors.

1.5 Common Use Cases

Vector databases have established themselves as foundational technology in various advanced computing applications, addressing the demand for high-dimensional data processing and management. Their adoption spans across multiple industries where complex data types and the need for rapid, accurate querying of feature-rich information play a central role. In this section, we explore the common use cases of vector databases, illustrating their adaptability and significant contributions to contemporary data-driven solutions.

One of the most prevalent applications for vector databases is in the field of recommendation systems. Leading platforms, including streaming services, e-commerce sites, and content providers, rely on recommendation systems to enhance user experience and engagement. By converting user behavior, preferences, and interaction patterns into high-dimensional vectors, these systems can determine the similarity between users and items, thereby providing personalized suggestions. Vector databases enable the rapid retrieval of similar vector representations, crucial for efficiently computing recommendations in real-time without compromising on performance.

Consider the following simplified example of building a recommendation system using vector data:

```python
from sklearn.metrics.pairwise import cosine_similarity
import numpy as np

# User and item feature vectors
user_features = np.random.rand(10, 50) # 10 users with 50-dimensional features
item_features = np.random.rand(100, 50) # 100 items with 50-dimensional features

# Calculate similarity between each user and each item
similarity_matrix = cosine_similarity(user_features, item_features)

# Retrieve top 5 item recommendations for each user
top_recommendations = np.argsort(similarity_matrix, axis=1)[:, -5:]
```

This example demonstrates how a vector database can underpin a recommendation engine by supporting efficient similarity calculations between user and item vectors.

Another fundamental use case for vector databases is in image and video recognition. Image recognition applications leverage convolutional neural networks to extract feature vectors from visual data, capturing essential patterns necessary for accurate classification, detection, and similarity search. Vector databases store these high-dimensional embeddings, facilitating rapid querying which is essential for both accurate retrieval and the high scalability demands of image-heavy applications like social media platforms, autonomous vehicles, and medical diagnostics.

To illustrate, consider the following example of indexing image embeddings for a large-scale image retrieval system:

```
from sklearn.neighbors import NearestNeighbors
import numpy as np

# Assume image embeddings for a collection of photos
image_embeddings = np.random.rand(5000, 2048) # 5000 images with 2048-
    dimensional embeddings

# Create a Nearest Neighbors model for the image dataset
nn_model = NearestNeighbors(n_neighbors=5, algorithm='auto').fit(
    image_embeddings)

# Query with a new image's embedding vector
query_embedding = np.random.rand(1, 2048)
distances, indices = nn_model.kneighbors(query_embedding)
```

In this code, the Nearest Neighbors model facilitates image retrieval by matching query embeddings with stored embeddings, highlighting the power of vector databases in handling extensive visual datasets efficiently.

The field of natural language processing (NLP) presents another domain where vector databases are indispensable. NLP applications use embeddings to capture the semantic essence of words, phrases, or documents, allowing for intelligent text analysis and understanding. This capability is crucial for tasks like semantic search, machine translation, sentiment analysis, and more. By storing word embeddings, document vectors, or complex contextual representations from models like BERT or GPT, vector databases enable efficient similarity retrieval and analysis tasks, forming the backbone of many APIs and NLP solutions.

Consider a basic implementation of storing and retrieving sentence embeddings using a pre-trained language model:

```
from transformers import BertModel, BertTokenizer
import torch
```

25

```
# Load pre-trained model and tokenizer for context embedding
tokenizer = BertTokenizer.from_pretrained('bert-base-uncased')
model = BertModel.from_pretrained('bert-base-uncased')

# Encode sentence inputs
sentences = ["Understanding NLP with vector databases", "Efficient retrieval of
      sentence vectors"]
inputs = tokenizer(sentences, return_tensors='pt', padding=True, truncation=True)

# Create sentence embeddings
outputs = model(**inputs)
sentence_embeddings = outputs.last_hidden_state.mean(dim=1)

# Assume simplified storage and retrieval using a vector database here
```

In this example, BERT encodes sentences into context-rich embeddings, which can then be efficiently stored and queried in a vector database to perform advanced NLP tasks.

Fraud detection in finance and insurance represents a critical use case for vector databases. Organizations must process transactions in real-time to identify and mitigate fraudulent activity, necessitating rapid pattern recognition and anomaly detection. Vector databases support these processes by storing and querying transaction vectors that embody user behavior or previous transaction profiles, enabling efficient comparison and flagging of anomalies within large datasets.

Consideration of the healthcare domain further highlights the importance of vector databases. Clinical diagnoses and medical research require the analysis and retrieval of genomic, phenotypic, and molecular data — all described as high-dimensional vectors. Vector databases store these vectors to facilitate efficient querying, pattern discovery, and patient similarity checks, supporting both the research side of genomics and patient healthcare delivery, including personalized treatment plans.

Vector databases are also critical in IoT (Internet of Things) deployments, including applications in smart cities, industrial automation, and environmental monitoring. IoT systems generate vast amounts of data from sensors, which can be encoded as vectors representing readings, locations, or states. Efficient storage, retrieval, and analysis of these vectors through vector databases ensure that IoT applications can offer real-time insights, predictive maintenance, and operational optimization.

Lastly, combating misinformation through content moderation and similarity detection relies heavily on vector databases. These systems detect near-duplicate content or similar patterns across vast web and media datasets, essential for ensuring authenticity in social media and combating the spread of false information. By storing content vectors and supporting real-time similarity checks, vector databases aid in the swift identification of misleading or non-original content.

In summary, vector databases are fundamental to a range of technology-driven applications across industries, facilitating advanced data processing on a scale once thought impractical. Through their high-dimensional indexing capabilities, optimized query speeds, and ability to interface seamlessly with AI and ML frameworks, vector databases provide the agility and efficiency needed to address the diverse challenges of modern data management. As industries continue to evolve and embrace data-centric strategies, the importance of vector databases in supporting intelligent, responsive applications will undoubtedly intensify.

1.6 Comparison with Traditional Databases

Vector databases emerge as a specialized solution capable of managing high-dimensional data efficiently, distinguishing themselves significantly from traditional database paradigms such as relational databases. Understanding the differences and potential benefits involves an examination of their architecture, data storage mechanisms, indexing strategies, query capabilities, and scalability considerations.

Traditional databases, primarily relational database management systems (RDBMS), have served as the backbone of data storage and retrieval for decades. These systems are designed around structured data models, where data is stored in tables consisting of rows and columns. The power of RDBMS lies in the structured query language (SQL) which facilitates complex queries across well-defined schemas consisting of linked tables. Key features of RDBMS include ACID (Atomicity, Consistency, Isolation, Durability) properties which ensure reliable transactions and data integrity.

In contrast, vector databases are engineered to handle unstructured and semi-structured data, with a focus on processing and storing vectorized data representations efficiently. Vector databases cater to tasks involving similarity searches, nearest neighbor queries, and operations on high-dimensional data, often found in machine learning (ML) applications and artificial intelligence (AI) pipelines.

One core distinction lies in the data models they support. While traditional databases excel in scenarios with well-defined schemas, vector databases operate on flexible data models that are adaptable, a requirement for managing high-dimensional vectors that result from feature extraction or embedding processes in ML.

Consider the following comparative exploration between an RDBMS and a vector database through example scenarios:

```sql
-- Example SQL for a traditional RDBMS
CREATE TABLE customers (
    customer_id INT PRIMARY KEY,
    name VARCHAR(100),
    age INT,
    email VARCHAR(255)
);

INSERT INTO customers (customer_id, name, age, email) VALUES (1, 'Alice', 30, '
    alice@example.com');

SELECT * FROM customers WHERE age > 25;
```

In this SQL example, a traditional RDBMS schema is demonstrated with structured data that is easy to query using SQL. This model is efficient for many business applications where data relations and integrity are paramount.

On the other hand, vector databases store data as vectors, which are arrays of numbers representing different dimensions of information. These vectors are often derived from raw data via model processing, commonly used in fields like image processing, text analysis, or recommendation systems. Vector databases require different indexing methods such as KD-trees or Locality Sensitive Hashing (LSH) to handle complex queries efficiently, as high-dimensionality poses challenges for traditional indexing strategies.

Here is a Python example using a vector database to manage high-dimensional vectors:

```
from sklearn.neighbors import NearestNeighbors
import numpy as np

# Feature vectors representing complex data
data_vectors = np.random.rand(1000, 100) # 1000 samples of 100-dimensional data

# Initialize and train the vector search index
nn_model = NearestNeighbors(n_neighbors=10, algorithm='auto').fit(data_vectors)

# Query the index with a new data point
query_vector = np.random.rand(1, 100)
distances, indices = nn_model.kneighbors(query_vector)
```

In this Nearest Neighbors example, a vector database efficiently handles similarity searches in high-dimensional space, beyond the scope of traditional indexing methods.

Indexing mechanisms further set vector databases apart. Traditional databases typically use B-trees or hash indexing to facilitate quick data retrieval in structured datasets. In contrast, vector databases rely on advanced indexing techniques like approximate nearest neighbor (ANN) algorithms to handle the curse of dimensionality, which becomes evident as data dimensions grow significantly.

The query capabilities of vector databases also diverge from traditional databases. SQL allows complex, multi-join queries over structured data with well-defined constraints. Conversely, vector databases focus on providing efficient insight into data through similarity measures. This includes cosine similarity, Euclidean distance, or custom-defined metrics for comparing data vectors, essential in applications like semantic search where effectiveness is measured by how closely retrieved results match intended meanings rather than strict data rules.

Another significant differential aspect involves scalability and performance optimization strategies. Traditional databases are optimized for vertical scaling, with a focus on robust transaction handling and maintaining integrity within centralized repositories. Vector databases, however, are often designed with horizontal scalability in mind, supporting distributed architectures to manage vast datasets accessed in real-time by AI applications.

The following example demonstrates the use of cosine similarity for querying vectors in a vector database:

```
from sklearn.metrics.pairwise import cosine_similarity

# High-dimensional vectors
vector_a = np.random.rand(1, 50)
vector_b = np.random.rand(1, 50)

# Perform cosine similarity to determine similarity measure
similarity_score = cosine_similarity(vector_a, vector_b)
```

In this example, the cosine similarity offers a measure of vector orientation, allowing fine-grained query capabilities based on the context of data vectors rather than straightforward attribute values.

An important operational distinction involves performance tuning and optimization. While traditional databases can leverage indexing optimization strategies and hardware tuning for improved performance, vector databases require specialized configurations to handle high-dimensional vectors optimally. These configurations include memory management for substantial vector datasets and using cache mechanisms to store frequently accessed vectors, essential for minimizing latency in real-time applications.

Finally, the practical use cases for vector databases veer into domains requiring complex pattern recognition and retrieval, such as recommendation systems, image recognition, and natural language understanding — areas often challenging for traditional RDBMS due to the nature of the data involved.

Overall, vector databases represent a departure from traditional paradigms by offering scalable, flexible solutions for high-dimensional data management. Their differences illuminate why, in an era where AI and ML are driving data innovation, vector databases become essential to address the diverse and intricate requirements of modern applications, complementing traditional databases by focusing on the complexity, semantics, and size of today's data landscape.

Chapter 2

Understanding Vectors and Their Importance

Vectors are fundamental components in the realm of data science and artificial intelligence, serving as essential elements for representing and processing information. This chapter delves into the mathematical foundation of vectors, including their representation in vector spaces and the operations that can be performed on them. By encoding information into vectors, we enable sophisticated computational tasks such as similarity measurements and data retrieval. Exploring the role of vectors in machine learning and AI, this chapter highlights their importance in facilitating advanced data analysis techniques and underscores their critical role in powering modern technologies and applications.

2.1 What are Vectors

In mathematics and applied fields such as physics, engineering, and computer science, vectors are essential constructs used to represent quantities with both magnitude and direction. They emerge from the need to encapsulate these two characteristics in various computational and theoretical models. This section provides an in-depth exploration of vectors, encompassing their mathematical foundation, properties, representation, and significance in computational contexts.

A vector is typically represented in either a geometric form, as an arrow in space, or in algebraic form, as an ordered list of numbers. The geometric interpretation emphasizes magnitude and directionality, while the algebraic view provides a basis for manipulation and computation.

Mathematically, an n-dimensional vector can be expressed as an ordered tuple $\mathbf{v} = (v_1, v_2, \ldots, v_n)$, where each v_i is a component of the vector $\mathbf{v}$. In a Cartesian coordinate system, this tuple corresponds to a point or directed line segment in space, oriented from the origin $(0, 0, \ldots, 0)$.

The addition of vectors is a fundamental operation, visually understood as the "tip-to-tail" method and algebraically as component-wise addition. For vectors $\mathbf{u} = (u_1, u_2, \ldots, u_n)$ and $\mathbf{v} = (v_1, v_2, \ldots, v_n)$, their sum is given by

$$\mathbf{u} + \mathbf{v} = (u_1 + v_1, u_2 + v_2, \ldots, u_n + v_n).$$

Scalar multiplication involves resizing vectors by a scalar quantity. For a scalar α and a vector $\mathbf{v} = (v_1, v_2, \ldots, v_n)$, the product $\alpha\mathbf{v}$ is determined component-wise:

$$\alpha\mathbf{v} = (\alpha v_1, \alpha v_2, \ldots, \alpha v_n).$$

The length or magnitude of a vector $\mathbf{v}$ is denoted by $|\mathbf{v}|$ or $\|\mathbf{v}\|$ and calculated using the Euclidean norm as:

$$\|\mathbf{v}\| = \sqrt{v_1^2 + v_2^2 + \cdots + v_n^2}.$$

Vectors can be normalized to a unit vector, retaining their direction but standardizing their magnitude to one:

$$\hat{\mathbf{v}} = \frac{\mathbf{v}}{\|\mathbf{v}\|}.$$

Vectors possess numerous characteristics that allow them to model abstract concepts and physical phenomena. Some essential properties include:

- **Commutativity**: Vector addition is commutative, meaning $\mathbf{u} + \mathbf{v} = \mathbf{v} + \mathbf{u}$.

- **Associativity**: Vector addition is associative: $(\mathbf{u} + \mathbf{v}) + \mathbf{w} = \mathbf{u} + (\mathbf{v} + \mathbf{w})$.

- **Distributivity**: Scalar multiplication sustains the distributive property with respect to vector addition: $\alpha(\mathbf{u} + \mathbf{v}) = \alpha\mathbf{u} + \alpha\mathbf{v}$.

In addition to these algebraic characteristics, vectors can be categorized based on their dimension. They may represent two-dimensional vectors (v_1, v_2), three-dimensional vectors (v_1, v_2, v_3), or extend to n-dimensional vectors in higher data spaces.

Consider extending this understanding with a simple code example, illustrating vector operations using Python, a widely used language for data science and mathematical computations.

```
import numpy as np

# Define two vectors
vector_u = np.array([1, 2, 3])
vector_v = np.array([4, 5, 6])

# Vector addition
vector_sum = vector_u + vector_v

# Scalar multiplication
scalar = 3
scalar_multiplication = scalar * vector_u

# Magnitude of a vector
magnitude_u = np.linalg.norm(vector_u)

# Normalize vector_u
unit_vector_u = vector_u / magnitude_u

print("Vector Sum:", vector_sum)
print("Scalar Multiplication:", scalar_multiplication)
print("Magnitude of vector_u:", magnitude_u)
print("Unit vector of vector_u:", unit_vector_u)
```

This code demonstrates core vector operations including addition, scalar multiplication, magnitude calculation, and normalization using the NumPy library. These operations serve as foundational moves in both mathematical reasoning and applied computational scenarios.

```
Vector Sum: [5 7 9]
Scalar Multiplication: [3 6 9]
```

33

Magnitude of vector_u: 3.7416573867739413
Unit vector of vector_u: [0.26726124 0.53452248 0.80178373]

Algebraic representation aside, vectors also possess significant utility in matrix form, often written as column or row vectors. For a vector $\mathbf{v} \in \mathbb{R}^3$, a common representation is:

$$\mathbf{v} = \begin{bmatrix} v_1 \\ v_2 \\ v_3 \end{bmatrix}$$

This orientation facilitates operations like the dot product (also known as the scalar product) and cross product, critical calculable measures in physics and engineering.

The dot product of $\mathbf{u} = (u_1, u_2, u_3)$ and $\mathbf{v} = (v_1, v_2, v_3)$ is given by:

$$\mathbf{u} \cdot \mathbf{v} = u_1 v_1 + u_2 v_2 + u_3 v_3$$

This product quantifies how parallel two vectors are and is used extensively in projections and determining orthogonality. The vectors are orthogonal if and only if their dot product equals zero.

Vectors further extend into cross product calculations in three-dimensional space, used to find a vector perpendicular to the plane formed by two input vectors:

$$\mathbf{u} \times \mathbf{v} = \begin{vmatrix} \mathbf{i} & \mathbf{j} & \mathbf{k} \\ u_1 & u_2 & u_3 \\ v_1 & v_2 & v_3 \end{vmatrix}$$

This matrix determinant expands to provide the vector product:

$$\mathbf{u} \times \mathbf{v} = (u_2 v_3 - u_3 v_2)\mathbf{i} - (u_1 v_3 - u_3 v_1)\mathbf{j} + (u_1 v_2 - u_2 v_1)\mathbf{k}$$

Implementing these operations through code augments understanding:

```
# Dot product
dot_product = np.dot(vector_u, vector_v)

# Cross product
cross_product = np.cross(vector_u, vector_v)

print("Dot Product:", dot_product)
print("Cross Product:", cross_product)
```

Dot Product: 32
Cross Product: [-3 6 -3]

Visualization is a crucial aspect when comprehending vector operations. Software and tools like MATLAB, Matplotlib (in Python), and others are widely used for graphical illustrations, progressing understanding from conceptual to visual.

Vectors serve as a cornerstone in numerous applications, spanning computer graphics, machine learning, and data science. In machine learning, vectors are often employed to encapsulate attribute features of datasets, facilitating operations within algorithmic models like support vector machines, neural networks, and clustering techniques.

Consider the transformation of data into vectors, a step vital for implementing machine learning models. For example, image processing hastens efficacy through pixel value vectors, whereas text analysis in natural language processing might use word embeddings where texts are vectorized for computational tractability.

Vectors have been standardized within computational frameworks due to their efficiency in encoding and processing structured and unstructured data. Libraries offering advanced interfaces for vector manipulations include NumPy for numerical computations and Pandas for data manipulation in Python, among others.

In summary, vectors are an indispensable component in both theoretical and applied mathematics, bridging concepts to their physical and computational manifestations. Their role as fundamental constructs in encoding, manipulating, and computing data accelerates the frontiers of modern technological advancements.

2.2 Vector Spaces

Vector spaces, often referred to as linear spaces, form a fundamental concept in linear algebra, presenting a framework within which vectors can be added, multiplied by scalars, and explored comprehensively through their properties. Understanding vector spaces is integral in various scientific and engineering applications, ranging from computational mathematics to quantum mechanics and beyond. This section

35

elaborates on the nature, structure, and significance of vector spaces, thereby enriching our comprehension of vectors' operational and theoretical dimensions.

A vector space V over a field F is a non-empty set equipped with two operations: vector addition and scalar multiplication. This algebraic structure satisfies eight axioms that characterize the behavior of elements—vectors—within the space. The field F conventionally refers to the set of real numbers $\mathbb{R}$ or complex numbers $\mathbb{C}$, facilitating arithmetic operations.

The defining axioms of vector spaces are as follows:

- **Closure under Addition**: For any two vectors $\mathbf{u}, \mathbf{v} \in V$, the sum $\mathbf{u} + \mathbf{v}$ is also in V.

- **Closure under Scalar Multiplication**: For any scalar $c \in F$ and vector $\mathbf{v} \in V$, the product $c\mathbf{v}$ is in V.

- **Associativity of Addition**: For all $\mathbf{u}, \mathbf{v}, \mathbf{w} \in V$, $(\mathbf{u} + \mathbf{v}) + \mathbf{w} = \mathbf{u} + (\mathbf{v} + \mathbf{w})$.

- **Commutativity of Addition**: For all $\mathbf{u}, \mathbf{v} \in V$, $\mathbf{u} + \mathbf{v} = \mathbf{v} + \mathbf{u}$.

- **Identity Element of Addition**: There exists an element $\mathbf{o} \in V$ such that for every vector $\mathbf{v} \in V$, $\mathbf{v} + \mathbf{o} = \mathbf{v}$.

- **Inverse Elements of Addition**: For every $\mathbf{v} \in V$, there exists an element $-\mathbf{v} \in V$ such that $\mathbf{v} + (-\mathbf{v}) = \mathbf{o}$.

- **Identity Element of Scalar Multiplication**: For every vector $\mathbf{v} \in V$, $1\mathbf{v} = \mathbf{v}$.

- **Distributive Properties**:

  - For all $c \in F$ and $\mathbf{u}, \mathbf{v} \in V$, $c(\mathbf{u} + \mathbf{v}) = c\mathbf{u} + c\mathbf{v}$.
  - For all $c, d \in F$ and $\mathbf{v} \in V$, $(c + d)\mathbf{v} = c\mathbf{v} + d\mathbf{v}$.
  - For all $c, d \in F$ and $\mathbf{v} \in V$, $(cd)\mathbf{v} = c(d\mathbf{v})$.

The elegance of vector spaces arises from these axioms' simplicity, combining to form a powerful framework underpinning numerous algebraic constructs. This foundational definition enables numerous computations, leading to deep insights into the algebraic structure and theories like linear independence, basis, and dimensions, discussed further.

The *dimension* of a vector space is defined as the number of vectors in a basis for the space. A *basis* is a set of linearly independent vectors that span the entire vector space. In simpler terms, any vector in the space can be expressed uniquely as a linear combination of the basis vectors.

Consider the three-dimensional vector space $\mathbb{R}^3$. A canonical basis is $\{\mathbf{e}_1, \mathbf{e}_2, \mathbf{e}_3\}$, where:

$$\mathbf{e}_1 = \begin{bmatrix} 1 \\ 0 \\ 0 \end{bmatrix}, \quad \mathbf{e}_2 = \begin{bmatrix} 0 \\ 1 \\ 0 \end{bmatrix}, \quad \mathbf{e}_3 = \begin{bmatrix} 0 \\ 0 \\ 1 \end{bmatrix}.$$

These vectors are orthogonal and span the space $\mathbb{R}^3$, meaning any vector $\mathbf{v} = (v_1, v_2, v_3)$ can be written as:

$$\mathbf{v} = v_1 \mathbf{e}_1 + v_2 \mathbf{e}_2 + v_3 \mathbf{e}_3.$$

To elucidate the concept of basis and linear independence, consider a Python example utilizing NumPy. This script verifies independence and calculates basis vectors for a subspace of $\mathbb{R}^3$.

```python
import numpy as np

# Define two vectors u and v in R^3
vector_u = np.array([1, 2, 3])
vector_v = np.array([4, 5, 6])

# Stack vectors to check independence
matrix = np.vstack((vector_u, vector_v))
rank = np.linalg.matrix_rank(matrix)

print("Rank of matrix formed by vectors u and v:", rank)

# Finding orthonormal basis using Gram-Schmidt process
def gram_schmidt(vectors):
    basis = []
    for v in vectors:
        # Subtract projections on previously found basis vectors
        for b in basis:
            v -= np.dot(v, b) / np.dot(b, b) * b
        if np.linalg.norm(v) > 1e-10: # Check for non-zero vector
            basis.append(v / np.linalg.norm(v))
    return basis
```

```
# Applying Gram-Schmidt to derive an orthonormal basis
basis_vectors = gram_schmidt([vector_u, vector_v])
print("Orthonormal basis:", basis_vectors)
```

Rank of matrix formed by vectors u and v: 2
Orthonormal basis: [array([0.26726124, 0.53452248, 0.80178373]), array([-0.87287156, -0.21821789, 0.43643578])]

The script first computes the rank to assess whether the vectors are linearly independent. With the Gram-Schmidt process, it determines an orthonormal basis for the subspace spanned by vectors **u** and **v**, confirming their linear independence.

The notions of linear combinations and span are central to vector spaces, reflecting how vectors can be composed or generated within the space.

A *linear combination* of vectors $\mathbf{v}_1, \mathbf{v}_2, \ldots, \mathbf{v}_k$ is expressed as:

$$c_1\mathbf{v}_1 + c_2\mathbf{v}_2 + \cdots + c_k\mathbf{v}_k,$$

where $c_1, c_2, \ldots, c_k$ are scalars.

The set of all possible linear combinations of a collection of vectors forms the *span* of those vectors, a crucial concept for identifying the subspace a set of vectors occupies.

Understanding these ideas can be facilitated through computation, allowing students to manipulate and investigate vector spaces experimentally. Use the following Python code to compute spans and verify linear dependencies:

```
# Define a set of vectors
vectors = np.array([[1, 2, 3], [4, 5, 6], [7, 8, 9]])

# Determine span using linear algebra rank
rank_span = np.linalg.matrix_rank(vectors)

print("The span (rank) of the given vectors:", rank_span)

# Check if a vector can be represented as a linear combination
target = np.array([3, 6, 9])
augmented_matrix = np.column_stack((vectors, target))

rank_augmented = np.linalg.matrix_rank(augmented_matrix)
if rank_span == rank_augmented:
    print("Target vector is within the span.")
```

38

```
else:
    print("Target vector is outside the span.")
```

```
The span (rank) of the given vectors: 2
Target vector is within the span.
```

Here, the rank of the matrix formed by the given vectors ($\mathbb{R}^3$ example) is calculated to determine the span or the dimensionality of the subspace they occupy. The example verifies that the target vector is a linear combination and thus within the span of the defining vectors.

Vector spaces model real-world phenomena and abstract mathematical theories. Across disciplines, vector spaces unveil various features and lead to solutions for complex systems:

- In machine learning, features of a dataset can be considered vectors in a multi-dimensional vector space, enabling tasks like classification, regression, and clustering.

- In quantum mechanics, states are often modeled as vectors in complex vector spaces (Hilbert spaces), providing a structure for studying particle behaviors and interactions.

- In control theory and robotics, vector spaces define spaces of possible states or configurations, aiding in modeling system dynamics and optimizations.

These applications demonstrate the manifold instances where vector spaces' foundational theoretical structures enhance understanding and problem-solving.

Vector spaces exhibit versatility, serving as the foundation for higher-dimensional data representations and computations. By examining them rigorously through mathematical axioms, vector operations, and computational illustrations, we appreciate their pivotal role in both theoretical explorations and applied advancements.

39

2.3 Vector Operations

Vector operations are foundational to the study of linear algebra and essential in various scientific and engineering disciplines. These operations facilitate the manipulation and analysis of vectors within vector spaces, supporting complex tasks such as optimization, modeling, and data processing. This section delves into key vector operations: addition, subtraction, scalar multiplication, dot product, and cross product, while illustrating their computational implementations and applications.

Addition and subtraction are primary operations, enabling the combination and differentiation of vector magnitudes and directions. For vectors $\mathbf{u} = (u_1, u_2, \ldots, u_n)$ and $\mathbf{v} = (v_1, v_2, \ldots, v_n)$ in an n-dimensional space, these operations are defined as:

$$\mathbf{u} + \mathbf{v} = (u_1 + v_1, u_2 + v_2, \ldots, u_n + v_n)$$

$$\mathbf{u} - \mathbf{v} = (u_1 - v_1, u_2 - v_2, \ldots, u_n - v_n)$$

The geometric representation of addition is captured by the parallelogram law, where the sum of two vectors corresponds to the diagonal of the parallelogram they form. Subtraction analogously involves tip-to-tail alignment of vectors. Computationally, these operations are efficiently performed using arrays, often implemented in languages like Python and MATLAB for their simplicity and performance.

```
import numpy as np

# Define vectors
vector_u = np.array([1, 3, 5])
vector_v = np.array([2, 4, 6])

# Perform vector addition
vector_addition = vector_u + vector_v

# Perform vector subtraction
vector_subtraction = vector_u - vector_v

print("Vector Addition:", vector_addition)
print("Vector Subtraction:", vector_subtraction)
```

Vector Addition: [3 7 11]

40

Vector Subtraction: [-1 -1 -1]

Through addition and subtraction, vectors are combined or differentiated, manifesting through various applications such as prediction errors in machine learning models and force calculations in physics.

Scalar multiplication involves resizing a vector by a scalar value. For a scalar a and vector $\mathbf{u} = (u_1, u_2, \ldots, u_n)$, the resulting vector $a\mathbf{u}$ is:

$$a\mathbf{u} = (au_1, au_2, \ldots, au_n)$$

This operation preserves the vector's direction if $a > 0$, or reverses it if $a < 0$, scaling the magnitude proportionally. Scalar multiplication is utilized in tasks such as normalizing vectors, adjusting magnitudes in physics, financial models, and more.

In practice, scalar multiplication is implemented straightforwardly:

```
# Scalar multiplication
scalar = 3
scaled_vector = scalar * vector_u

print("Scaled Vector:", scaled_vector)
```

Scaled Vector: [3 9 15]

Scalar multiplication adjusts vectors to desired magnitudes or standardized forms, essential in data scaling strategies employed within machine learning preprocessing stages.

The dot product (or scalar product) quantifies the similarity between two vectors, calculated as:

$$\mathbf{u} \cdot \mathbf{v} = u_1 v_1 + u_2 v_2 + \cdots + u_n v_n$$

This operation returns a scalar and reflects the degree to which vectors align, being maximal when vectors point in the same direction and zero when orthogonal. The dot product is critical for computing angles, projections, and in the context of machine learning for measuring feature correlations.

To compute the dot product in Python:

```
# Dot product using numpy
dot_product = np.dot(vector_u, vector_v)

print("Dot Product:", dot_product)
```

Dot Product: 44

Applications of dot products are ubiquitous, ranging from projecting forces in physics to determining document similarity using term vectors in natural language processing.

The cross product, applicable in $\mathbb{R}^3$, results in a vector perpendicular to two input vectors, given by:

$$\mathbf{u} \times \mathbf{v} = \begin{vmatrix} \mathbf{i} & \mathbf{j} & \mathbf{k} \\ u_1 & u_2 & u_3 \\ v_1 & v_2 & v_3 \end{vmatrix} = (u_2 v_3 - u_3 v_2)\mathbf{i} - (u_1 v_3 - u_3 v_1)\mathbf{j} + (u_1 v_2 - u_2 v_1)\mathbf{k}$$

The magnitude of the cross product vector equals the area of the parallelogram that can be formed by the original vectors, providing a measure of vector orthogonality and spatial span.

Calculating the cross product within Python:

```
# Cross product using numpy
cross_product = np.cross(vector_u, vector_v)

print("Cross Product:", cross_product)
```

Cross Product: [-2 4 -2]

Cross products support torque calculations in physics, rotational transformations in 3D space, and in determining perpendicularity within spatial environments.

The power and versatility of vector operations extend into diverse fields where they play crucial roles in advancing technology and understanding phenomena:

- Physics and Engineering: Vectors model forces, velocities, and fields, utilizing operations for resultant computations and balance equations.

42

- Computer Graphics: Vector operations render textures and simulate movements efficiently, integral to transformations applied
  during graphical processing.

- Data Science and Machine Learning: Vectors represent features,
  with operations facilitating data normalization, transformation,
  and in the operation of algorithms like the k-nearest neighbors,
  where distances are computed using various norms.

- Economics and Finance: Vector mathematics form the backbone
  of optimization models, predicting market trends while ensuring
  effective resource allocation algorithms.

Let us delve further into a practical example illustrating the fit of vector operations in machine learning, specifically in the domain of linear
regression—a simple yet potent model.

```
# Hypothetical dataset
X = np.array([1, 2, 3, 4, 5])
y = np.array([2, 4, 5, 4, 5])

# Simple linear regression model
# Convert data to vectors
X_vector = np.vstack((np.ones_like(X), X)).T # Add bias (intercept)
y_vector = y

# Calculate coefficients using normal equation
# = (X^T X)^(-1) X^T y
beta = np.linalg.inv(X_vector.T @ X_vector) @ X_vector.T @ y_vector

print("Regression coefficients:", beta)
```

Regression coefficients: [2.2 0.6]

In this example, vector operations are pivotal in computing regression
coefficients—the vector of weights and intercept in the linear model.
The use of vectorization and matrix operations in predictive modeling underscores vectors' importance in computational efficiencies and
model accuracies.

Collectively, vector operations form a cohesive system, underpinning
methodologies that abstract and solve problems in elegant, computationally effective manners. From basic arithmetic to intricate model
adjustments, these operations set the stage for deciphering relationships across dimensions and fields, reflecting a profound simplicity
that leads to stronger insights and advanced applications.

43

2.4 Encoding Information in Vectors

Encoding information in vectors is a critical concept in computer science, especially in areas like data processing, machine learning, and artificial intelligence. This process involves transforming diverse types of data into a standardized numerical form that can be easily manipulated by algorithms. Vectors, being ordered lists of numbers, serve as effective structures for information encoding, supporting operations that facilitate pattern recognition, classification, and decision-making.

When data, whether structured or unstructured, is encoded into vector form, it becomes amenable to a variety of mathematical manipulations and computational analyses. This transformation involves mapping each piece of data to a set of numerical values, enabling algorithms to process data points consistently. Such conversions are crucial for:

- Handling Structured Data: Directly converting categorical and numerical features from tabular datasets into vectors.

- Textual Data Processing: Encoding text into vectors for tasks like sentiment analysis and translation.

- Image Processing: Translating pixel values into vectors, which can then be fed into neural networks for recognition tasks.

To illustrate, consider a common example from machine learning: transforming categorical and continuous data into features for models.

For structured data, the conversion frequently involves feature engineering, an essential preparatory step that bridges raw datasets and computational models. Within this framework, both continuous and categorical variables are transformed into vectors. Continuous variables often remain unchanged, while categorical data may require techniques like one-hot encoding.

Consider a dataset with mixed types, such as:

- Age (Continuous)

- Gender (Categorical - Male, Female)

44

- Occupation (Categorical - Doctor, Engineer, Artist)

Initially, for numerical features like age, direct encoding into vectors is feasible, while categorical features require transformation. We'll showcase feature vectorization, particularly one-hot encoding, through this Python example:

```python
import numpy as np
import pandas as pd

# Illustrative dataset
data = pd.DataFrame({
    'Age': [25, 32, 47],
    'Gender': ['Male', 'Female', 'Male'],
    'Occupation': ['Doctor', 'Engineer', 'Artist']
})

# One-hot encode categorical variables
encoded_data = pd.get_dummies(data, columns=['Gender', 'Occupation'])

# Data in vector form
feature_vectors = encoded_data.values

print("Encoded Feature Vectors:\n", feature_vectors)
```

```
Encoded Feature Vectors:
 [[25  1  0  1  0  0]
  [32  0  1  0  1  0]
  [47  1  0  0  0  1]]
```

The provided code demonstrates how tabular data converts into a numerical matrix suited for input into machine learning models. Each row corresponds to an entity and each column a feature, enabling various computationally viable manipulations.

Text data is inherently unstructured, necessitating sophisticated encoding methods to produce meaningful vectors. The most recognized techniques in this realm are:

- Bag of Words (BoW): A simple approach involving term frequency.

- Term Frequency-Inverse Document Frequency (TF-IDF): A refinement over BoW, emphasizing rare but informative terms.

- Word Embeddings: Advanced techniques embedding semantic meanings into fixed-length vectors.

45

Each method encodes text differently, suited to various applications, influencing computational performance and model interpretability.

In a Bag of Words model, a document is represented as a set of words, disregarding grammar and structure but capturing vocabulary presence. TF-IDF enhances this by weighing words, decreasing the impact of common words (e.g., "the", "and") across documents. An example using TF-IDF:

```
from sklearn.feature_extraction.text import TfidfVectorizer

# Sample documents
documents = [
    "The quick brown fox jumps over the lazy dog.",
    "Never jump over the sleeping dog swiftly."
]

# Initialize TF-IDF Vectorizer
tfidf_vectorizer = TfidfVectorizer()

# Encode documents
tfidf_matrix = tfidf_vectorizer.fit_transform(documents)

# Transform into array format
tfidf_array = tfidf_matrix.toarray()

print("TF-IDF Vectors:\n", tfidf_array)
```

```
TF-IDF Vectors:
 [[0.         0.37997836 0.37997836 0.37997836 0.37997836 0.         0.
   0.37997836 0.37997836 0.37997836]
  [0.51785612 0.         0.         0.         0.41428875 0.51785612
   0.51785612 0.         0.         0.         ]]
```

In neural language models, word embeddings like Word2Vec and GloVe enable nuanced word vector representations, capturing semantics and analogical relations by training on vast corpuses. Results are vectors positioning words in multi-dimensional space, useful for linguistic predictions and semantic analyses.

Images, traditionally perceived as arrays of pixels, can be encoded into vectors for machine vision tasks. Each pixel, often a trio of RGB values, contributes to a flattened vector representation, subsequently processed in classifiers or neural networks.

```
from skimage import io
import matplotlib.pyplot as plt

# Load an image from file
```

```
image = io.imread('example.jpg')

# Flatten image into a vector
image_vector = image.flatten()

print("Image Vector Shape:", image_vector.shape)

# Display the image
plt.imshow(image)
plt.axis('off')
plt.show()
```

Understanding images as vectorized forms extends into applications like object detection and classification, where sophisticated neural networks, such as Convolutional Neural Networks (CNNs), leverage these encodings.

Beyond traditional data types, vectors are employed to represent more complex structures, such as graphs, which capture interconnected entities or nodes. Graph encoding addresses applications like social network analysis or protein interactions in bioinformatics.

Node2Vec and Graph2Vec are notable algorithms in transforming graph-based data into vector embeddings, conserving the structure and relevance of nodes or entire graphs.

The translation of varied data types into informational vectors plays a pivotal role across industries and technologies:

- Natural Language Processing: Vectorized text underpins systems like chatbots, automating and streamlining language understanding and response generation.

- Image Recognition and Generation: Vectors encoded as images drive facial recognition software and creative AI in generating synthetic images.

- Recommendation Systems: User profiles and preferences vectorized improve recommendation precision across e-commerce and streaming platforms.

- Genomic Research and Precision Medicine: Genomic sequences encoded into vectors empower personalized medicine, enhancing treatment targeting and efficacies.

47

Encoding methodologies balance the preservation of information fidelity with computational tractability, determining model comprehensiveness and accuracy. As data dimensionality and complexity expand, encoding paradigms continue to evolve, accommodating the growing intricacies of modern data landscapes.

Encoding information into vectors allows the intersection of raw data with computational models. With innovations in vectorization techniques, this alignment propels not only technical advancements but also reshapes how we harness information towards knowledge discovery and intelligent applications.

2.5 Vectors in Machine Learning and AI

Vectors are fundamental to the design, implementation, and functioning of machine learning (ML) and artificial intelligence (AI) systems. They represent data inputs and outputs, parameters of models, and intermediate computations. Understanding how vectors operate within ML and AI frameworks is crucial to leveraging these technologies for tasks such as data analysis, pattern recognition, and decision-making. This section explores their role, delving into vector usage in feature representation, model parameterization, gradient computations, and more.

- **Feature Representation**

In ML and AI, vectors serve as a primary medium for feature representation. Features are essentially measurable characteristics or properties used by algorithms to learn patterns and make predictions. The process of encoding these features into vectors allows ML algorithms to process data effectively.

- **Numerical Data**

Transforming numerical data into a vector format is relatively straightforward, as each feature can be directly incorporated as a vector's component. Consider a simple example of house pricing, where features such as square footage, number of bedrooms, and age are used:

$$\mathbf{x} = \begin{bmatrix} \text{Square Footage} \\ \text{Number of Bedrooms} \\ \text{Age in Years} \end{bmatrix} = \begin{bmatrix} 2000 \\ 3 \\ 10 \end{bmatrix}$$

This vector representation facilitates input into models like linear regression or decision trees. Python's NumPy library is often used to handle these vector transformations:

```
import numpy as np

# Feature vector for a single data point
features = np.array([2000, 3, 10])

print("Feature Vector:", features)
```

Feature Vector: [2000   3   10]

- **Categorical Data**

Categorical data requires special handling before incorporation into vectorized models. Techniques such as one-hot encoding or embeddings transform categories into numerical vectors. For example, for a categorical feature like "Color" with possible values of "Red," "Green," and "Blue," one-hot encoding represents these as:

$$\text{Red} = [1, 0, 0], \quad \text{Green} = [0, 1, 0], \quad \text{Blue} = [0, 0, 1]$$

Embedding techniques, widely used in natural language processing, map dimensions to vectors of lesser size while capturing relational semantics and hierarchies.

- **Model Parameterization**

In the design of ML models, vectors encompass parameters such as weights and biases. These parameters adapt during training to minimize the objective function, optimizing model predictions.

- **Linear Models**

49

For linear models like linear regression or logistic regression, model parameters are represented as vectors. The weight vector **w** represents the influence of each feature, with the model learning these weights through the process of training:

$$y = \mathbf{w}^T \mathbf{x} + b$$

Where **w** is the weight vector, **x** is the feature vector, and b is the bias. Training involves optimizing **w** and b to minimize errors between predictions and actual output.

```
from sklearn.linear_model import LinearRegression

# Hypothetical data
X = np.array([[2000, 3, 10], [1500, 2, 15], [2500, 4, 5]])
y = np.array([300000, 150000, 450000])

# Linear regression model
model = LinearRegression().fit(X, y)

print("Model Weights:", model.coef_)
print("Model Bias:", model.intercept_)
```

```
Model Weights: [100. 50000. -5000.]
Model Bias: -99999.99999999977
```

Here, the derived weights represent each feature's contribution to predicting housing prices, simplifying decision boundaries and classifications in regression analyses.

- **Neural Networks**

In neural networks, vectors model numerous parameters across multiple layers. Weights that connect neurons in adjacent layers are often stored and updated as matrices during forward and backward propagation. Each layer's output, likewise, is represented as a vector of activations, feeding into subsequent layers.

Convolutional neural networks (CNNs), widely exploited for image processing, use multidimensional arrays (tensors) extending vector concepts to learn spatial hierarchies within images. By feeding forward vectors of pixel data and adjusting weights through learned gradients,

50

CNNs can abstract complex features from simple edge detectors to complex patterns.

Deep learning frameworks like TensorFlow and PyTorch facilitate vector operations at scale, leveraging GPU optimizations to efficiently manage extensive parameter spaces.

- **Gradient Computation and Optimization**

Gradients in vector form guide optimization in training models. Frequently, models optimize a cost function by adjusting parameters iteratively, using algorithms like gradient descent. The gradient vector indicates the direction in which each parameter should move to decrease the cost function:

$$\nabla J(\mathbf{w}) = \frac{\partial J}{\partial \mathbf{w}}$$

Where J is the cost function and $\mathbf{w}$ the parameter vector. Optimizers adjust weights in accordance with the gradient, refined further using variations like stochastic and mini-batch gradients that enhance convergence rates and stability.

```
# Gradient calculation using autograd
import autograd.numpy as anp
from autograd import grad

# Quadratic cost function example
def cost_function(w):
    return anp.dot(w, w)

# Compute the gradient
gradient = grad(cost_function)

weights = anp.array([3.0, 4.0])
grad_value = gradient(weights)

print("Gradient Value:", grad_value)
```

Gradient Value: [6. 8.]

Gradient vectors are pivotal in optimizing objective functions, directing models to minimize errors iteratively while adapting weights and biases.

- **Application Areas**

Vectors facilitate diverse ML and AI deployments across industries:

- **Natural Language Processing (NLP)**: Vectors enable languages and meanings to be captured and compared. Embeddings map sentences and words into lower-dimensional vector spaces, powering models for translation, sentiment analysis, and summarization.

- **Computer Vision**: Images transformed into vectors inform models detecting objects, faces, and actions within frames, utilized in security, automotive, and health industries.

- **Reinforcement Learning**: State vectors model environments, guiding agents in simulations where decisions are made iteratively, solving sequence prediction and optimization tasks.

- **Recommendation Systems**: User and item vectors facilitate collaborative filtering, predicting user preferences and assisting services like e-commerce by enhancing personalized experiences.

Beyond these tasks, vectors are integral to statistical analysis, biological data interpretations, and even financial optimizations, where patterns in stock indices or gene sequences are abstracted and modeled mathematically.

- **Future Directions and Innovations**

The adaptation of vectors in ML and AI continues to evolve. Transformations like attention mechanisms in language models treat sentence vectors dynamically, emphasizing relevant parts of inputs. Frameworks expanding to quantum computing envision qubit vectorizations, adapting fundamental operations to accommodate exponentially more information due to superposition and entanglement properties.

AutoML platforms embodying vectors streamline the design and tuning phase by exploring vast model architectures and hyperparameter spaces, elevating vector processing efficiencies. As computational power escalates with advancements in processors and storage, the holistic integration of vectors into AI paradigms promises new break-throughs, fostering systems that learn more naturally and intuitively.

Vectors form an indispensable element of ML and AI systems, fundamentally structuring data representation, parameterization, and optimization. Their inherent attributes and evolving implementations promise ongoing advancements that reshape the trajectory of intelligent technological landscapes.

2.6 Importance of Vectors in Data Retrieval

Vectors play a pivotal role in the domain of data retrieval, forming the backbone of retrieval algorithms and the representation of data within systems tasked with searching, indexing, and organizing information efficiently. Data retrieval, an integral component of information systems, covers practices from document retrieval and multimedia information retrieval to web search and recommendation systems.

At the heart of many retrieval systems lies the Vector Space Model (VSM), a foundational framework for representing text documents as vectors in a multi-dimensional space. In this model, documents and queries are transformed into vectors, and the similarity between them is measured to determine relevance, commonly using cosine similarity.

Given a document corpus, each document d_i is represented as a vector $\mathbf{d}_i$, with dimensions corresponding to terms in the vocabulary. A term can be weighted by its term frequency (TF) and often refined with inverse document frequency (IDF) to form the TF-IDF vector representation. Thus, each document can be expressed as:

$$\mathbf{d}_i = [w_1, w_2, \ldots, w_n]$$

where w_j denotes the weight of term j in document d_i. Mathematically, this vectorization facilitates comparison between documents and queries $\mathbf{q}$, seeking a vector space representation for any information retrieval application.

The effectiveness of the VSM is intrinsically linked to the methods employed for similarity comparison between vectors. The cosine similarity measure is typically used for this:

$$\text{cosine}(\mathbf{d}_i, \mathbf{q}) = \frac{\mathbf{d}_i \cdot \mathbf{q}}{\|\mathbf{d}_i\| \|\mathbf{q}\|}$$

This metric evaluates the cosine of the angle between two vectors in vector space, serving as an indicator of their orientation. A cosine similarity of 1 indicates that vectors are identical in direction, while a similarity of 0 implies orthogonality.

Example implementation with cosine similarity using Python:

```
from sklearn.feature_extraction.text import TfidfVectorizer
from sklearn.metrics.pairwise import cosine_similarity

# Example documents
documents = [
    "The sky is blue.",
    "The sun is bright today.",
    "The sky is bright and blue today."
]

# Initialize TF-IDF Vectorizer
vectorizer = TfidfVectorizer()

# Fit and transform the documents
tfidf_matrix = vectorizer.fit_transform(documents)

# Compute cosine similarity between documents
similarity_matrix = cosine_similarity(tfidf_matrix)

print("Cosine Similarity Matrix:\n", similarity_matrix)
```

```
Cosine Similarity Matrix:
 [[1.         0.11378749 0.62952301]
  [0.11378749 1.         0.40319033]
  [0.62952301 0.40319033 1.        ]]
```

This matrix illustrates the pairwise cosine similarity between documents, grounding the decision of rankings in information retrieval tasks.

As datasets expand and evolve, the dimensionality of vector spaces frequently grows, creating challenges such as the "curse of dimensionality" where performance and accuracy degrade due to increased complexity and data sparsity. Techniques like dimensionality reduction and embeddings address these challenges by mapping high-dimensional vectors into more compact representations, preserving essential qualities.

Dimensionality reduction techniques like Principal Component Analysis (PCA) and t-distributed Stochastic Neighbor Embedding (t-SNE) effectively reduce vector space dimensions while retaining variance or structure, facilitating efficient retrieval. PCA, for example, projects high-dimensional vectors into a lower-dimensional subspace by retaining principal components:

```
from sklearn.decomposition import PCA

# Reduce dimensionality of tf-idf matrix
pca = PCA(n_components=2)
pca_result = pca.fit_transform(tfidf_matrix.toarray())

print("PCA Reduced Dimensions:\n", pca_result)
```

```
PCA Reduced Dimensions:
 [[-0.54779471  0.10271531]
 [-0.06574462 -0.60334437]
 [ 0.61353932  0.50062906]]
```

PCA outcomes enable retrieval systems to contend with complex, multi-dimensional data while mitigating computational loads and improving storage efficiency.

Vector embeddings, like word embeddings for text or deep embeddings for images, offer learned representations that maintain semantic meanings and can drastically improve retrieval outcomes. Embeddings trained using deep learning models learn structured relationships within data and incorporate contextual nuances beyond purely syntactic constructs.

Learning to Rank (LTR) approaches apply machine learning to retrieval tasks leveraging vectorized features to order documents according to relevance, capitalizing on training data with known outcomes to construct robust ranking systems adapted for web search engines and personalized recommendations.

Modern data retrieval frameworks utilize vector representations to enhance accuracy and speed. Notable applications include search engines, recommendation systems, and content delivery networks:

- Search Engines: Vectors translate user queries and web content into comparable forms within vast indices, enabling search engines like Google to effectively retrieve and rank web results.

- Information Filtering: Systems that filter digital communications and content (e.g., emails, social media feeds) implement vectorization strategies to flag spam or prioritize pertinent messages.

- Recommendation Systems: Collaborative and content-based filtering methods applied in platforms like Netflix or Spotify use vectors to map user preferences, effectively suggesting content by computing similarities and projecting trends.

Despite their effectiveness, vector-based retrieval systems contend with challenges of freshness, diversity, and scalability. Maintaining updated indices that reflect new content and user behaviors remains non-trivial, requiring continuous advancements in latency optimizations and model updating routines.

The field continues to develop, driven by trends like:

- Self-supervised Learning: Enhanced models that understand data semantics without explicitly labeled datasets facilitate more robust vector embeddings for retrieval tasks.

- Federated Learning: Secure and decentralized learning architectures incorporate vector-based retrieval techniques that respect privacy, distributing data processing across devices without centralized data collection.

- Quantum Information Retrieval: Quantum computing explores exponential speed-ups using vectorization adaptations, promising enhanced retrieval systems capable of handling burgeoning information depths through principles like superposition and entanglement.

Vectors, through their integration in retrieval systems, propel technologies that underpin knowledge dissemination and surface data in actionable forms. With ongoing advancements, their importance across varied contexts will continue to expand, ushering in an era where intelligent data handling adapts seamlessly to evolving informational landscapes.

2.7 Challenges in Vector Representation

Vector representation is a central concept in computing and data science, widely employed in applications ranging from natural language processing (NLP) to computer vision. However, despite their robustness and versatility, vectors also present challenges in their representation and manipulation. These challenges can arise from high dimensionality, data sparsity, interpretability issues, and scalability in processing, especially in large-scale data environments. This section explores these challenges in detail, along with potential solutions and improvements that aim to mitigate them.

High dimensionality often leads to the "curse of dimensionality". As dimensionality increases, the volume of the space grows exponentially, making the available data sparse. This scarcity can lead to difficulties in clustering, classification, and other tasks, as algorithms struggle with the increased computational complexity and the higher potential for overfitting.

Consider, for instance, a dataset used for image recognition. Each image can be represented as a vector where each pixel contributes to a dimension. For a 100×100 pixel image, the feature vector is already 10,000 dimensions before applying any transformations or combinations of color channels.

To combat high dimensionality, dimensionality reduction techniques are employed. These methods aim to reduce the number of random variables under consideration by obtaining a set of principal variables:

- **Principal Component Analysis (PCA)**: Transforms the data to a new coordinate system, reducing dimensions while retaining variance.

- **t-Distributed Stochastic Neighbor Embedding (t-SNE)**: Useful for visualization, t-SNE reduces dimensions while preserving the dataset's structure and relationships.

The following Python code demonstrates PCA applied to a high-dimensional dataset:

```
from sklearn.decomposition import PCA
```

```
import numpy as np

# Simulate high-dimensional data
np.random.seed(0)
data = np.random.rand(100, 500) # 100 samples with 500 features

# Apply PCA
pca = PCA(n_components=2)
pca_result = pca.fit_transform(data)

print("Reduced Dimensions via PCA:\n", pca_result)
```

```
Reduced Dimensions via PCA:
 [[-0.03895202 -0.12204315]
 [-0.05170769  0.02463333]
 [ 0.0072145  -0.11848742]
 ...
 [-0.05193946 -0.09096463]
 [-0.08194436  0.08054784]
 [-0.04347744 -0.0217068 ]]
```

By retaining only the top principal components, PCA offers a viable solution to high-dimensional datasets, providing computationally efficient and interpretable results.

Embedding represents another effective solution to high-dimensionality issues. These are used extensively in NLP and machine vision, mapping high-dimensional space to lower dimensions amenable to learning systems. For example, word embeddings like Word2Vec or GloVe transform large vocabulary sizes into dense vectorial forms that capture semantic similarities and relations.

Data sparsity often arises in vector representations, particularly in text analysis, where vector dimensions represent vocabulary terms that may not appear frequently across documents. Sparse vectors can cause inefficiencies in storage and processing because most elements in these vectors are zero.

Sparse representations offer solutions by storing only non-zero elements, thus optimizing memory usage and computational efficiency. Libraries like SciPy in Python offer data structures to manage sparse matrices effectively:

```
from scipy.sparse import csr_matrix

# Example of sparse representation
```

58

```
dense_vector = np.random.rand(500) * (np.random.rand(500) > 0.95)
sparse_vector = csr_matrix(dense_vector)

print("Original Density:", dense_vector)
print("Sparse Representation:\n", sparse_vector)
```

```
Original Density: [0. 0. 0. ... 0. 0. 0.]
Sparse Representation:
    (0, 64)        0.5722519057908734
    (0, 74)        0.8556404695309484
    (0, 204)       0.06232622999524821
    ...
    (0, 498)       0.5442512629173706
```

Sparse vectors conserve resources and improve processing time in large-scale datasets, where non-zero entries are significantly outnumbered by zero entries.

Another substantial challenge in vector representation arises in the interpretability and transparency of vectors, especially when employed in complex models like neural networks. Understanding what each dimension or a combination of dimensions represents in the original data can be difficult.

Models such as deep neural networks produce hidden layer activations, which are vectors capturing intricate data interactions. However, these activations often lack straightforward interpretability, complicating efforts to understand model decisions.

To address interpretability, models like LIME (Local Interpretable Model-agnostic Explanations) and SHAP (SHapley Additive exPlanations) offer actionable insights by approximating model predictions as interpretable vectors:

```
import xgboost as xgb
import shap

# Train a simple model
X, y = shap.datasets.boston()
model = xgb.train({"learning_rate": 0.01}, xgb.DMatrix(X, label=y), 100)

# Explain the model's predictions
explainer = shap.TreeExplainer(model)
shap_values = explainer.shap_values(X)

shap.summary_plot(shap_values, X)
```

Interpretable AI tools reveal dimensions associated with predictions, enabling users to discern influential attributes within vector representations, fostering transparency and trust.

Scalability is a persistent challenge, particularly when processing massive metadata or real-time data streams. As data scales, systems must efficiently manage and execute vector operations within the constraints of time, storage, and computational resources.

Parallel processing frameworks like Apache Kafka and Spark facilitate large-scale vector operations by distributing tasks across clusters. When vectors are processed in parallel, anxieties surrounding scalability diminish, improving efficiency across data retrieval and processing functionalities.

Tackling the challenges of vector representation, advancements continue to emerge across computational efficiencies and innovative algorithmic structures:

- **Quantum Computing**:   Offers potential advancements in processing capabilities, allowing high-dimensional vector operations at quantum speeds with principles like qubit superposition and entanglement.

- **Federated Learning**: Provides avenues to process vectors securely and privately on decentralized devices, maintaining scalable solutions without centralizing data, benefiting sectors with stringent privacy demands.

- **Adaptive Machine Learning Models**: Novel models dynamically adjust vector spaces, utilizing reinforcement learning to adapt dimensions and features during operational tasks.

In the context of optimizing vector representations, adopting these evolving techniques and frameworks aligns with the modern landscape's demands for efficient, interpretable, and scalable data processing capabilities.

While challenges in vector representation persist across high dimensionality, sparsity, interpretability, and scalability, continued innovation mitigates these issues. Through advanced techniques like dimensionality reduction, sparse representations, interpretability tools, and scalable computing solutions, vectors remain at the forefront, driving data-intensive technologies and solutions forward.

Chapter 3

Core Concepts of Vector Databases

Vector databases are built on a foundation of core concepts that distinguish them from traditional database systems, primarily focusing on handling high-dimensional data through vectors. This chapter outlines key elements such as data modeling paradigms unique to vector databases, indexing structures designed for efficient data retrieval, and similarity measures critical for vector operations. It also addresses challenges associated with managing high-dimensional data and the methodologies employed to optimize query processing. Explaining these fundamental principles provides a comprehensive understanding of the capabilities and advantages of vector databases in managing complex datasets.

3.1 Data Modeling in Vector Databases

Data modeling within vector databases represents a paradigm shift from traditional relational and NoSQL databases by focusing on the encapsulation of data as vectors. These vectors are pivotal in representing data in a way that enhances the ability to manipulate and retrieve high-dimensional information with efficiency. The methodology behind this structure is foundational to understanding the power and versatility of vector databases, especially as they are applied to complex and data-rich environments.

At the core of data modeling in vector databases lies the concept of a vector as a data object. A vector in this context is a one-dimensional array of numerical values, each representing a particular feature or attribute of the data object it describes. This allows for not only a compact representation of complex data but also facilitates the application of mathematical operations to assess relationships and patterns within large datasets.

Vectors are constructed by encoding the characteristics of data into a format that can be computationally manipulated. Let us consider a practical example involving image data. An image can be transformed into a vector by using various feature extraction techniques, such as histograms of oriented gradients, scale-invariant feature transform, or, more recently, embeddings from convolutional neural networks. Each image, then, is represented as a vector in a high-dimensional space where each dimension corresponds to an extracted feature.

```
from keras.applications.vgg16 import VGG16, preprocess_input
from keras.preprocessing.image import img_to_array, load_img
import numpy as np

# Load the VGG16 model
model = VGG16(weights='imagenet', include_top=False)

# Load an image file and convert it to a matrix
image = load_img('path/to/image.jpg', target_size=(224, 224))
image = img_to_array(image)
image = np.expand_dims(image, axis=0)
image = preprocess_input(image)

# Extract features using the model
features = model.predict(image)
feature_vector = features.flatten()

print('Feature vector shape:', feature_vector.shape)
```

Vectors serve as the building blocks of vector databases, where each entry in the database corresponds to a unique vector representation of a data object. The primary benefit of this approach is that it enables operations such as similarity search, clustering, and classification to be performed rapidly due to the inherently mathematical nature of vector operations. Importantly, vector spaces enable the application of various distance and similarity measures, which are central to many machine learning and data retrieval tasks.

Data integration into vector databases follows a series of stages that ensure efficient retrieval and manipulation. Initially, the data is transformed into vector form through processes like those illustrated above. Subsequently, indexing structures optimized for handling high-dimensional data, such as KD-trees and locality-sensitive hashing (LSH), are employed to organize these vectors within the database. These structures are designed to efficiently locate vectors within the high-dimensional space based on proximity measures.

The challenge of handling high-dimensional data lies in the "curse of dimensionality," a phenomenon where the volume of the space increases exponentially with the number of dimensions, rendering many data mining processes inefficient or ineffective. Vector databases address this issue through dimension reduction techniques such as Principal Component Analysis (PCA) or Autoencoders, which reduce the number of dimensions while preserving the intrinsic properties of the data.

```
from sklearn.decomposition import PCA

# Suppose 'data' is a matrix where each row is a feature vector
pca = PCA(n_components=50)
reduced_data = pca.fit_transform(data)

print('Reduced matrix shape:', reduced_data.shape)
```

The capability of vector databases to handle complex associations and operations arises from their mathematical grounding, particularly in linear algebra and vector calculus. Operations such as vector addition, dot product, and cross product provide a basis for computing relationships between data entries, thus enabling complex analytical operations. For instance, cosine similarity, defined as the cosine of the angle between two vectors in a multi-dimensional space, is a popular similarity measure in vector databases.

$$\text{Cosine Similarity} = \frac{\mathbf{A} \cdot \mathbf{B}}{\|\mathbf{A}\|\|\mathbf{B}\|}$$

Multi-dimensional data is effectively managed through vector databases by employing various indexing techniques that ensure

65

scalability and performance efficiency. For instance, Annoy and FAISS are indexing libraries designed to handle approximate nearest neighbor searches in large high-dimensional datasets. Such tools exemplify the architectural strategies adopted by vector databases to maintain agility under demanding data processing requirements.

Vector-based modeling also supports fault tolerance and distributed computing paradigms, essential for managing large-scale deployments. By distributing vector representations across multiple nodes, a vector database can take advantage of parallel processing techniques to handle exceedingly large data volumes, achieving both robustness and increased processing throughput.

Modeling data as vectors ties directly into the realm of data analysis and machine learning, where vectors form the underpinning for models utilized in prediction and classification tasks. Neural networks, for example, inherently operate on vectorized data inputs, and their architectures can be seamlessly integrated into vector database environments to facilitate real-time learning and adaptation.

Data modeling in vector databases offers an advanced framework for managing and analyzing data characterized by complex, high-dimensional relationships. This approach benefits from the synergy between mathematical rigor and computational efficiency, enabling a wide array of practical applications in modern data-intensive fields such as machine learning, computer vision, and natural language processing. As the demand for processing larger and more sophisticated datasets grows, the principles behind vector-based data modeling promise to unlock new capabilities and insights.

3.2   Vector Index Structures

In vector databases, the efficacy of data retrieval hinges significantly on the structure and efficiency of indexing methods employed. Indexing structures are essential for the rapid retrieval of data from high-dimensional spaces, where the volume and complexity of data can present significant challenges. Generating efficient vector index structures remains a focal point in database research, as the capability to search, query, and manipulate vector data directly influences the performance and scalability of these systems.

At the heart of vector index structures is the challenge posed by the "curse of dimensionality," where the geometrical space increases exponentially with each added dimension, making traditional data retrieval approaches less effective. To navigate this complexity, vector databases employ specialized indexing methods designed to provide approximate solutions that are both fast and resource-efficient, allowing effective navigation of these vast multidimensional spaces.

- **Locality-Sensitive Hashing (LSH):** Locality-Sensitive Hashing is one of the most prominent techniques designed for efficiently querying high-dimensional data. LSH works by hashing input items so that similar items map to the same "buckets" with high probability. This is achieved by creating multiple hash functions tailored to capture different aspects of data similarity, improving the precision of queries in miss-match scenarios.

```python
from sklearn.metrics.pairwise import cosine_similarity
import numpy as np

class LSH:
    def __init__(self, num_planes, num_tables):
        self.num_planes = num_planes
        self.num_tables = num_tables
        self.tables = [{} for _ in range(num_tables)]
        self.planes = [np.random.randn(num_planes, 1) for _ in range(num_tables)]

    def hash(self, vector):
        hashes = []
        for plane_set in self.planes:
            hash_value = ''.join(['1' if np.dot(vector, plane) >= 0 else '0' for plane in
                plane_set])
            hashes.append(hash_value)
        return hashes

    def add(self, vector, label):
        for i, hash_value in enumerate(self.hash(vector)):
            if hash_value not in self.tables[i]:
                self.tables[i][hash_value] = []
            self.tables[i][hash_value].append(label)

    def query(self, vector):
        seen_labels = set()
        for i, hash_value in enumerate(self.hash(vector)):
            if hash_value in self.tables[i]:
                seen_labels.update(self.tables[i][hash_value])
        return list(seen_labels)

# Usage of LSH for a vector database
```

```
lsh = LSH(num_planes=10, num_tables=5)
# Add vectors and query
```

The primary strength of LSH is its ability to quickly narrow down candidate sets from which nearest neighbors can be identified, making it suitable for applications requiring rapid approximate queries, such as media retrieval and recommendation systems.

- **KD-Trees and Ball Trees:** KD-Trees and Ball Trees are two other influential indexing structures that partition data space to improve query performance. KD-Trees work by recursively partitioning the space into axis-aligned hyper-rectangles, resulting in a binary tree representing the spatial distribution of the vector data. This allows for efficient range and nearest-neighbor queries in low to moderately high dimensions.

- In comparison, Ball Trees utilize M-ball partitioning to offer increased efficiency in higher-dimensional querying tasks. By creating hierarchical groupings of data points into nested hyperspheres, Ball Trees improve search efficiency in higher-dimensional spaces where KD-Trees tend to degrade.

```
from sklearn.neighbors import KDTree, BallTree
import numpy as np

# Suppose data is an array of vectors
data = np.random.random((1000, 10))

# Construct KD-Tree
kd_tree = KDTree(data)

# Construct Ball Tree
ball_tree = BallTree(data)

# Query the nearest neighbors
point = data[0]
kd_neighbors = kd_tree.query([point], k=5)
ball_neighbors = ball_tree.query([point], k=5)

print('KD-Tree Neighbors:', kd_neighbors)
print('Ball Tree Neighbors:', ball_neighbors)
```

Both KD-Trees and Ball Trees offer practical algorithms for low to moderately high-dimensional data, although the complexity grows as dimensions increase, at which point approximate methods like LSH become more effective.

- **Hierarchical Navigable Small World (HNSW) Graphs:**
  HNSW Graphs represent a cutting-edge indexing structure applied primarily in vector databases for efficient high-dimensional search. These graphs are based on the paradigm of proximity graphs, where every data point is connected to a set of neighbors, forming a graph that can be navigated quickly to find approximate nearest neighbors. The HNSW algorithm enhances this by constructing a multi-layered graph where higher layers provide coarser levels of search locality.

- The efficiency of an HNSW graph derives from its logarithmic local navigational property, which ensures a small number of hops to traverse through nodes in even extensive data collections. Through informed parallelization and increased navigational improvisation, HNSW is capable of addressing large-scale similarity search requirements.

```
import faiss

# Suppose data is an array of vectors
data = np.random.random((10000, 100)).astype('float32')

# Construct HNSW index
d = data.shape[1]
index = faiss.IndexHNSWFlat(d, 32) # Dimension = d, M = 32
index.add(data)

# Query the nearest neighbor
D, I = index.search(data[:5], 10)

print('HNSW neighbors indices:', I)
```

HNSW has found applications in domains such as image recognition, genomics, and recommendation systems, where the speed and accuracy of vector retrieval are paramount. Its innovative hierarchical design and navigational shortcuts offer a substantial improvement over traditional nearest neighbor structures.

- **Efficient Index Updates and Maintenance:** A crucial facet of vector indexing is the maintenance and updating of the index as data evolves. Dynamic environments where data is frequently updated, added, or deleted require adaptive index structures that can sustain performance despite fluctuations in vector space.

69

- Dynamic maintenance entails balancing indexing operation costs with query performance. Methods that allow incremental updating, such as lazy updates or batch reindexing, preserve system efficiency. More sophisticated techniques might involve automated re-tuning of index parameters based on workload changes, thus guaranteeing steady operational throughput over time.

- Furthermore, distributed computing capabilities integrated into indexing strategies further enhance scalability. By partitioning vector datasets across distributed nodes and maintaining independent or loosely coupled indexes, vector databases leverage parallel processing resources, achieving efficient high-scale data management.

In summary, vector index structures lie at the core of vector databases, enabling efficient querying and managing high-dimensional data. Techniques like Locality-Sensitive Hashing, KD-Trees, Ball Trees, and Hierarchical Navigable Small World Graphs optimize retrieval by focusing on proximity and arrangement within vector spaces. The implementation of these structures directly influences the performance and scalability of vector databases, positioning them as crucial technologies in handling modern data-centric applications. As technological advancements continue, vector indexing methods are expected to evolve, continually enhancing the capability to handle vast and complex datasets.

3.3 Vector Similarity Measures

In vector databases, the ability to measure the similarity between vectors is fundamental to numerous applications such as clustering, classification, and recommendations. Vector similarity measures quantify the likeness between data points encapsulated as vectors and are pivotal in identifying patterns, making predictions, and extracting meaningful insights from data.

The choice of similarity measure depends on the nature of the dataset and the specific requirements of the application. Each method offers unique advantages and is suited for different types of data and

70

tasks. The most commonly utilized measures include cosine similarity, Euclidean distance, Manhattan distance, and more sophisticated approaches like the Mahalanobis distance.

Cosine Similarity

Cosine similarity is a popular measure that assesses the cosine of the angle formed between two vectors in multidimensional space. It is defined mathematically as:

$$\text{Cosine Similarity} = \frac{\mathbf{A} \cdot \mathbf{B}}{\|\mathbf{A}\| \|\mathbf{B}\|}$$

This metric is particularly effective for text mining and information retrieval tasks due to its ability to measure orientation over magnitude. It is invariant to the scale of the vectors, making it ideal for data where the direction of features is more significant than their length.

```
from sklearn.metrics.pairwise import cosine_similarity
import numpy as np

# Define two example vectors
vector_a = np.array([1, 2, 3])
vector_b = np.array([2, 4, 6])

# Calculate cosine similarity
similarity = cosine_similarity([vector_a], [vector_b])

print('Cosine Similarity:', similarity[0][0])
```

Cosine similarity values range from -1 to 1, where a value closer to 1 indicates greater similarity. The measure is remarkable for applications where data sparsity is prevalent, such as in document-term matrices used in natural language processing.

Euclidean Distance

Euclidean distance, often intuitive, measures the "straight line" or direct distance between two vectors in Euclidean space. The Euclidean distance between two vectors **A** and **B** is given by:

$$\text{Euclidean Distance} = \sqrt{\sum_{i=1}^{n} (A_i - B_i)^2}$$

71

It provides a tangible metric for determining the absolute difference between data points, making it suitable for clustering and anomaly detection when the size difference is meaningful.

```
import numpy as np

# Define two example vectors
vector_a = np.array([1, 2, 3])
vector_b = np.array([4, 5, 6])

# Calculate Euclidean distance
euclidean_dist = np.linalg.norm(vector_a - vector_b)

print('Euclidean Distance:', euclidean_dist)
```

Euclidean distance is sensitive to the scale of the data. In tasks where different features vary widely in range, normalization is often required to provide meaningful results.

Manhattan Distance

Manhattan distance, also known as L1 norm, measures the distance between two points along a path strictly aligned with the axis directions. It is calculated as:

$$\text{Manhattan Distance} = \sum_{i=1}^{n} |A_i - B_i|$$

This measure is beneficial when dealing with grid-like path distances or in applications where absolute differences per dimension are desired.

```
from scipy.spatial import distance

# Define two example vectors
vector_a = np.array([1, 2, 3])
vector_b = np.array([4, 5, 6])

# Calculate Manhattan distance
manhattan_dist = distance.cityblock(vector_a, vector_b)

print('Manhattan Distance:', manhattan_dist)
```

The simplicity of Manhattan distance is particularly useful in high-dimensional spaces, where the Euclidean measure may exaggerate the distance due to a large number of dimensions.

Mahalanobis Distance

The Mahalanobis distance considers correlations within a dataset, offering a multivariate measure that accounts for the variance in each dimension and the covariance among dimensions. This distance is defined as:

$$\text{Mahalanobis Distance} = \sqrt{(\mathbf{A} - \mathbf{B})^T \mathbf{S}^{-1} (\mathbf{A} - \mathbf{B})}$$

where $\mathbf{S}^{-1}$ is the inverse covariance matrix of the feature space. Mahalanobis distance is particularly useful for identifying outliers or analyzing datasets with correlated variables.

```python
from scipy.spatial import distance
import numpy as np

# Define two example vectors and their covariance matrix
vector_a = np.array([1, 2])
vector_b = np.array([2, 4])
cov_matrix = np.cov(np.array([vector_a, vector_b]).T)

# Calculate Mahalanobis distance
mahalanobis_dist = distance.mahalanobis(vector_a, vector_b, np.linalg.inv(
    cov_matrix))

print('Mahalanobis Distance:', mahalanobis_dist)
```

The Mahalanobis measure is valuable in multivariate anomaly detection, cluster analysis, and classification, offering a robust method of comparing data points against statistical distributions.

Jaccard Similarity

In scenarios where feature sets rather than continuous values characterize data, Jaccard similarity provides an effective means of quantification. This measure compares two sets to quantify their overlap, defined as:

$$\text{Jaccard Similarity} = \frac{|A \cap B|}{|A \cup B|}$$

Jaccard similarity is widely used in applications such as recommendations, where itemsets are compared rather than individual features.

```python
from scipy.spatial import distance

# Define two binary vectors
vector_a = [0, 1, 1, 0, 1]
```

73

```
vector_b = [1, 1, 0, 0, 1]

# Calculate Jaccard similarity
jaccard_sim = 1 - distance.jaccard(vector_a, vector_b)

print('Jaccard Similarity:', jaccard_sim)
```

Jaccard similarity offers direct insight into the degree of overlap, making it ideal for deduplication tasks, binary classification analysis, and binary input feature spaces.

Vector similarity measures form the bedrock of vector analysis, providing essential metrics to discern relationships among data entries in vector databases. Each method possesses unique strengths and is suited to specific forms of analysis, from accounting for scale variations to overcoming data sparsity challenges. As the diversity of datasets and applications grows, the array of similarity measures continues to expand, facilitating deeper insights and enhanced decision-making through robust data analysis techniques. Encapsulating and leveraging rich data relationships through these measures enables vector databases to underpin advanced computational and analytical paradigms.

3.4 High-Dimensional Data Management

In vector databases, managing high-dimensional data is paramount, owing to the complexity and scale implicated when handling multidimensional datasets. Traditional database systems struggle with high-dimensional data due to exponential increases in the volume of the space, which complicates search, retrieval, and analysis processes. This dimension-related complexity is often referred to as the "curse of dimensionality." Effective management of high-dimensional data encompasses strategies and techniques designed to optimize the processing, storage, and retrieval of data characterized by large numbers of dimensions.

High-dimensional data appears ubiquitously across various fields, including genomics, image and video processing, and machine learning applications. Each field demands tailored strategies to manage the intricate data relationships and extraction of meaningful insights without exorbitant computational costs. The goal is to enable efficient data handling and maintain rapid query performance, even under the weight of thousands of dimensions.

- **Dimensionality Reduction Techniques** - Dimensionality reduction techniques are central to high-dimensional data management. These methods reduce the number of random variables under consideration by creating a set of principal variables. The motivation behind dimensionality reduction is dual: to improve computational efficiency and to aid in data visualization by reducing the clutter in data representation.

- **Principal Component Analysis (PCA)** - PCA is a quintessential dimensionality reduction method that transforms data to a new coordinate system. The transformation is achieved by converting the original variables into a new set of uncorrelated variables, ordered by variance. These new coordinates, known as principal components, capture the greatest variance in the data.

```
from sklearn.decomposition import PCA
import numpy as np

# Assuming 'data' is a matrix where each row is a high-dimensional vector
data = np.random.rand(100, 50) # 100 samples in 50 dimensions

# Apply PCA to reduce dimensions to 10
pca = PCA(n_components=10)
reduced_data = pca.fit_transform(data)

print('Reduced Data Shape:', reduced_data.shape)
```

- **t-Distributed Stochastic Neighbor Embedding (t-SNE)** - t-SNE is another dimensionality reduction technique used for exploring high-dimensional data. Unlike PCA, t-SNE is particularly suited for visualizing high-dimensional datasets by modeling similarities of data points in high-dimensional space as preserving proximity in low-dimensional space.

```
from sklearn.manifold import TSNE
import numpy as np

# Assuming 'data' is a matrix where each row is a high-dimensional vector
data = np.random.rand(100, 50) # 100 samples in 50 dimensions
```

```
# Apply t-SNE to reduce dimensions to 2 for visualization
tsne = TSNE(n_components=2)
embedded_data = tsne.fit_transform(data)

print('Embedded Data Shape:', embedded_data.shape)
```

Dimensionality reduction improves data management by simplifying the dataset, which eases computational requirements and enhances the interpretability of data analytics and visualization.

- **Indexing in High-Dimensional Spaces** - Managing high-dimensional data also involves efficient indexing structures to facilitate quick and accurate data retrieval. With the increase in dimensions, traditional indexing techniques such as B-trees become inefficient due to sparsity in high-dimensional spaces. Therefore, advanced indexing strategies are crucial.

- **Approximate Nearest Neighbor (ANN)** - search algorithms, such as Locality-Sensitive Hashing (LSH) and trees like KD-Trees and Ball Trees, are typically used to address these challenges. These algorithms aim to balance between search accuracy and computational efficiency.

```
from annoy import AnnoyIndex
import numpy as np

# Create an Annoy index for Euclidean distance
f = 100 # number of dimensions
t = AnnoyIndex(f, 'euclidean')

# Add items to the index
for i in range(1000):
    v = np.random.random(f)
    t.add_item(i, v)

# Build the index
t.build(10) # 10 trees

# Perform a query to find the nearest neighbors
nearest_neighbors = t.get_nns_by_item(0, 10)

print('Nearest Neighbors:', nearest_neighbors)
```

- **Feature Selection Strategies** - Feature selection is a pivotal strategy in high-dimensional data management, focusing on

76

identifying and utilizing the most relevant dimensions, thereby reducing the dimensionality. Feature selection helps reduce over-fitting, enhances generalization performance, and significantly diminishes computational load.

- **Filter Methods** - Filter methods leverage statistical measures to score each feature for its relevance with the response variable. Methods such as correlation coefficients or mutual information are employed to filter out less informative features before model training.

```
from sklearn.feature_selection import SelectKBest, f_regression
import numpy as np

# Sample data
X = np.random.rand(100, 50)
y = np.random.rand(100)

# Apply SelectKBest to choose top 10 features based on correlation
best_features = SelectKBest(score_func=f_regression, k=10)
X_new = best_features.fit_transform(X, y)

print('Selected Features Shape:', X_new.shape)
```

- **Wrapper Methods** - Wrapper methods involve using a predictive model to score feature subsets, searching through the space of possible features and evaluating them based on model performance. Recursive feature elimination is an example where features are recursively pruned, keeping the best-performing subset.

```
from sklearn.feature_selection import RFE
from sklearn.linear_model import LinearRegression
import numpy as np

# Sample data
X = np.random.rand(100, 50)
y = np.random.rand(100)

# Use linear regression as the model
model = LinearRegression()

# Apply RFE to select top 10 features
selector = RFE(model, n_features_to_select=10, step=1)
X_rfe = selector.fit_transform(X, y)

print('Selected Features Shape:', X_rfe.shape)
```

77

- **Scalability Strategies in High-Dimensional Data Management** - Effective high-dimensional data management entails developing systems that can scale with data growth. Scalability challenges are particularly evident when handling vast datasets characterized by massive dimensions, which demand resources beyond the capacity of standard sequential processing.

- To address scalability, one approach is to distribute data across multiple nodes using parallel and distributed computing frameworks such as Apache Spark. By distributing data and tasks, it is possible to reduce the time complexity of computations and accommodate larger datasets efficiently.

- **Parallel Processing with Spark** - offers an environment to execute large-scale data processing tasks. Data is distributed across a cluster, and computations are parallelized, allowing for the efficient handling of immense datasets.

```
from pyspark import SparkContext
from pyspark.sql import SparkSession
import numpy as np

# Initialize Spark session
spark = SparkSession.builder.appName("HighDimensionalDataProcessing").
    getOrCreate()

# Create a Spark DataFrame
data = np.random.rand(10000, 100) # 10,000 samples in 100 dimensions
df = spark.createDataFrame(data.tolist())

# Example processing: selecting the first column
df_selected = df.selectExpr("_1 as feature1")

print('Data processing complete with Spark.')
```

- **Challenges and Future Outlook** - Despite advances in algorithms and processing capabilities, high-dimensional data management continues to face challenges related to computational efficiency, storage capacity, and the complexity of querying across sparse data spaces. The need to balance between exactness, approximation, and performance remains critical.

- Future approaches in high-dimensional data management will likely revolve around further optimizing existing algorithms and

78

architecture innovations to handle data efficiently. Hybrid approaches integrating machine learning and traditional database methods may evolve to prioritize intelligent data summarization, metadata-driven indexing, and real-time processing capabilities.

- Advancements in quantum computing may offer paradigms for exponentially accelerating high-dimensional computations, while developments in AI could drive autonomous indexing and real-time error correction among vast datasets. As technology evolves, so will the strategies for handling the ever-increasing volume and dimensionality of data, enabling more robust and insightful data management capabilities across varied fields.

3.5 Query Processing Techniques

Query processing is a critical aspect of vector databases, responsible for executing and optimizing queries efficiently to provide relevant data results swiftly. The challenges inherent in high-dimensional vector data necessitate sophisticated techniques to ensure performance and accuracy. Effective query processing involves a balance between minimizing computational resources and maximizing retrieval accuracy across potentially vast and complex datasets.

In vector databases, query processing can encompass various operations, including similarity search, range queries, and nearest neighbor queries. Due to the unique structure of vector data, traditional query processing techniques often fall short, necessitating the development of specialized strategies designed to capitalize on the mathematical properties inherent in vector spaces.

Similarity Search and Nearest Neighbor Queries

Similarity search is a core function in vector databases, aimed at finding vectors similar to a given query vector based on a defined similarity measure. Nearest neighbor search is the most common form of similarity search, targeting data points closest to the query vector in terms of a given distance metric.

One effective method for performing nearest neighbor searches in vector spaces is utilizing Approximate Nearest Neighbors (ANN) algorithms. Techniques such as Locality-Sensitive Hashing (LSH), KD-Trees, and more sophisticated Hierarchical Navigable Small World (HNSW) graphs are frequently employed due to their ability to balance speed and precision.

```
import faiss
import numpy as np

# Create random high-dimensional data
data = np.random.random((10000, 128)).astype('float32')

# Construct the index
index = faiss.IndexFlatL2(128)
index.add(data)

# Perform a query
query = np.random.random((1, 128)).astype('float32')
distances, indices = index.search(query, k=10)

print('Nearest neighbors by index:', indices)
print('Distances:', distances)
```

FAISS, developed by Facebook AI Research, is a library highly optimized for similarity search and dense vector clustering. It provides state-of-the-art implementations to perform queries with large datasets efficiently.

Range Queries in Vector Spaces

Range queries allow users to retrieve data points within a specific distance or similarity threshold relative to a query vector. These queries are crucial when the aim is to identify clusters or areas in the vector space that share common features at varying degrees of similarity.

One technique for optimizing range queries is the use of space-filling curves, such as the Hilbert or Z-order curve, which linearize multi-dimensional spaces to preserve locality. By converting high-dimensional coordinates into one-dimensional values, it is feasible to apply binary search techniques to expedite query processing.

```
import numpy as np

# Define a threshold distance
threshold = 0.2

# Function to perform range query based on Euclidean distance
def range_query(data, query_vector, threshold):
    return [i for i, vector in enumerate(data) if np.linalg.norm(vector - query_vector) <
        threshold]
```

80

```
# Generate random data and query
data = np.random.random((1000, 128))
query_vector = np.random.random((128))

# Find vectors within the threshold
result = range_query(data, query_vector, threshold)
print('Indices within range:', result)
```

While simple threshold methods can be used, they are computationally expensive for very large databases, and thus indexing methods that can prune the search space more efficiently are often desirable.

Query Optimization Techniques

Query optimization is the process of enhancing the execution plan for database queries to improve processing time and resource utilization. In vector databases, optimization can be achieved at the algorithmic level as well as through the leverage of advanced indexing structures.

- **Algorithmic Optimization** involves modifications to the search algorithms themselves to improve performance. For example, leveraging hierarchical indexes like HNSW allows the queries to start from coarse-grained searches and iteratively drill down to finer precision, reducing unnecessary distance calculations.

- **Caching Mechanisms**, including result caching and metadata caching, can significantly reduce the need for repeated computations by storing the results of frequent queries or pre-calculated distances, particularly in environments where the same queries recur regularly.

- **Cost-based Optimization** evaluates various query execution plans and selects the most efficient one based on cost estimations of processing times and resource usage. Analyzing the computational expense, such as CPU, memory usage, and disk I/O, aids in refining which paths a query could take through indexed data.

Parallel Query Execution

Given the computational demands of querying high-dimensional data, parallel processing techniques are crucial for maintaining performance and scalability. By decomposing the query workload across multiple

81

processors or nodes, the load can be distributed, considerably reducing execution time.

Frameworks such as Apache Spark provide robust infrastructure for parallelizing data operations. Utilizing Spark's built-in functionality allows vector databases to implement distributed query processing, leveraging data partitioning and parallel task execution capabilities.

```
from pyspark.sql import SparkSession
import numpy as np

# Initialize Spark session
spark = SparkSession.builder.appName("VectorQueryProcessing").getOrCreate()

# Create random high-dimensional data
data = np.random.random((100000, 128)).tolist()

# Create a DataFrame in Spark
df = spark.createDataFrame(data)

# Example: perform map operation to compute vector norms
norms = df.rdd.map(lambda row: np.linalg.norm(row)).collect()

print('Data norms computed with Spark.')
```

Parallel query execution not only enhances performance but also supports greater fault tolerance, as distributed systems can route around node failure, ensuring continuity in query processing.

Challenges in Query Processing for Vector Databases

The primary challenge in query processing for vector databases lies in efficiently addressing the computational intensity of high-dimensional spaces. Complexity grows significantly with increased dimensions, leading to potential performance bottlenecks.

- Scalability: Handling growth in data dimensions while ensuring response times remain within acceptable limits.

- Accuracy vs. Performance: Balancing computational accuracy against the need for quick response times, especially in approximation-based retrieval methods.

- Resource Utilization: Ensuring efficient CPU, memory, and I/O usage, especially in distributed environments where resources are shared among various processes.

Emerging Trends and Future Directions

As the fields relying on vector data expand, query processing techniques will need to evolve to accommodate increasingly diverse demands. Among the trends and anticipated advancements are:

- Machine Learning Integration: The integration of machine learning models for predictive query optimization, potentially allowing databases proactively to reindex or cache data based on expected future queries.

- Quantum Computing: Harnessing quantum computing's potential to facilitate high-dimensional computations exponentially faster than classical methods.

- Adaptive Index Structures: Development of adaptive indexing strategies that dynamically tune parameters based on workload shifts, maintaining optimal query performance with minimal manual intervention.

Continuous research and development in query processing techniques promise to enhance the capability and efficiency of vector databases, ensuring they can meet the demands of ever-increasing data complexity and scale effectively. These innovations will be integral to empowering data-driven discoveries and applications across diverse domains reliant on rich, high-dimensional data.

3.6 Data Storage and Retrieval

The design and implementation of data storage and retrieval mechanisms are vital elements in the architecture of vector databases. As data operations increasingly leverage high-dimensional vector representations, the chosen strategies significantly influence the system's performance, scalability, and flexibility. Vector databases are engineered to facilitate rapid access, efficient storage, and precise management of vast datasets characterized by numerous dimensions and complex relationships.

High-dimensional vector data demands storage solutions that can maintain structural integrity and allow for fast retrieval. Maximizing

storage efficiency without compromising data accuracy poses technical challenges, necessitating innovative solutions for optimal data management.

- **Columnar Storage Architecture** is one approach employed
  for storing vector data, which involves organizing data in
  columns instead of rows. This architecture is particularly
  advantageous for analytical queries, as it allows for the efficient
  scanning of relevant dimensions without the need to access
  entire rows, reducing the I/O load.

```
import pyarrow as pa
import numpy as np

# Create high-dimensional data
data = {'feature_' + str(i): list(np.random.rand(100000)) for i in range(128)}
table = pa.table(data)

# Store columnar data with PyArrow
with pa.OSFile('data.arrow', 'wb') as sink:
    with pa.RecordBatchFileWriter(sink, table.schema) as writer:
        writer.write_table(table)

print('Columnar storage complete with PyArrow.')
```

- **Distributed File Systems**, such as Hadoop Distributed File
  System (HDFS), are integral to managing large-scale vector
  databases by distributing data across clusters of nodes. By
  partitioning data effectively, distributed systems enhance both
  fault tolerance and parallel processing capabilities.

```
import pyarrow as pa
import pyarrow.hdfs as hdfs

# Establish connection to HDFS
hdfs_client = hdfs.connect('hdfs://namenode:8020')

# Path to store data in HDFS
path = '/user/hadoop/vector_data.parquet'
hdfs_client.mkdir('/user/hadoop')

# Write table to HDFS
with hdfs_client.open(path, 'wb') as sink:
    with pa.RecordBatchFileWriter(sink, table.schema) as writer:
        writer.write_table(table)

print('Data storage in HDFS complete.')
```

- **Vector Data Compression**

Given the potentially large size and high dimensionality of vector datasets, effective compression techniques are essential to reduce storage requirements and increase retrieval speed. Compression enables the storage of data in a more compact form, significantly decreasing the space needed while maintaining the ability to quickly decompress as needed for operations.

- **Dimensionality Reduction** can serve as a form of compression, where techniques like Principal Component Analysis (PCA) reduce the dimensions of vector data without significant loss of information, inherently compressing the data.

- **Run-Length Encoding (RLE)**, **Delta Encoding**, and **Dictionary Encoding** are other columnar storage compression techniques that optimize storage by exploiting redundancy within columns, important for memory optimization, especially in columnar databases.

```
import pyarrow.parquet as pq

# Compress and write parquet file
pq.write_table(table, 'compressed_data.parquet', compression='snappy')

print('Data compression with Parquet completed.')
```

Snappy, GZIP, and LZO are commonly used algorithms in vector databases for their lightweight yet efficient compression capabilities, making them suitable for real-time querying and analytics.

- **Efficient Data Retrieval Techniques**

Efficient retrieval of high-dimensional vector data is critical, requiring methods that can quickly locate and access required data points. The ability to search efficiently is often contingent on the careful indexing of data and the development of retrieval algorithms that exploit these indexes.

- **Inverted Indexes** are widely used for fast searching in vector databases, mapping terms (or vector components) to the docu-

85

ment or item identifiers containing them. This allows quick data retrieval based on specific feature queries.

- **Vector Approximation** techniques are applied to simplify retrieval operations. By approximating data vectors into more searchable forms such as embeddings or centroids, these algorithms enable fast yet accurate searches.

- **Caching strategies**, including query result caching and intermediate data caching, can effectively reduce repetitive processing times by storing and reusing previously computed results, significantly improving retrieval speed, especially in environments where similar queries occur frequently.

- **Real-time Retrieval Applications**

Real-time applications, such as online recommendation systems and personalized search engines, exist within a growing realm of use cases benefiting from efficient vector data retrieval. Such systems require rapid access to the most relevant vector data, demanding both speed and accuracy to sustain user interaction.

- **Vector Embeddings** are often leveraged in these environments, where complex items like images or texts are converted into dense vectors. Retrieval algorithms match user queries to these embeddings to identify the closest or most similar data points efficiently.

```
import faiss

# Simulating vector embeddings for a dataset
embedding_dimension = 128
embeddings = np.random.random((5000, embedding_dimension)).astype('float32')

# Creating a FAISS index
index = faiss.IndexFlatL2(embedding_dimension)
index.add(embeddings)

# Real-time query example
query_vector = np.random.random((1, embedding_dimension)).astype('float32')
distances, indices = index.search(query_vector, k=5)

print('Real-time retrieval indices:', indices)
```

- **Backup and Recovery Mechanisms**

The availability and resilience of vector databases hinge on robust backup and recovery strategies. As organizations depend increasingly on the integrity of data within these systems, strategies that ensure data can be quickly and safely restored in the event of loss or corruption are integral.

Snapshotted backups capture the current state of the database at scheduled intervals. These backups are stored on secure, distributed systems, ensuring redundancy and availability. Recovery plans involve automated scripts to restore data from snapshots, supporting rapid resumption of operations.

- **Differential and Incremental Backups** offer refined backup strategies, capturing only changes since the last backup. These methods optimize storage and minimize data transfer requirements, crucial for databases dealing with constant data updates or insertions.

```bash
#!/bin/bash

# Directory paths
SRC_DIR=hdfs://namenode:8020/user/hadoop/vector_data
BACKUP_DIR=hdfs://namenode:8020/user/hadoop/backup

# Creating a timestamped backup
current_time=$(date +"%Y-%m-%d_%H-%M-%S")
hadoop distcp $SRC_DIR $BACKUP_DIR/$current_time

echo "Backup completed for $current_time"
```

These backup solutions support business continuity and safeguard against data loss, providing organizations with confidence in their data infrastructure.

Data storage and retrieval in vector databases represent a convergence of modern storage architectures, efficient retrieval algorithms, and robust data management principles. High-dimensional vector data introduces specific challenges that are expertly addressed through innovations in storage, compression, and retrieval methodologies. As the demand for real-time data accessibility and scalable storage solutions continues to grow, vector databases are poised to play an increasingly

87

pivotal role in enabling advanced data-intensive applications, ensuring quick, reliable, and efficient data operations.

3.7 Consistency and Reliability

In the ecosystem of vector databases, ensuring consistency and reliability is fundamental for maintaining data integrity, accuracy, and trustworthiness in the face of operations critical to modern applications. As vector databases are leveraged increasingly in fields requiring high-dimensional data handling—such as artificial intelligence, data analytics, and real-time recommendations—these databases must uphold stringent standards to avoid discrepancies, ensure data availability, and prevent loss.

Consistency in databases refers to the guarantee that data remains in a valid state across various operations, ensuring that all users see the same view of the data over time. In the context of vector databases, consistency is particularly vital due to the complexity and high interconnectivity of vector data.

Strong Consistency ensures that after a transaction is completed, all future queries will reflect the outcome of that transaction. This model is akin to the atomicity, consistency, isolation, durability (ACID) properties in traditional databases, and is often implemented through two-phase commit protocols and locks.

```
from threading import Lock

data = {}
lock = Lock()

def update_vector(key, new_value):
    with lock:
        # Transaction begin
        data[key] = new_value
        # Additional consistency checks can be done here
        # Transaction end

update_vector('vector_key', [0.1, 0.2, 0.3])
```

Eventual Consistency is typically adopted in distributed systems when it is acceptable for different nodes to hold inconsistent states temporarily, provided they converge to a single consistent state eventually. This model is beneficial for systems focusing on availability and partition tolerance, as in the CAP theorem, and is common in systems requiring high throughput and low latency.

Causal Consistency strengthens eventual consistency by maintaining order for related updates, ensuring that causally related writes are seen by all nodes in the same sequence. This is particularly advantageous in collaborative environments where tracking the order of operations matters.

Reliability in vector databases guarantees that the data is persistently available and correct, even in the face of system failures, network losses, or other unexpected events. Ensuring reliability involves the implementation of protocols and systems that can detect, compensate for, and recover from failures.

Replication involves creating multiple copies of data across different nodes or locations. This redundancy supports not only fault tolerance in the event of node failure but also aids in load balancing and reduces latency by bringing data closer to users across geographical distances.

```
replica_data_center = {}

def replicate_data(key, value, datacenters):
    for dc in datacenters:
        if dc not in replica_data_center:
            replica_data_center[dc] = {}
        replica_data_center[dc][key] = value

datacenters = ['us-west', 'us-east', 'eu-central']
replicate_data('vector_key', [0.1, 0.2, 0.3], datacenters)
```

Data Sharding is a method of database partitioning that splits vector data across multiple databases or servers. Sharding helps in distributing the data load, enhancing performance, and facilitating horizontal scaling. By segmenting data, sharding allows databases to handle larger datasets without degrading performance, ensuring reliability as the dataset grows.

```
def shard_vector_data(data, num_shards):
    sharded_data = [[] for _ in range(num_shards)]
    for i, vector in enumerate(data):
        shard_id = i % num_shards
        sharded_data[shard_id].append(vector)
    return sharded_data

# Simulate vector data
vector_data = [list(range(10)) for _ in range(30)]
```

```
sharded = shard_vector_data(vector_data, 3)
print('Sharded Data:', sharded)
```

Continuous monitoring and well-defined failure recovery protocols are vital for maintaining consistency and reliability. Monitoring tools capture system metrics, data integrity, and query performance in real time, allowing immediate detection of anomalies or failures.

Automated Recovery Systems employ strategies such as checkpoints, snapshots, and transactional logs to automate recovery processes, minimizing downtime and data loss in the wake of failures. Systems often utilize logs to replay transactions up to a failure point, ensuring the database can revert to a consistent state efficiently.

The distributed nature of many vector databases, necessary for handling large-scale data operations, introduces challenges in maintaining consistency and reliability:

- **Network Partitions**: In distributed databases, network failures can isolate nodes, resulting in inconsistent data views. Effective partition tolerance strategies are essential to maintain operations during these partitions.

- **Replica Divergence**: Ensuring all replicas reflect the latest data changes is a challenge. Systems must efficiently manage conflicts and coordinate updates across replicas to maintain consistency.

Ensuring data integrity requires an emphasis on atomicity in database transactions. Atomic transactions ensure that all operations within a transaction are completed successfully or none at all, crucial for maintaining database integrity amidst complex data manipulations.

Multi-version Concurrency Control (MVCC) is a concurrency control method used in many databases to manage transactions without locking, enhancing system throughput and scalability while maintaining atomic transactions.

```
class MVCCDatabase:
    def __init__(self):
        self.data = {}
        self.versions = {}
```

```
def write__data(self, key, version, value):
    if key not in self.versions or self.versions[key] < version:
        self.data[key] = value
        self.versions[key] = version

def read__data(self, key):
    return self.data.get(key, None)

database = MVCCDatabase()
database.write__data('vector__key', 1, [0.1, 0.2, 0.3])
database.write__data('vector__key', 2, [0.4, 0.5, 0.6])
print('Current version:', database.read__data('vector__key'))
```

MVCC allows multiple versions of a data item to exist, supporting concurrent read and write actions without immediate locking, and assuring data integrity by controlling transaction version conflict.

As datasets grow exponentially, future trends in consistency and reliability will likely involve advances in several areas:

- **Blockchain for Data Integrity**: Employing blockchain technology for immutable data logs and decentralized consensus mechanisms could add robust layers of integrity and tamper-proofing to vector databases.

- **Machine Learning for Anomaly Detection**: Utilizing machine learning to intelligently monitor systems and predict failures before they occur could significantly bolster reliability by activating preemptive responses.

- **Graph-based Consistency Models**: Leveraging graph-based methods for tracking dependency and causal relationships among data can maintain consistency in complex and dynamic data environments.

Ensuring consistency and reliability in vector databases is crucial for data-intensive applications and networked systems dependent on the timely and accurate retrieval of quality data. As these systems continue to evolve, deploying advanced algorithms and technologies will become foundational to managing the growing scale and complexity of vectorized data environments, ensuring that databases not only maintain their robustness but also advance in their capabilities.

Chapter 4

Indexing and Querying in Vector Databases

Effective indexing and querying in vector databases are crucial for optimizing data retrieval and ensuring efficient performance. This chapter examines various indexing techniques, including tree-based and hash-based methods, designed to improve the speed and accuracy of query responses. It also explores strategies for processing both exact and approximate queries, particularly focusing on nearest neighbor searches in high-dimensional spaces. The discussion emphasizes the importance of scalable indexing solutions and query optimization techniques, essential for managing the complexity and demands of modern data-driven applications.

4.1 Basics of Indexing in Vector Databases

Indexing in vector databases is pivotal for the efficient retrieval of data, particularly given the rising popularity of machine learning and artificial intelligence applications. In vector databases, data is often stored in high-dimensional spaces, which poses unique challenges for indexing and querying. As opposed to traditional databases that manage scalar values, a vector database deals with complex data types like images, audio, text, and other forms that are often represented as vectors. To handle the complexities of these data types efficiently, robust indexing approaches are employed.

The primary goal of indexing is to reduce the time complexity of query operations by organizing data for quick lookups. This is especially important in vector databases, where brute-force search is computationally expensive due to the high dimensionality of data. The curse of dimensionality typically manifests as increased computational costs and reduced accuracy of search results. Hence, a well-structured indexing mechanism is essential to mitigate these issues.

High-dimensional vectors are commonly used to represent data in vector databases, as they capture essential features of the datasets they model. Consider, for instance, image recognition systems where each image is converted into a feature vector representing various aspects of that image, such as color histograms or edge concentrations. When indexing these vectors, several techniques can be employed to accommodate their complexity and improve query responses.

Data indexing in vector databases involves several tasks, such as:

- Data Partitioning: Segmenting the dataset into manageable partitions that can be processed independently.

- Data Clustering: Grouping data based on similarity so that similar data points are located close to each other, facilitating efficient search and retrieval.

- Efficient Storage Structure: Optimizing the data layout on disk to minimize access time and make use of caching phenomena.

- Fast Lookup Algorithms: Using algorithmic optimizations to quickly locate data points relevant to a given query.

The role of indexing becomes crucial when dealing with nearest neighbor searches, a common operation in vector databases. Nearest neighbor search aims to find data points in the database that are closest to a given query point, according to some distance metric. Without efficient indexing, such searches become prohibitively expensive in high-dimensional spaces due to the requirement to compute distances to many or all points in the dataset. An effective indexing strategy, therefore, greatly improves the performance of nearest neighbor searches by pruning the search space significantly.

```python
from scipy.spatial import KDTree

def build_kd_tree(data):
    """Build a k-d tree from given data points."""
    return KDTree(data)

def nearest_neighbor_search(tree, query_point):
    """Find the nearest neighbor of query_point in the k-d tree."""
    distance, index = tree.query(query_point)
    return distance, index

# Example Usage
data_points = [[2.0, 3.0], [5.0, 4.0], [9.0, 6.0], [4.0, 7.0], [8.0, 1.0], [7.0, 2.0]]
kd_tree = build_kd_tree(data_points)
query = [2.0, 4.5]
nearest = nearest_neighbor_search(kd_tree, query)
print(f"Nearest neighbor: {data_points[nearest[1]]}, Distance: {nearest[0]}")
```

In the above example, a k-d tree, one of the simplest and most effective indexing strategies for low to moderate dimensions, is constructed using the scipy library. This data structure supports efficient retrieval of the nearest neighbors to a query point by recursively partitioning the data space into nested regions, thereby reducing the number of points that need to be examined.

For multidimensional data of significantly higher dimensionality, however, k-d trees become inefficient, necessitating the development and use of other specialized data structures and algorithms, such as Locality-Sensitive Hashing (LSH) and Approximate Nearest Neighbor (ANN) techniques.

The concept of LSH is particularly notable in handling high-dimensional data efficiently. Rather than attempting to partition the entire data space into definitive regions, LSH uses hash functions to map similar input vectors to the same or nearby bins more likely. This results in reduced computational resources being expended for both space and time when performing nearest neighbor queries.

```python
import numpy as np
from sklearn.neighbors import LSHForest
```

```
def build_lsh_forest(data, n_estimators=10, n_candidates=50):
    """Build a Locality-Sensitive Hashing forest."""
    lshf = LSHForest(n_estimators=n_estimators, n_candidates=n_candidates)
    lshf.fit(data)
    return lshf

def approximate_nn_search(lsh, query_point):
    """Approximate nearest neighbor search using LSH."""
    distances, indices = lsh.kneighbors([query_point])
    return distances[0], indices[0]

# Example Usage
data_points = np.random.rand(100, 128) # Suppose we have 100 points in 128
    dimensions
lsh_forest = build_lsh_forest(data_points)
query = np.random.rand(128)
nearest_distances, nearest_indices = approximate_nn_search(lsh_forest, query)
print(f"Nearest neighbors indices: {nearest_indices}, Distances: {nearest_distances}")
```

One of the essential characteristics of efficient indexing systems is their ability to adapt to dynamic datasets. As vector databases often encounter frequent updates, deletions, and insertions, the underlying indexing structures must support operations without necessitating a complete rebuild. For this reason, many state-of-the-art indexing systems use dynamic structures, such as R-trees and their variants, which support adjustments in response to structural changes.

Another advanced indexing concept crucial in vector databases is the use of inversion indexing methods, mainly derived from text retrieval systems, yet finding applications in vector spaces — especially sparse ones. Inverted indices facilitate rapid query execution by mapping features to their corresponding data point identifiers. While frequently used for sparse vector representations, they can be adapted to dense data scenarios through techniques like Product Quantization (PQ) which enable dense vectors to be interpreted in a sparse fashion through quantization.

Modern vector databases also leverage combinations of these strategies, utilizing layered architectures to handle varying workloads and performance constraints effectively. For instance, combining approximate techniques like LSH with precise methods like tree-based indexing can balance query accuracy with speed, allowing for flexible responses to dynamic user needs.

In practice, deciding upon an indexing strategy often involves extensive benchmarking across different possible configurations and workload types to find the optimal balance between indexing speed, query performance, and storage costs. By understanding the specific characteristics of the dataset, including dimensionality, vector sparsity, and query frequency, developers can tailor their indexing strategies to meet the demands of their application environment efficiently.

Vector databases, an integral part of advanced computational frameworks, are increasingly leveraging the prowess of machine learning. Incorporating learned indexes, which utilize machine learning models to predict the location of index entries, has been shown to outperform traditional index techniques in various scenarios by reducing both lookup times and storage overhead.

Such integration of machine learning techniques with classical index strategies fosters hybrid systems that adapt dynamically to changes in both data and query distribution. It presages a future where indexes continue to evolve rapidly, adopting intelligent systems that learn and improve over time, thus continuously optimizing performance.

The fundamentals of indexing in vector databases are multi-faceted, comprising several advanced concepts and methodologies that together constitute the toolkit required for robust database management in the context of high-dimensional data retrieval. The ability to tailor these strategies to the specificities of individual use cases will remain a key determinant of the effectiveness of vector databases in fulfilling the needs of increasingly data-intensive applications across industries.

4.2 Types of Indexing Techniques

Indexing techniques are critical for optimizing data retrieval in vector databases, especially given the complex nature of the data that these systems typically handle. The choice of indexing method can significantly impact the efficiency of query execution, data organization, and overall system performance. Various indexing techniques cater to different aspects of vector database requirements, each with its unique strengths and trade-offs.

The primary types of indexing techniques can be broadly categorized into tree-based, hash-based, and inverted index methods. Each of these approaches serves distinct purposes, offering particular advantages applicable to specific data structures and query types.

Tree-based indexing techniques are among the most common methods used in vector databases due to their intuitive data partitioning capabilities. In this category, we discuss k-d trees, R-trees, and B-trees, among others. These structures are particularly useful for multidimensional data management:

- **k-d Trees (k-dimensional Trees)**: A k-d tree is a binary tree that partitions space in k-dimensional space, making it well-suited for range queries and nearest neighbor searches. The tree is constructed by recursively splitting the dataset along one dimension at each level of the tree. By alternating the splitting dimension, a balanced tree with efficient search properties can be created.

```
import numpy as np
from scipy.spatial import KDTree

# Sample data points in 2D
data_points = np.random.rand(100, 2)

# Constructing a k-d Tree
kd_tree = KDTree(data_points)

# Querying for nearest neighbors
query_point = np.random.rand(2)
dist, index = kd_tree.query(query_point, k=3)
print(f"Nearest neighbors: {data_points[index]}")
```

  k-d trees are primarily effective in low-dimensional spaces; performance can degrade due to the curse of dimensionality for datasets with high dimensions, where the probability of many points being equidistant in space increases.

- **R-trees**: R-trees are another tree-based structure designed to manage multidimensional spatial data. Unlike k-d trees, R-trees utilize bounding rectangles to create hierarchical structures. Each node represents the minimum bounding rectangle (MBR) that contains its children, allowing overlap, which can contribute to query complexity.

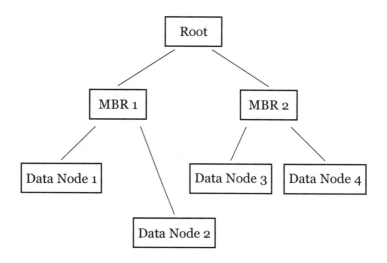

Though R-trees are designed to handle overlapping regions better, this characteristic can slow down the query if the overlap increases, necessitating visits to multiple branches during a search.

- **B-trees and their Variants**: B-trees are balanced tree data structures that maintain sorted data and allow for searches, sequential access, insertions, and deletions in logarithmic time. They are not ideal for highly complex vector data due to lack of multidimensional partitioning capability but remain an essential underpinning for disk-based storage, providing efficient indexing for more traditional database systems.

Hash-based indexing methods are particularly advantageous when dealing with operations that need constant time complexity. Locality-Sensitive Hashing (LSH) is one prominent technique in this category:

- **Locality-Sensitive Hashing (LSH)**: This technique effectively handles high-dimensional data by hashing input items in such a way that similar items map to the same "buckets" with high probability. The underlying principle involves using hash functions sensitive to local similarities, hence facilitating approximate nearest neighbor search.

99

```
from sklearn.random_projection import SparseRandomProjection

# Example data points in high dimensions
data_points = np.random.rand(1000, 128)

# Applying random projection
transformer = SparseRandomProjection(n_components=128)
data_projected = transformer.fit_transform(data_points)

# Hash points to bins
hash_buckets = {}
for i, point in enumerate(data_projected):
    hash_key = tuple(np.round(point))
    if hash_key not in hash_buckets:
        hash_buckets[hash_key] = []
    hash_buckets[hash_key].append(i)
```

LSH is particularly beneficial in scenarios where significant computational resources are required for exhaustive search, enabling reductions in search time while tolerating a degree of approximation.

Lastly, inverted indexes form an essential part of indexing techniques, predominantly used in document retrieval systems and information retrieval settings, adapted for vector databases.

- **Inverted Index**: An inverted index maintains mappings from content, typically words or features, to their locations in a dataset, allowing quick search and retrieval. In vector databases, this approach can be adapted for sparse vectors, where each dimension corresponds to features or codes derived using techniques like Product Quantization.

  The flexibility in mapping and retrieval operations makes inverted indexes attractive in scenarios where quick, repeated queries against the same dataset are crucial. The inversion process allows for extreme query optimization by narrowing down search scopes quickly.

Despite these indexing methods offering substantial capabilities, it is important to note that, in vector databases, hybrids or ensembles of these techniques are often used to achieve desirable performance outcomes.

100

For example, combining the robust partitioning of tree-based models with the speed of hash-based approaches can provide an effective solution in both query execution acceleration and dimensionality management. Additionally, the integrity of an index technique's performance is frequently influenced by preprocessing steps like dimensionality reduction (using PCA or t-SNE) or data transformation (normalization).

Moreover, with advancements in computing technologies such as GPU-based processing, real-time indexing, and search facilities have become feasible, further augmenting these indexing techniques with a layer of computational efficiency that was previously unattainable.

In vector databases, the design of these indexing systems dictates their scalability, response to growth, and ability to accommodate expanding datasets or increasing dimensions. A comprehensive understanding of these indexing techniques will enable practitioners to tailor their database systems best suited to work integrally with their specific operational requirements and datasets, optimizing query processes and ensuring robust database functionality.

4.3   Efficient Query Processing

Efficient query processing in vector databases is critical to managing and analyzing large volumes of high-dimensional data. Vector databases, which cater to a variety of applications from recommendation systems to image recognition, rely heavily on robust querying capabilities for retrieving relevant data promptly. Given the complexity inherent in multidimensional datasets, optimizing query processing requires a careful consideration of algorithms, data structures, and execution strategies that are specifically designed to handle the unique challenges of vector data.

The primary challenge in processing queries efficiently lies in the high dimensionality of vector data. This situation, often referred to as the "curse of dimensionality," results in increased computational cost and decreased efficiency of traditional search techniques. Addressing this efficiently involves leveraging advanced techniques such as approximate query processing, dimensionality reduction, parallel processing, and machine learning-based enhancements.

Key strategies for efficient query processing include:

- **Approximate Query Processing (AQP)**: AQP techniques focus on providing fast, approximate answers to queries, which are often satisfactory for practical applications. These approaches trade off some precision for improved computational speed and reduced resource consumption. AQP is particularly beneficial in exploratory data analysis and situations where speed is prioritized over perfect accuracy.

- **Dimensionality Reduction**: Reducing the number of dimensions in vector data helps diminish the complexity and computational cost associated with querying high-dimensional spaces. Techniques such as Principal Component Analysis (PCA) and t-distributed Stochastic Neighbor Embedding (t-SNE) transform high-dimensional data into lower-dimensional forms while preserving essential characteristics. Reduced-dimensional spaces facilitate faster and more efficient querying.

```
from sklearn.decomposition import PCA
import numpy as np

# Sample high-dimensional data
data_points = np.random.rand(1000, 128)

# Applying PCA to reduce dimensions to 10
pca = PCA(n_components=10)
reduced_data = pca.fit_transform(data_points)

# Efficient querying can be performed on reduced_data
```

- **Parallel Query Execution**: Modern vector databases can utilize parallel processing capabilities of contemporary hardware, such as multi-core CPUs and GPUs, to execute queries concurrently. This approach increases throughput and efficiency, especially for complex queries that involve large scans or calculations.

- **Data Partitioning and Indexing**: Properly partitioning data and maintaining efficient index structures dramatically enhance query execution speed. By reducing the volume of data that needs to be scanned at query time, indices such as k-d trees, R-trees, and hash-based methods enable focused searches in pertinent data subsets. The adoption of these structures should consider the query patterns and typical workload to accommodate expected operations effectively.

- **Query Optimization Techniques**: Techniques like query rewriting, automatic query plan generation, and heuristic optimization methods aim to refine query execution plans. Optimal algorithms not only improve execution speed but also ensure that resource usage is managed efficiently.

- **Caching and Materialized Views**: Caching common query results and utilizing materialized views can significantly improve repeated query performance. By maintaining query results over time, systems can deliver quick responses to frequently executed queries without reprocessing them fully.

```
CREATE MATERIALIZED VIEW fast_access_view AS
SELECT product_id, AVG(score) as avg_score
FROM product_ratings
GROUP BY product_id;
-- This view can be refreshed periodically or updated incrementally to keep data
    current
```

- **Utilizing Query Acceleration Features**: Leveraging specialized hardware capabilities, such as GPU-accelerated databases, facilitates high-speed data processing suitable for vector operations. These accelerators can process large amounts of vector data in parallel, reducing computation times for queries that involve complex calculations.

In implementing these practices, an effective system must reconcile the differences between the precision of returned results and the complexity of operations executing under potentially stringent performance requirements. For applications that demand real-time performance such as recommendation services, balancing execution latency with computation cost is particularly significant.

The foundation of efficient query processing also hinges on understanding the workload and query patterns typical to the application context. Adaptive systems that learn and predict usage patterns can dynamically optimize queries, routing them through optimized execution paths. Machine learning models play an instrumental role in simulating these adaptive techniques, predicting query evaluations, and optimizing database systems' tuning through recommendations based on both historical and contextual data.

```
from sklearn.linear_model import LinearRegression

# Assuming previous query time data is available
features = np.array([[query1_features], [query2_features], ...]) # feature vectors for
    different queries
exec_times = np.array([query1_time, query2_time, ...]) # recorded execution times

# Train a model on historical query times
regressor = LinearRegression()
regressor.fit(features, exec_times)

def predict_query_time(query_features):
    """Predict the execution time for a new query."""
    return regressor.predict([query_features])

# Use model predictions to choose optimal query configurations
```

Advanced query optimizers may incorporate such models into their query planning phases, creating richly annotated plans that align closely with resource availability and specific operational statistics. This artificially intelligent approach can reduce execution times and enhance the scalability of query-processing engines, providing comprehensive solutions to the challenges outlined by the high-dimensionality complex data inherent in vector databases.

Efficient query processing in vector databases encompasses the intricate synthesis of algorithmic principles, hardware capabilities, and strategic methodologies designed to scale databasing challenges effectively. As dataset sizes and dimensionality continue to grow, the role of query optimization in ensuring responsive and reliable access to data becomes ever more pivotal, underscoring the strategic direction of modern vector database systems toward fully optimized, artificially intelligent infrastructures. Through ongoing advancements in computational techniques, these systems will continue evolving, playing an integral role in processing the extensive and intricate datasets of future applications.

4.4 Approximate Nearest Neighbor Search

Approximate Nearest Neighbor (ANN) search is a crucial technique for querying high-dimensional data in vector databases efficiently. In various applications—such as recommender systems, computer vision, and natural language processing—performing rapid and scalable searches for nearest neighbors is essential. However, exact nearest neighbor search, which entails a linear scan through the dataset, is often prohibitive in terms of computational costs in high-dimensional spaces. ANN searches provide an efficient alternative by trading off a small degree of accuracy for substantial improvements in performance.

The primary aim of ANN search is to identify points in a dataset that are close to a given query point according to a specific distance metric, usually the Euclidean distance or cosine similarity. By focusing on speed and approximate results, ANN techniques excel where exact solutions would consume excessive time or resources.

The foundation of ANN entails several key elements:

- **Distance Measures**: Selection of an appropriate distance metric is fundamental to any nearest neighbor search. Euclidean distance is preferred in continuous spaces, while cosine similarity is often used for textual and high-dimensional data where direction rather than magnitude is significant.

- **Indexing Structures**: Effective data structures designed to expedite search operations are critical. Examples include Locality-Sensitive Hashing, k-d trees, and clustering-based approaches. These structures partition the data space to minimize search costs efficiently.

- **Dimensionality Reduction**: Transforming datasets into lower-dimensional spaces simplifies the search process by enhancing the computational feasibility of distance calculations, often using PCA, t-SNE, or UMAP (Uniform Manifold Approximation and Projection).

- **Hashing Techniques**: Hashing, especially LSH, is valuable for

105

partitioning data into buckets where similarity is retained prob-
abilistically. It enhances query speed when high precision is unnecessary but rapid response is paramount.

Locality-Sensitive Hashing (LSH) is one of the most popular ANN techniques:

```
import numpy as np
from sklearn.random_projection import GaussianRandomProjection
from collections import defaultdict

# Generate sample data
data_points = np.random.randn(1000, 128)

# Reducing dimensionality using Gaussian Random Projection
dim_reducer = GaussianRandomProjection(n_components=50)
reduced_data = dim_reducer.fit_transform(data_points)

# Implement LSH with random hash functions
def hash_function(x, a, b, bucket_size):
    return int((np.dot(a, x) + b) // bucket_size)

bucket_size = 10
hash_tables = [defaultdict(list) for _ in range(5)]
random_vectors = [np.random.randn(50) for _ in range(5)]
offsets = [np.random.rand() * bucket_size for _ in range(5)]

for idx, point in enumerate(reduced_data):
    for i in range(5):
        h = hash_function(point, random_vectors[i], offsets[i], bucket_size)
        hash_tables[i][h].append(idx)

# Example query point processing
query_point = np.random.randn(128)
reduced_query = dim_reducer.transform([query_point])[0]
candidates = set()

for i in range(5):
    h = hash_function(reduced_query, random_vectors[i], offsets[i], bucket_size)
    candidates.update(hash_tables[i][h])

# Compute best match from candidates
best_match = None
best_distance = float('inf')
for idx in candidates:
    dist = np.linalg.norm(reduced_data[idx] - reduced_query)
    if dist < best_distance:
        best_distance = dist
        best_match = idx

print(f"Best match index: {best_match}, Distance: {best_distance}")
```

This Python demonstration highlights how LSH efficiently narrows
potential matches in early stages, significantly improving search run-

times by correlating input vectors to similar hashcodes.

Further to LSH, alternative methods such as **Approximate Nearest Neighbors Oh Yeah (ANNOY)** or **Hierarchical Navigable Small World (HNSW)** graphs demonstrate significant advantages in specific data contexts:

- **ANNOY**: Employs random projections of vectors and tree structures for fast, approximate searching. ANNOY's efficient construction and querying make it ideal for dense, high-dimensional datasets.

- **HNSW Graphs**: Leverage navigable small world graphs for highly scalable and efficient searches, making them suitable for real-time applications and large-scale datasets.

Despite the strengths of these ANN techniques, system architects must thoroughly consider the precision demands of their specific application contexts. While a multimedia retrieval application may tolerate some approximation in similarity matches, real-time cybersecurity systems may not.

Moreover, accuracy, construction, and the handling of dynamic data (frequent insertions/deletions) vary amongst ANN techniques:

- **Precision-Performance Tradeoff**: Configurable parameters allow tuning these methods to desired tradeoffs—balancing between speed and the likelihood of retrieving true nearest neighbors.

Algorithm 1 Construction and Search Parameters in HNSW

1: Choose $ef_{construction}$ - Trade-off parameter that affects index construction complexity and index size.
2: Choose M - Maximum number of links per element, influences index memory use and query efficiency.

A thoughtful combination of these strategies—emphasizing precision where critical while maximizing response speeds where feasible—bestows a robust method of customizing the ANN implementation to meet specific needs.

The worldly impact of ANN techniques aligns closely with sectors where rapid, approximate search capability in massive high-dimensional spaces is the defining characteristic of an application's utility. Given markers such as growing data scale and algorithmic sophistication, ANN systems continue to evolve, encompassing paradigms seamlessly connecting their operational design to dynamic and demanding data contexts.

Lastly, as technology trends further acclimate to cognitive systems and AI-driven applications, ANN approaches are expected to evolve in tandem. These systems will increasingly incorporate hybrid methodologies that integrate deep learning models for feature extraction and similarity learning, promising even greater accuracy and efficiency in capturing and leveraging the complexities inherent in high-dimensional datasets.

4.5   Scalable Indexing Solutions

In vector databases, the fundamental challenge is how to design and implement indexing solutions that not only facilitate fast lookup and retrieval operations but also scale effectively as data volumes and dimensions increase. Scalable indexing solutions are critical for maintaining performance in the face of rapid data growth, supporting the dynamic needs of modern applications ranging from big data analytics to machine learning and AI.

Scalability in indexing solutions can be approached from several perspectives, including algorithmic scalability, infrastructure-level scalability, and application-specific scalability. Each of these aspects involves leveraging different technologies and methods to ensure that the system can efficiently handle increasing loads without compromising on speed or accuracy.

Algorithmic Scalability refers to the development of indexing methods that maintain efficiency with growing data sizes. This often involves innovations in existing algorithms or the creation of entirely new methodologies. Key approaches under this umbrella include:

1. **Dynamic Indexing**: Algorithms that can adapt to changes in data without requiring complete re-indexation are essential. Dynamic in-

dexing supports operations such as insertions, deletions, and updates, making it suitable for environments where data is continuously evolving.

2. **Hierarchical Data Structures**: Hierarchical indexing structures such as M-trees and cover trees enhance scalability by organizing data into layers, reducing the number of comparisons required during search operations.

3. **Distributed Data Structures**: These offer parallel processing capabilities across multiple nodes, handling large-scale datasets by distributing the indexing task across a cluster of machines.

Consider the example of a distributed k-d tree, which partitions data across multiple nodes. This approach benefits from parallel querying, where each node processes its partition independently, combining results for efficient retrieval.

The implementation of distributed k-d trees in practice involves:

```
class DistributedKDTree:
    def __init__(self, data_splits):
        self.local_trees = [KDTree(data) for data in data_splits]

    def query(self, query_point, k=1):
        from concurrent.futures import ThreadPoolExecutor
        with ThreadPoolExecutor() as executor:
            futures = [executor.submit(tree.query, query_point, k)
                       for tree in self.local_trees]
            results = [f.result() for f in futures]
        return min(results, key=lambda x: x[0])
```

Infrastructure-Level Scalability involves optimizing backend resources and architecture to support large data operations. Techniques to achieve this include:

1. **Sharding and Replication**: These are essential techniques in distribution architectures, where sharding involves partitioning the dataset into smaller parts stored across multiple nodes, and replication involves creating copies of data to ensure availability and reliability.

2. **Load Balancing**: Distributing workload across resources to ensure no single resource becomes a bottleneck, which is key in maintaining high throughput and reducing latency.

3. **Cloud Integration and Elastic Scaling**: Using cloud resources to dynamically allocate additional resources based on workload require-

ments, allowing databases to scale seamlessly as demand increases.

Application-Specific Scalability can be tailored using domain-specific knowledge to tune indexing systems for particular use cases. For instance, machine learning pipelines with integrated vector databases might use quantization techniques specifically designed for scaling similarity search:

```python
import numpy as np
from sklearn.cluster import KMeans

class ProductQuantization:
    def __init__(self, num_centroids):
        self.num_centroids = num_centroids
        self.centroids = []

    def fit(self, data):
        # Breaking data into subvectors and clustering each part
        subvectors = np.split(data, self.num_centroids, axis=1)
        for subvector in subvectors:
            kmeans = KMeans(n_clusters=self.num_centroids).fit(subvector)
            self.centroids.append(kmeans.cluster_centers_)

    def encode(self, vector):
        # Encoding a vector into quantized indices
        code = []
        subvectors = np.split(vector, self.num_centroids)
        for i, subv in enumerate(subvectors):
            idx = np.argmin(np.linalg.norm(self.centroids[i] - subv, axis=1))
            code.append(idx)
        return code

# Example usage
data = np.random.randn(1000, 128)
pq = ProductQuantization(num_centroids=16)
pq.fit(data)

# Encode a vector into quantized indices
encoded_vector = pq.encode(np.random.randn(128))
print(f"Quantized Indices: {encoded_vector}")
```

Such quantization reduces the dataset's effective size, accelerating both storage and retrieval operations, making them profoundly suitable for high-throughput requirements, particularly in vector search applications within AI systems.

As data continues to grow exponentially, being scalable also implies being adaptable. Indexing systems designed with adaptation in mind function in agile environments, adjusting strategies based on observed data patterns, resource availability, and evolving query types.

Emerging technologies such as in-memory databases offer tremendous scalability advantages, where storing indices in volatile memory allows extremely fast data access times. These environments readily take advantage of advanced hardware capabilities, including NVMe storage interfaces and high-thread-count processors.

Further, machine learning models are increasingly employed to predict the best strategies for indexing, effectively tuning index parameters based on anticipated workload dynamics. Systems leveraging such predictive analytics dynamically create index structures that avoid computation overhead on less critical operations while bolstering caching schemes for high-demand queries.

In concluding this exposition on scalable indexing solutions, it underscores the foundational nature of building adaptive, highly robust systems capable of enduring the computational and data size challenges anticipated with the future trends in data consumption. Collaborating across these algorithmic, infrastructural, and domain-specific modalities furnishes comprehensive coverage towards sustainable scalability solutions in vector databases, a cornerstone in the architecture of data-driven decision-making frameworks pervasive in today's digital economy.

4.6 Managing Multidimensional Data

Managing multidimensional data efficiently is pivotal in the context of vector databases, as modern datasets often encompass extensive features that characterize the data in high-dimensional spaces. Such data is prevalent in many domains, including genomics, image and video analysis, financial markets, recommender systems, and beyond. The complexities inherent in handling multidimensional data stem from not only the volume but also the intricacies involved in structuring, storing, and querying these data effectively.

Data Representation: At the heart of managing multidimensional data is its representation. Effective representation schemes are essential for reducing storage requirements, enhancing query efficiency, and maintaining accuracy. Fundamental representation techniques might include raw feature vectors, transformed feature spaces, or encoded representations using quantization.

- **Normalization and Scaling**: Prior to processing, data is typically normalized or scaled to ensure that each dimension contributes fairly to distance computations, avoiding bias towards larger scales. Techniques such as min-max scaling or Z-scoring are standard practices.

```
import numpy as np
from sklearn.preprocessing import MinMaxScaler, StandardScaler

# Sample multidimensional data
data_points = np.random.rand(100, 128)

# Min-Max Scaling
scaler = MinMaxScaler()
scaled_data = scaler.fit_transform(data_points)

# Standardization (Z-score normalization)
standardizer = StandardScaler()
standardized_data = standardizer.fit_transform(data_points)
```

- **Feature Engineering**: Transforming raw input data into meaningful representations via feature engineering enhances the quality and efficacy of subsequent analyses. Techniques such as polynomial features, interaction effects, and custom transformations cater to specific domain needs.

Dimensionality Reduction: A cornerstone in managing high-dimensional data involves dimensionality reduction, which aims to condense data into a lower-dimensional space without significant loss of information. This reduces computation and simplifies models.

- **Principal Component Analysis (PCA)**: PCA is a linear technique that projects data onto a reduced feature space where variance is maximized. It is particularly beneficial for eliminating collinear dimensions, thereby simplifying the data structure.

```
from sklearn.decomposition import PCA

# Apply PCA to reduce dimensions to 10
pca = PCA(n_components=10)
pca_data = pca.fit_transform(data_points)

print(f"Explained variance ratios: {pca.explained_variance_ratio_}")
```

- **T-distributed Stochastic Neighbor Embedding (t-SNE)**: t-SNE is a non-linear method that preserves local similarities in data, making it ideal for visualization purposes more than direct analysis.

- **Autoencoders**: Neural network-based methods that involve encoding and decoding data, autoencoders learn concise data representations crucial for feature understanding and subsequent processing.

```
from keras.layers import Input, Dense
from keras.models import Model

# Input layer and encoding network
input_dim = data_points.shape[1]
encoding_dim = 32

input_layer = Input(shape=(input_dim,))
encoder = Dense(encoding_dim, activation='relu')(input_layer)

# Decoding layer
decoder = Dense(input_dim, activation='sigmoid')(encoder)
autoencoder = Model(inputs=input_layer, outputs=decoder)

# Compile autoencoder
autoencoder.compile(optimizer='adam', loss='mse')

# Train autoencoder
autoencoder.fit(data_points, data_points, epochs=50, batch_size=32, shuffle=True)
```

Efficient Data Storage and Retrieval: Managing storage efficiently is paramount in high-dimensional spaces, where both disk space and memory footprints can rapidly expand.

- **Hierarchical Data Formats**: Using hierarchical data formats such as HDF5 allows for efficient storage and retrieval, compressing data effectively without significant loss.

- **Sparse Storage Solutions**: Sparse matrices conserve space by only recording non-zero values explicitly, facilitating storage efficiencies in inherently sparse datasets.

- **Multihashing Techniques**: Storing data through hashing reduces the effective dimensionality needed for retrieval, optimizing query speed and efficiency. This involves techniques like Product Quantization, leveraging cluster centers to approximate vector placements.

Advanced Indexing Techniques: Effective indexing schemes bolster the retrieval systems in vector databases, ensuring that queries resolve swiftly even with scaling dimensional complexity.

- **k-d Trees**: Ideal for low to moderate dimensions, k-d trees reduce search complexity through spatial partitioning.

```
from scipy.spatial import KDTree

# Create K-D Tree
kd_tree = KDTree(data_points)

# Example query
query_point = np.random.rand(128)
distance, idx = kd_tree.query(query_point)

print(f"Closest point index: {idx}, Distance: {distance}")
```

- **Multi-probe LSH**: Enhances typical Locality-Sensitive Hashing by probing multiple hash spaces simultaneously, catering to complex data patterns.

- **Cover Trees and R-trees**: Utilize hierarchical partitions for high-dimensional datasets, each offering unique advantages in specific operational contexts.

Data Management with Relational and Non-relational Models: Balancing between traditional relational paradigms and modern non-relational models provides comprehensive handling of multidimensional data needs.

- **Relational Databases**: Employ structured query languages and table-based formats suitable for clearly defined multidimensional data with fixed schemas.

- **NoSQL and Column-Family Stores**: Leverage flexible schema definitions and distributed storage infrastructures to manage variable-dimension features across expansive datasets.

- **Graph Databases**: Use graph representations to interconnect dimensions meaningfully, ideal for datasets with intricate relational aspects.

114

Handling High-Dimensional Query Complexity: Managing queries effectively within high-dimensional databases necessitates the development of sophisticated query planners and optimizers.

- **Use of Query Rewrites and Execution Plans**: Frameworks that transform queries into optimized operations, reducing redundant or high-cost computations.

- **Caching Mechanisms**: Using cache layers to store intermediate results and popular queries improves response times significantly in dynamic query environments.

- **Adaptive Query Execution**: Systems that adapt execution strategies based on real-time performance metrics and computational loads increase efficiency and responsiveness.

In sum, managing multidimensional data necessitates a concerted approach that synergizes data representations, efficient storage mechanisms, advanced indexing, and strategic data models. The interplay of these elements maximizes performance while adapting nimbly to new challenges as data scales. A holistic understanding and deployment of these practices ensure that vector databases remain robust and scalable, ready to meet the increasing demands of diverse applications across every sector utilizing high-dimensional datasets.

4.7 Query Optimization Techniques

Query optimization is an essential component of database management systems, particularly within vector databases that deal with large-scale, high-dimensional data. The aim of query optimization is to improve the efficiency and effectiveness of query execution, minimizing the response time and resource usage while maximizing throughput. In a modern vector database, query optimization involves employing both algorithmic strategies and system-level enhancements to address the specific challenges posed by complex queries and multidimensional data.

Efficient query processing is not just about selecting fast execution paths but also about understanding the underlying data distribution, workload characteristics, and system configuration. Thus, query optimization techniques are particularly multifaceted, involving aspects ranging from the design of the database schema to the run-time execution plans.

- **Cost-Based Optimization**: This technique involves estimating the resource cost of different query execution plans and selecting the least expensive path for execution. Cost-based optimization considers various factors such as I/O operations, CPU resources, memory usage, and the statistical distribution of data.

  The steps involved in cost-based optimization include:

  - **Parsing**: The query is parsed into an initial structure, usually a syntax tree, which is the input for the optimization phase.

  - **Logical Plan Generation**: A representation of the query without physical details, focusing purely on the logical sequence of operations.

  - **Physical Plan Generation**: Here, the database management system evaluates different algorithms and access methods to perform the query operations outlined in the logical plan.

  - **Cost Estimation**: The optimizer assigns a cost to each physical plan based on estimates of required resources, selecting the most efficient option.

```
EXPLAIN ANALYZE SELECT * FROM high_dimensional_table WHERE
    vector_feature @> 'value';
```

This command suggests a query planner to assess and display the execution strategy of a query, helping identify bottlenecks and opportunities for optimization.

- **Rule-Based Optimization**: Rather than evaluating cost, rule-based optimizers apply predefined transformations known to improve query performance. Essential rules might include query rewriting techniques such as:

- **Predicate Pushdown**: Reordering predicates to filter data at the earliest opportunity, reducing the amount of data carried through the query execution.

- **Join Reordering**: Modifying the order of joins to minimize intermediate results, based on estimated data sizes and selectivity.

- **Common Subexpression Elimination**: Identifying repeated expressions within a query and computing them once, storing results temporarily.

```
# Optimizing through predicate pushdown
def optimized_query(dataframe):
    return dataframe[dataframe['feature'] > 100][['feature']].sort_values(by='feature')
```

In this example, filtering is performed before the sorting operation to minimize the data workload during sorting.

- **Adaptive Query Processing**: This involves building systems that adjust processing strategies based on real-time performance feedback. Unlike traditional optimization, which relies on static, pre-execution predictions, adaptivity allows for dynamic changes to execution plans contingent on observed data characteristics and system conditions.

  - **Feedback Loops**: Continually collecting execution metrics to refine future query plans.

  - **Runtime Reoptimization**: Adjusting the execution strategy if initial plans are underperforming due to underestimated costs or unexpected data skew.

  - **Progressive Query Engines**: Executing parts of a query incrementally, refining estimations and adjusting strategies on-the-fly.

- **Index Utilization**: Efficient use of indices can significantly affect query performance, reducing the need for full-table scans.

  - **Selective Index Creation**: Establishing indices on columns with high selectivity, enhancing the speed of common and critical queries.

117

- **Index Hints**: Using hints within queries to guide the database engine to utilize or ignore specific indices or strategies.

```
SELECT * FROM indexed_table USE INDEX (idx_column) WHERE column = '
    value';
```

This approach can be particularly effective when the optimizer's default selection does not meet specific query performance expectations.

- **Parallel Execution**: Deploying parallelism to exploit multi-core processors and distributed systems aims to improve query throughput and reduce response time.

  - **Partitioned Parallelism**: Dividing a large query into smaller subqueries that can be executed in parallel across different partitions of the data.
  - **Pipeline Parallelism**: Stages of query processing operate in parallel, streaming data between operations without idle time.

```
from multiprocessing import Pool

def process_partition(partition):
    # Perform query operations on this partition
    return sum(partition)

# Assuming data is partitioned into segments
partitions = [[...], [...], ...] # Example data partitioning

with Pool(processes=4) as pool:
    results = pool.map(process_partition, partitions)

total_result = sum(results)
```

- **Query Caching and Materialization**: Storing results of expensive queries or common subqueries can significantly cut down processing times for repeated queries.

  - **Result Caching**: Keeping the outcomes of frequent queries in memory for rapid retrieval.
  - **Materialized Views**: Persisting computation results in a fixed table format, updated periodically to reflect changes in the underlying data.

118

- **Use of Advanced Hardware**: Tapping into novel hardware architectures to expedite query operations, leveraging capabilities such as:

  - **GPU Acceleration**: For parallelizable vectorized operations, utilizing the massively parallel architecture of GPUs can accelerate data processing.
  - **In-Memory Processing**: Minimizes the latency associated with disk I/O, allowing for faster processing using large amounts of RAM.

Optimizing query performance is a multi-layered process that demands an integrated approach, combining foundational principles with sophisticated, adaptive algorithms designed to suit changing data landscapes. Modern vector databases harness these optimizations, fostering environments where insightful analytics over extensive datasets can be conducted efficiently, supporting increasingly data-intensive applications in real time.

The continual enhancement of query optimization strategies is indispensable for facilitating the robust, efficient data handling capabilities demanded by contemporary data management applications. By enabling quick and precise query response times, these techniques not only support scalability but also ensure that vector databases can serve as reliable backbone systems for complex and dynamic analytical workloads.

Chapter 5

Integration of Vector Databases with AI

The integration of vector databases with AI technologies significantly enhances the capabilities of modern applications by efficiently managing and processing large-scale vector data critical for AI tasks. This chapter discusses how vector databases support AI-driven functions such as model training, semantic search, and natural language processing, showcasing their indispensable role in creating intelligent systems. It highlights the benefits of using vector databases to improve data retrieval processes and AI model performance while addressing integration challenges. The chapter also includes case studies illustrating successful implementations, underscoring the transformative impact of this integration on various AI applications.

5.1 Role of Vector Databases in AI

The integration of vector databases in artificial intelligence (AI) has become pivotal as AI systems increasingly rely on large-scale parallel data processes. Vector databases provide an optimized structure for storing and retrieving high-dimensional data that is prevalent in AI applications. Their ability to efficiently manage and query such data enhances the performance of AI models, enabling more sophisticated and nuanced AI-driven functionalities.

Vector databases are highly relevant in AI due to their specialized design aimed at managing data points that can be represented as vectors. These vectors can encompass features extracted from various data types, including images, text, and numerical data, thereby forming a fundamental element of modern AI systems. Given the diverse nature of input data for AI tasks, vector databases provide a universally adaptable and robust storage and retrieval solution.

At the core of vector databases is the ability to handle similarity searches in high-dimensional space. Unlike traditional scalar databases, which focus on discrete data retrieval based on exact key matches, vector databases excel in proximity-based searches. This capability is critical for applications such as recommendation systems, image recognition, and natural language processing, where understanding the degrees of similarity or semantic resemblance between data points is essential.

The notion of similarity in vector spaces is mathematically grounded in metrics such as Euclidean distance, cosine similarity, or inner product measures. These metrics govern the underlying algorithms that drive vector database search efficiencies. For instance, the approximate nearest neighbor (ANN) search algorithm aids in expediting the retrieval of data points that closely resemble a specified query vector. This is particularly useful in AI where computational efficiency is crucial due to the typically vast scale of data involved. Here is an example of how the ANN algorithm is employed to find similar vectors:

```
import faiss
import numpy as np

# Create a random dataset
d = 64 # vector dimension
nb = 10000 # database size
nq = 5 # number of queries
np.random.seed(1234) # for reproducibility
xb = np.random.random((nb, d)).astype('float32')
xq = np.random.random((nq, d)).astype('float32')

# Configure the index
index = faiss.IndexFlatL2(d) # L2 is Euclidean
index.add(xb) # add vectors to the index
```

```
print("Index contains", index.ntotal, "vectors")

# Perform a search
k = 5 # we want to see 5 nearest vectors
D, I = index.search(xq, k) # search
print(I) # indices of nearest neighbors
```

For scenarios in which real-time data processing is critical, such as in streaming data environments, vector databases enhance performance through efficient indexing mechanisms. They utilize advanced data structures, such as KD-trees, VP-trees, and inverted file systems, that are optimized for high-speed data retrieval operations. The use of such hierarchical data structures enables rapid searches on multidimensional data, providing an infrastructural backbone for real-time AI decision-making processes.

While vector databases significantly expedite data handling operations, they also support the computational demands of deep learning algorithms used in AI. Many deep learning architectures, including Convolutional Neural Networks (CNNs) and Recurrent Neural Networks (RNNs), operate on high-dimensional tensor data that can be effectively managed within a vector database framework. By facilitating swift access to these high-volume data arrays, vector databases streamline the model training phase, reducing latency and improving overall efficacy.

Moreover, vector databases enable AI models to better capitalize on feature-rich datasets through efficient utilization of embeddings, which are dense vector representations of data that encode semantic information. This is particularly essential in Natural Language Processing (NLP) where text embeddings such as Word2Vec or BERT convert textual input into vector forms that capture syntactic and semantic nuances. This capability is leveraged in tasks such as semantic search and text classification, where AI models require a deep contextual understanding of language input.

Vector embeddings operate as the transformational layer between raw data formats and the abstracted intelligence delivered by AI models. For instance, embeddings applied in recommender systems can denote user preferences through vector similarity analysis, revealing based user-item interactions at a semantically rich level. The following example illustrates how text embeddings can be stored and queried using a

123

vector database:

```
from sentence_transformers import SentenceTransformer
import faiss
import numpy as np

# Define a list of sentences
sentences = ["Vector databases enhance AI efficiency.",
             "Deep learning relies on feature-rich datasets.",
             "Efficient data retrieval is crucial for AI."]

# Load a pre-trained model
model = SentenceTransformer('paraphrase-MiniLM-L6-v2')

# Encode sentences to get corresponding embeddings
sentence_embeddings = model.encode(sentences)

# Use FAISS for indexing
d = sentence_embeddings.shape[1]
index = faiss.IndexFlatL2(d)
index.add(np.array(sentence_embeddings).astype('float32'))

# Query with a new sentence
query = "AI benefits from rapid data retrieval."
query_embedding = model.encode([query])

# Search the index
D, I = index.search(np.array(query_embedding).astype('float32'), 2)
print("Most similar sentences are:\n", [sentences[idx] for idx in I[0]])
```

The utility of vector databases is further underscored in supporting AI interpretability and explainability, a significant aspect in deploying AI models. By accessing intermediate data layers and transformations stored efficiently within a vector database, practitioners can trace model decision pathways, thus optimizing model evaluations and ensuring adherence to policy compliance.

Combining vector database infrastructure with distributed systems and parallel computation frameworks further bridges the gap between AI-powered solutions and scalable real-world applications. Leveraging Distributed AI (D-AI), processing capacity is amplified across nodes that concurrently execute data-intensive tasks. Vector databases exhibit remarkable compatibility with these frameworks, being well-versed in both sharded and partitioned architectures that essentialize distributed information sharing.

The synergy of vector databases with AI extends into cutting-edge domains such as autonomous systems, where real-time response, high availability, and fault tolerance are imperatives. For instance, autonomous vehicles employ sensor data encapsulated as vectors to make rapid navigational decisions, relying on vector databases to provide instantaneous access to vast accumulated experience points from prior sensor data readouts.

It is equally vital to understand that while the role of vector databases in AI is transformative, it also presents integration challenges such as ensuring data quality, managing dimensionality trade-offs, and handling vector sparsity. Efficient vectorization practices and leveraging techniques like Principal Component Analysis (PCA) for dimensionality reduction help mitigate high dimensionality concerns. Balancing algorithm complexity and computation time is crucial for optimizing vector database performance in AI applications.

Understanding and implementing the role of vector databases in AI involve recognizing their inherent capacity for conflict resolution, handling concurrent updates, and ensuring transactional safety across AI models. Such operations are critical for maintaining the integrity and consistency of data ecosystems in which vector databases reside.

Vector databases represent a fundamental advancement in data architecture aligned with AI progression. As AI systems grow in complexity, the nuanced role of vector databases in managing data flow effectively and enabling rapid retrieval of semantically meaningful data will continue to expand. These databases underpin the evolution of AI systems, contributing to their scalability, effectiveness, and ability to deliver real-world solution applicability through enhanced data management frameworks.

5.2   Training AI Models with Vector Data

The process of training AI models fundamentally revolves around transforming raw data into structured representations suitable for learning algorithms, of which vector data plays an instrumental role. Vector data, entailing numerical values organized into tuples, encapsulates features extracted from various modalities, such as text, image, or numerical data, translating them into a format that AI models can effectively process and learn from.

One of the primary uses of vector data in AI training regimes is feature extraction, where inputs are converted into vector forms that highlight key properties relevant for prediction or classification tasks. Machine learning models, such as Support Vector Machines (SVM), neural networks, and decision trees, utilize these vectorized inputs to discern patterns and make predictive decisions.

Vectorization is a critical preprocessing step that involves encoding input features into numerical, typically real-valued, vectors. In the context of natural language processing (NLP), for example, vector embeddings such as word2vec, glove, or fastText translate words or sentences into vectors that capture grammatical meanings and semantic similarities. This transformation is vital for training language models, enabling them to perform tasks such as text classification, sentiment analysis, and machine translation.

The use of vector data in image processing and computer vision is another illustrative example. Images are inherently high-dimensional data structured as tensor arrays. By converting pixel data into feature vectors through methods like convolutional operations, vectorized representations render deep learning models capable of executing complex tasks such as object recognition, image segmentation, and image synthesis. Consider the following Python code snippet that illustrates vectorizing an image dataset using Convolutional Neural Network (CNN) in PyTorch:

```python
import torch
import torch.nn as nn
import torch.optim as optim
from torchvision import datasets, transforms

# Define transformations for the training data
transform = transforms.Compose([
    transforms.ToTensor(),
    transforms.Normalize((0.5,), (0.5,)) # Min-max normalization
])

# Load the dataset
train_dataset = datasets.MNIST(root='./data', train=True, transform=transform,
    download=True)
train_loader = torch.utils.data.DataLoader(dataset=train_dataset, batch_size=64,
    shuffle=True)

# Define a simple CNN model
class SimpleCNN(nn.Module):
    def __init__(self):
        super(SimpleCNN, self).__init__()
        self.conv1 = nn.Conv2d(1, 32, kernel_size=3)
        self.conv2 = nn.Conv2d(32, 64, kernel_size=3)
```

126

```
    self.fc1 = nn.Linear(64*12*12, 128)
    self.fc2 = nn.Linear(128, 10)

def forward(self, x):
    x = torch.relu(self.conv1(x))
    x = torch.relu(self.conv2(x))
    x = x.view(-1, 64*12*12)
    x = torch.relu(self.fc1(x))
    x = self.fc2(x)
    return x

# Model instantiation
model = SimpleCNN()
criterion = nn.CrossEntropyLoss()
optimizer = optim.SGD(model.parameters(), lr=0.01)

# Training loop
for epoch in range(5): # iterate over epochs
    for images, labels in train_loader:
        optimizer.zero_grad()
        outputs = model(images)
        loss = criterion(outputs, labels)
        loss.backward()
        optimizer.step()
    print(f"Epoch {epoch+1}/{5}, Loss: {loss.item()}")
```

Vector data lends itself to mathematically grounded operations, empowering model training through statistical learning paradigms. High-dimensional data vectors facilitate linear algebra computations central to gradient descent and backpropagation algorithms utilized in weight updates during the training phase. Such operations ensure that AI models iteratively adjust their internal parameters towards minimizing prediction errors.

Training models with vector data necessitates handling complexities intrinsic to high-dimensional spaces, often referred to as the "curse of dimensionality." The challenge lies in maintaining computational efficiency and preventing model overfitting as dimensions increase. Strategies such as dimensionality reduction techniques—Principal Component Analysis (PCA), t-distributed Stochastic Neighbor Embedding (t-SNE), or Autoencoders—are essential. These techniques retain informative features while reducing computational burden, allowing models to learn effectively.

In practice, the deployment of vector data extends into sophisticated machine learning architectures like Transformers. These models, characterized by their attention mechanisms, leverage vector representations to process sequential inputs as seen in NLP applications. By transforming words or tokens into vectors through embeddings, transformers achieve state-of-the-art performance in language modeling tasks. The following example demonstrates how vector embeddings are utilized in a transformer model using the Hugging Face Transformers library:

```
from transformers import BertTokenizer, BertModel
import torch

# Load pre-trained model tokenizer
tokenizer = BertTokenizer.from_pretrained('bert-base-uncased')

# Tokenize input text
text = "Training AI models with vector data is essential."
input_ids = torch.tensor([tokenizer.encode(text, add_special_tokens=True)])

# Load pre-trained model
model = BertModel.from_pretrained('bert-base-uncased')

# Get vector embeddings
with torch.no_grad():
    outputs = model(input_ids)
    last_hidden_states = outputs.last_hidden_state

# Display the vector embedding for the first token
print(last_hidden_states[0][0])
```

Vector data plays a crucial role in augmenting AI model generalizability. By capturing the latent space within data, vectors enable models to transfer learned characteristics across different, but related, data domains. This becomes particularly significant in transfer learning scenarios where pre-trained vector representations are fine-tuned to tackle new tasks with limited labelled data.

The versatility of vector data in multimodal learning cannot be overstated, where disparate data types—visual, auditory, textual—are integrated within unified learning frameworks. Here, vectors act as the common denominator, allowing interoperability between modalities. Such intricate representations underpin applications like speech-to-text systems, visual question answering, and autonomous navigation.

Furthermore, AI systems leveraging vector data often operate synergistically with vector databases to optimize data manipulation and retrieval. During training, vector databases can provide efficient batch retrieval of training samples, align data loading with computational workloads, and ensure consistent accessibility alongside multi-threaded operations.

The journey from raw data to vector-based AI models encompasses a methodical application of both domain knowledge and computational prowess, relying heavily on precision engineering of data pipelines, robust vector encodings, and strategic model architectures.

Practical implementations necessitate an ecosystem that extends beyond mere algorithm deployment. Handling environmental constraints—ranging from hardware capacities, data storage modalities, to network bandwidth—dictate how effectively models capitalize on vector data in real-time settings.

It is also important to stress the paradigmatic shift vector data induces in AI ethics and governance. By inadvertently embedding biases through vectorized data, there exists a tangible risk of bias propagation in AI decisions. Comprehensive auditing of vector processes, transparent vector transformations, and the inclusion of fairness criteria within training pipelines is therefore vital for upholding the ethical tenets of AI practice.

As AI systems become increasingly reliant on vector data, the symbiosis between AI and vector representations fosters innovation across disciplines, promoting the emergence of more intelligent, perceptive, and predictive systems. These systems, grounded in the intricacies of vectorized understanding, are reshaping our engagement with technology, guiding the evolution of smarter and more autonomous computational entities.

5.3 Vector Databases for Natural Language Processing

In the domain of Natural Language Processing (NLP), vector databases have emerged as crucial enablers of enhanced data manipulation and retrieval, supporting a wide array of linguistic tasks by facilitating efficient management of high-dimensional text embeddings. As NLP applications grow more sophisticated, the need for robust and scalable vector storage solutions becomes apparent, particularly as language models increase in complexity and dataset sizes multiply.

Vector databases specifically cater to storing and query operations on vector embeddings derived from textual data, making them indispensable for tasks such as semantic search, document classification, sentiment analysis, and machine translation. These embeddings transform textual information into a numerical format, maintaining semantic and syntactic properties encoded in dense vector representations. Well-known techniques such as Word2Vec, Global Vectors for Word Representation (GloVe), and Bidirectional Encoder Representations from Transformers (BERT) produce these embeddings, capturing rich linguistic information suitable for storage within vector databases.

Central to vector databases' effectiveness in NLP is their ability to efficiently perform similarity searches, an essential operation for numerous NLP tasks. Such searches often utilize metrics like cosine similarity, which measures the cosine of the angle between two n-dimensional vectors, providing a measure of semantic similarity between text inputs. The efficiency of vector databases in executing similarity searches makes them valuable for applications like information retrieval, where the objective is to fetch documents or text segments most relevant to user queries.

To illustrate, consider a semantic search application where the task is to retrieve passages closest in meaning to an input query. Utilizing embeddings stored within a vector database, the application can rapidly identify and rank text segments that exhibit high semantic similarity to the query. This mechanism underlies many modern search engines and digital assistants, enhancing user interaction by delivering more contextually relevant results. Here's an illustrative example using Python to perform semantic search with stored embeddings:

```python
from sentence_transformers import SentenceTransformer
import faiss
import numpy as np

# Define text corpus
documents = ["The field of NLP is evolving rapidly.",
             "Vector databases support efficient similarity searches.",
             "Advanced techniques are utilized in semantic search applications."]

# Load a model for sentence embeddings
model = SentenceTransformer('all-mpnet-base-v2')

# Encode documents to create embeddings
document_embeddings = model.encode(documents)

# Initialize a FAISS index for similarity search
d = document_embeddings.shape[1]
```

```
index = faiss.IndexFlatIP(d) # using Inner Product
index.add(np.array(document_embeddings).astype('float32'))

# Define a query
query = "What is the role of vector databases in language tasks?"
query_embedding = model.encode([query])

# Perform the search
D, I = index.search(np.array(query_embedding).astype('float32'), k=2)
print("Most semantically similar documents:", [documents[idx] for idx in I[0]])
```

Storing NLP embeddings in vector databases also facilitates acceler-
ated model training and deployment processes by providing a centralized and efficient vector management system. This is particularly beneficial for large-scale NLP models, where vectorized word representations enable enhanced processing speeds and model performance.

Additionally, vector databases are adept at supporting the demands of
multilingual NLP applications. By storing embeddings across multiple languages, they enhance cross-linguistic capabilities, facilitating
tasks such as cross-language information retrieval and multilingual
sentiment analysis. This is crucial in globalized environments where
language models must understand and process content across diverse
linguistic landscapes.

A significant advantage of vector databases in NLP is their scalability and flexible indexing capabilities, which accommodate the growing
abundance and variety of textual data. Layered indexing structures,
such as HNSW (Hierarchical Navigable Small World) graphs, enable
rapid retrieval even in expansive data environments, ensuring consistent performance and low-latency operations.

Moreover, the integration of vector databases in NLP workflows extends to real-world deployments within conversational AI systems. Virtual assistants and chatbots rely on rapid access to knowledge bases,
where vector databases store conversational history and pre-encoded
responses. This enables these systems to provide contextually aware
and responsive interactions with users, improving conversational flow
and user satisfaction.

In the construction of recommendation systems, vector databases
leverage NLP embeddings to analyze textual user reviews or comments,
forming the basis for personalized content recommendations. By aligning reviews with product descriptions or similar user opinions, these

systems deliver tailored suggestions that enhance user engagement and satisfaction.

In the broader context of Information Retrieval (IR), vector databases contribute significantly to building intelligent search systems capable of capturing nuances in user queries to provide accurate results. They achieve this by leveraging embeddings to discern the deeper meanings behind search terms, thereby refining the matching process beyond keyword-based searches.

Furthermore, vector databases inherently support privacy-preserving AI methodologies in NLP through techniques like differential privacy or homomorphic encryption applied in vector computations. These mechanisms ensure that sensitive data is protected while maintaining the operability and utility of NLP models.

Utilizing vector databases, NLP frameworks adopt a more refined approach when dealing with domain-specific languages or jargon. By training language models on specialized text corpora and storing the resulting embeddings, these databases facilitate detailed understanding and processing within niche domains, such as medical, legal, or scientific texts.

While vector databases in NLP prove remarkably effective and versatile, challenges remain. Ensuring data integrity during embedding transformations, handling text disambiguation, and managing storage efficiency in voluminous vector datasets are critical considerations. Addressing these issues through optimal embedding strategies and sophisticated database logging mechanisms is key to sustainable NLP advancements.

The interplay between vector databases and NLP crafts a compelling narrative of efficiency, scalability, and enhanced understanding. These databases underpin vast and intelligent language systems transforming how textual data is interpreted, analyzed, and leveraged in AI applications. As NLP technologies expand into diverse sectors, vector databases will continue to play an integral role in unlocking the complete potential of linguistic models, reshaping information extraction, and ultimately influencing how language understanding coalesces into tangible business and societal value.

5.4 AI-driven Data Retrieval Techniques

AI-driven data retrieval techniques have revolutionized the way we access, manage, and interpret vast oceans of data. Augmented by advancements in artificial intelligence (AI) and machine learning (ML), these techniques enable rapid, efficient, and contextually relevant retrieval of information, surpassing traditional keyword-based approaches.

The core principle behind AI-driven data retrieval is the deployment of intelligent algorithms that can process and understand content at a semantic level, thereby enhancing the accuracy and relevance of retrieved data. This is achieved through the use of sophisticated models that leverage both supervised and unsupervised learning paradigms, utilizing large datasets to identify patterns and deduce latent structures within the data.

Vector embeddings form the backbone of many AI-driven retrieval systems, translating diverse data types, such as text, images, and audio, into high-dimensional vector representations. This translation is essential for enabling similarity-based searches, where the aim is to retrieve data points that are closely aligned in the vector space with a given query. The following Python example demonstrates how vector embeddings are used in an AI-driven data retrieval setup for images using a pre-trained deep learning model:

```
import torch
from torchvision import models, transforms
from PIL import Image
import json

# Load a pre-trained ResNet model
model = models.resnet50(pretrained=True)
model.eval()

# Define a transformation process for the images
transform = transforms.Compose([
    transforms.Resize(256),
    transforms.CenterCrop(224),
    transforms.ToTensor(),
    transforms.Normalize(mean=[0.485, 0.456, 0.406], std=[0.229, 0.224, 0.225]),
])

# Function to compute the embedding of an image
def generate_embedding(image_path):
    image = Image.open(image_path)
    image_tensor = transform(image).unsqueeze(0)
```

133

```
with torch.no_grad():
    embedding = model(image_tensor)
return embedding

# Generate embeddings for a query image
query_embedding = generate_embedding('path/to/query_image.jpg')
```

In text-based data retrieval, language models such as BERT and GPT-3 provide powerful embeddings that facilitate semantic search operations. These models understand context and disambiguate user intents, resulting in semantic richness superior to traditional search mechanisms. Intelligent processing of user queries is vital, enabling systems to infer user context, preferences, and nuanced meaning.

AI-driven retrieval systems also employ natural language understanding (NLU) techniques to further enhance data interaction. By leveraging syntactic parsing and sentiment analysis, these systems can dynamically adjust retrieval strategies according to the sentiment and structure of user input, permitting more agile and responsive data access pipelines.

Real-world applications of AI-driven data retrieval are wide-ranging and impactful. Recommendation systems across e-commerce and content streaming platforms harness retrieval algorithms to suggest products or media content aligned with user preferences and past interactions. They rely heavily on collaborative filtering and content-based filtering approaches, supported by vectorized user and item representations that articulate relationships in a multi-dimensional preference space.

Knowledge graphs offer another dimension to AI-driven data retrieval by linking information across domains, entities, and relationships in structurally explicit ways. They provide a semantic foundation for data retrieval, allowing AI systems to draw inferences based on the interconnectedness of information in the graph.

An effective demonstration of knowledge graph utilization in data retrieval can be illustrated through a Python example that uses the Neo4j library to query interconnected nodes representing related concepts:

```
from neo4j import GraphDatabase

class Neo4jRetrieval:

    def __init__(self, uri, user, password):
```

134

```
        self.driver = GraphDatabase.driver(uri, auth=(user, password))

    def close(self):
        self.driver.close()

    def fetch_related_entities(self, entity):
        with self.driver.session() as session:
            result = session.run(
                "MATCH (e {name: $entity})-[:RELATED_TO]->(related) RETURN
                    related.name", entity=entity)
            return [record['related.name'] for record in result]

retrieval = Neo4jRetrieval("bolt://localhost:7687", "neo4j", "password")
related_entities = retrieval.fetch_related_entities("Artificial Intelligence")
print("Related entities:", related_entities)
retrieval.close()
```

Furthermore, machine vision has made significant advances, with AI-driven techniques enhancing object recognition, medical imaging, and security surveillance. AI systems exhibit heightened capabilities for detecting anomalies or extracting critical features, contributing to improved decision-making processes across various sectors.

In the domain of bioinformatics, AI-driven retrieval techniques provide targeted access to biomolecular data by identifying structural similarities in complex datasets. Retrieval systems utilizing vector representations aid in the discovery of potential drug compounds, offering new opportunities for research and development.

While AI-driven data retrieval presents transformative benefits, it is coupled with challenges that necessitate strategic considerations. Issues such as data privacy, ethical use of AI, and algorithmic transparency demand attention. Analyzing and resolving potential biases embedded within training data is essential, as biases can propagate into retrieval outputs, affecting fairness and equity.

Effective data governance practices and applied guideline frameworks ensure that AI-driven retrieval systems are not only technologically advanced but also ethically sound. Incorporating user consent mechanisms, audit trails, and explainability features further strengthens trust in these systems.

In the pursuit of innovation, data retrieval techniques continue to evolve. Future advancements envision the integration of AI with quantum computing technologies, offering heightened computational capabilities that can process vast data repositories at unprecedented speeds.

This convergence promises to further refine retrieval accuracy and efficiency.

To harness the full potential of AI-driven data retrieval requires ongoing developments in algorithmic design, data infrastructure, and interdisciplinary collaboration. By embedding adaptability and innovation at every stage, retrieval techniques will continue to extend their impact, facilitating smarter, more informed interactions with data that underpin progress across diverse walks of life.

5.5 Integration Challenges

Integrating vector databases with AI systems presents a set of complex challenges that necessitates careful consideration and strategic resolution. These challenges arise due to the intricate nature of data handling, the computational demands of AI, and the evolving technological landscape where such integrations occur. Addressing these challenges requires an in-depth understanding of both vector database management and AI algorithms, combined with robust infrastructure design and implementation strategies.

One of the foremost challenges in integrating vector databases with AI is ensuring data consistency and quality. In AI applications, the quality of data used for training and inference directly influences the performance and reliability of the models. Inconsistencies or errors in vector data can propagate through AI systems, leading to inaccurate predictions or unintended biases. Ensuring data consistency involves rigorous data validation and cleaning processes before data is stored in the vector database. This includes handling missing data, outliers, and ensuring data follows a consistent schema.

The scalability of vector databases is another significant challenge. As AI systems scale, they generate enormous volumes of data, necessitating databases that can efficiently store, index, and retrieve high-dimensional vectors. Ensuring that vector databases can scale horizontally by adding more nodes or via distributed architectures is crucial. Implementations such as sharding, where a database is partitioned to distribute the data across multiple servers, and replication, where data is duplicated across multiple nodes for redundancy, are strategies employed to handle scalability issues.

Integration requires managing the computational demand AI places on vector databases. AI algorithms, particularly deep learning models, often require real-time access to large datasets. Ensuring low-latency retrieval and high throughput from vector databases requires optimizing both the hardware and software layers. This can involve using high-performance computing resources, optimizing query execution plans, and utilizing caching mechanisms to store frequently accessed data vectors temporarily.

Effective indexing and retrieval of vectors are perennial challenges in integration. Creating efficient indices that allow rapid querying of high-dimensional vectors is essential. Index structures like KD-trees, R-trees, VP-trees, and more recent advancements like Index Flat, and Product Quantization utilized in libraries such as FAISS are designed to enhance retrieval performance. Here's an example demonstrating the complexity of indexing vectors using the FAISS library to optimize retrieval:

```
import faiss
import numpy as np

# Generate random vectors for database
dimensions = 128
num_vectors = 10000
random_data = np.random.random((num_vectors, dimensions)).astype('float32')

# Initialize the FAISS index with IndexFlatL2 (Euclidean)
index = faiss.IndexFlatL2(dimensions)

# Add vectors to the index for searching
index.add(random_data)

# Define a query vector
query_vector = np.random.random((1, dimensions)).astype('float32')

# Search for the nearest neighbors with optimized index
k = 5 # number of nearest neighbors to search
distances, indices = index.search(query_vector, k)

print("Top 5 nearest neighbors in database:", indices)
```

Interoperability with existing systems poses a challenge due to diverse technological stacks and data ecosystems employed within organizations. Different systems employ varied data formats, programming languages, and communication protocols, which can complicate the seamless integration of vector databases. Developing APIs, drivers,

137

and middleware that can facilitate communication across disparate systems is critical. Standardizing data exchange formats and adopting message brokers or service buses ensures smooth interoperability.

Security of data throughout the integration process is another major concern. As vector databases often store sensitive and high-value data that contribute to AI's decision-making capabilities, ensuring its protection from unauthorized access and breaches is of utmost importance. Employing robust encryption mechanisms for data at rest and in transit, implementing stringent access controls, and regular security audits help in mitigating security risks.

Latency and timing constraints present further challenges, especially in real-time AI applications. Applications require the retrieval and processing of vector data within strict time frames. Implementing efficient data pipelines, leveraging asynchronous processing, and optimizing network protocols to reduce latency is essential. Techniques such as edge computing, where processing is partially done closer to the data source or end users, can alleviate network-induced delays.

Balancing trade-offs between computational complexity and energy efficiency is vital, particularly as AI models grow in size and sophistication. Ensuring efficient use of computational resources while maintaining optimal performance requires careful architecture design and code optimization. Adjusting models to run efficiently on hardware with limited resources, such as Internet-of-Things (IoT) devices, involves utilizing techniques like model pruning, quantization, and leveraging specialized hardware such as TPUs or FPGAs.

Ensuring compatibility with emerging AI architectures and methodologies represents a forward-looking challenge. As AI techniques evolve—such as the move towards explainable AI (XAI) and ethical AI practices—vector databases need to adapt to support these new paradigms, which may require additional data points and attributes to be stored and retrieved efficiently. This might include metadata related to model decision processes or fairness metrics.

Involving a human-centric perspective, addressing biases that may be introduced during the integration process remains critical. Biases can emerge from the data itself, the way vector databases are structured, or how AI systems interpret vector data. Implementing fairness checks, involving diverse datasets, explicating AI decision-making processes,

138

and regular evaluations against ethical benchmarks mitigate these issues.

Moreover, tackling these challenges requires not only technical solutions but also organizational, cultural, and process-oriented adaptations. Encouraging collaboration between data engineers, AI researchers, database administrators, and domain experts ensures alignment in understanding the integration challenges and their potential impacts on business objectives.

Engaging in continuous learning, keeping abreast of the latest advances in vector databases and AI research, actively participating in open-source communities, and leveraging cloud-based solutions for distributed computing resources fortifies the strategic capability to surmount integration challenges effectively.

As AI technologies continue their rapid advancement, successful integration of vector databases will be a crucial determinant of the effectiveness, scalability, and reliability of AI systems across sectors seeking to harness the power of intelligent data insights. By addressing the multifaceted challenges of integration pragmatically and innovatively, organizations pave the path toward a seamless operational synergy between state-of-the-art technologies and insightful AI-driven solutions.

5.6   Real-time AI Applications

The development and deployment of real-time AI applications have grown exponentially with the advancement of computing technologies and algorithms, enabling the rapid processing of data as it arrives. Real-time AI involves systems designed to respond instantly or near-instantly to input, updating decisions and predictions while continuously interacting with their environment. These applications span various domains, from healthcare and finance to automotive and augmented reality, highlighting the transformative impact of real-time AI on contemporary technological landscapes.

Real-time AI systems require a constellation of technologies that integrate data acquisition, preprocessing, model inference, and decision-making into seamless workflows with minimal latency. Achieving real-time performance necessitates optimizing each component, balancing computational demands with the latency requirements of the intended context. Often, this involves the strategic deployment of hardware accelerators, sophisticated algorithms, and specialized data structures.

A fundamental element of real-time AI applications is their reliance on stream processing frameworks that manage continuous data flows. These frameworks enable the rapid ingestion and processing of data, applying models in real-time to maintain up-to-date insights. Tools like Apache Kafka, Apache Flink, and Apache Spark Streaming exemplify the robust infrastructure supporting real-time analytics, providing scalable and fault-tolerant processing capabilities. The implementation of such frameworks frequently involves distributed computing principles to manage workload across multiple nodes.

Consider the following example illustrating real-time streaming using Apache Kafka. In this setup, a producer sends data to a Kafka topic, which a consumer receives and processes in real-time:

```python
from kafka import KafkaProducer, KafkaConsumer
import json

# Initialize a Kafka producer
producer = KafkaProducer(
    bootstrap_servers='localhost:9092',
    value_serializer=lambda v: json.dumps(v).encode('utf-8')
)

# Send data to a Kafka topic
producer.send('realtime_topic', {'sensor_id': 1, 'value': 100})
producer.flush()

# Initialize a Kafka consumer
consumer = KafkaConsumer(
    'realtime_topic',
    bootstrap_servers='localhost:9092',
    value_deserializer=lambda v: json.loads(v.decode('utf-8'))
)

# Consume data in real-time
for message in consumer:
    print("Received data:", message.value)
    # Real-time processing logic goes here
```

In real-time AI, the deployment of machine learning models necessitates inference engines that can perform predictions at high speeds without compromising accuracy. Models optimized for real-time applications often undergo extensive processes such as quantization, which reduces model size and computation by approximating real-valued weights with lower precision arithmetic. This optimization is crucial for running models on edge devices or systems with constrained resources.

One of the quintessential domains benefiting from real-time AI is autonomous vehicles, where systems must constantly process sensory inputs to make instantaneous decisions, such as object detection, trajectory planning, and collision avoidance. These applications employ a combination of LIDAR, radar, and camera data, requiring sophisticated perception algorithms like Convolutional Neural Networks (CNNs) running on real-time inference frameworks.

In healthcare, real-time AI paves the way for continuous patient monitoring systems that alert clinicians to critical changes in vital signs. By analyzing physiological data from wearable sensors in real-time, these systems aid in early diagnosis and timely intervention, improving patient care outcomes.

For the finance sector, real-time AI is a cornerstone of algorithmic trading systems that analyze market data to execute trades swiftly, responding to fluctuations and emerging patterns before competitors. These systems utilize predictive models and anomaly detection algorithms to optimize trading strategies, requiring architectures that deliver low-latency processing.

In augmented reality (AR), real-time AI underpins applications that enhance physical environments with adaptive virtual overlays. Using real-time computer vision techniques, AR systems recognize and track objects in the user's surroundings, seamlessly integrating contextual information to enhance user experiences.

Real-time AI also powers advanced natural language processing in conversational agents, facilitating dynamic, ongoing dialogue with users. These systems process input in real-time, implementing decision trees, intent recognition, and sentiment analysis to deliver coherent and contextually appropriate responses. The following Python snippet demonstrates how such a real-time conversational agent might operate using the Natural Language Toolkit (NLTK):

```python
import nltk
from nltk.chat.util import Chat, reflections

# Define pairs for pattern matching and responses
pairs = [
```

```
    ['hi|hello|hey', ['Hello!', 'Hey there!']],
    ['how are you?', ['I am a real-time bot, always running!', 'Doing great, thank you!']],

    ['exit', ['Goodbye!', 'Have a great day!']],
]

# Initialize the Chat
chatbot = Chat(pairs, reflections)

# Start the conversation
print("Chatbot ready. Type 'exit' to end conversation.")
while True:
    user_input = input("You: ")
    if user_input.lower() == 'exit':
        break
    response = chatbot.respond(user_input)
    print("Bot:", response)
```

Implementing real-time AI systems invariably involves addressing challenges such as latency, throughput, and scalability. Maintaining low latency is critical, where even minor delays can impact system efficacy, particularly in time-sensitive applications. Leveraging caching, data prefetching, and efficient data structures can minimize access and computation delays.

Ensuring high throughput is essential for handling extensive data inputs typical of real-time streams. Systems must be designed to scale horizontally, dynamically adjusting resources to accommodate variations in data volume. Techniques like load balancing and distributed database architectures support scalable and reliable operations.

Real-time AI applications also necessitate considerations around data consistency and integrity, particularly when integrating with external data sources or APIs. Ensuring accurate and time-aligned data aggregation from multiple feeds requires robust synchronization and conflict resolution mechanisms.

Furthermore, real-time AI systems must be resilient to network and hardware failures, maintaining uninterrupted service and consistent performance. Incorporating redundancy, failover strategies, and monitoring tools enables quick recovery and ensures that services remain operational.

Security and privacy represent crucial aspects, given the dynamic nature of data in real-time systems. Implementing robust authentication, data encryption, and access controls protect against unauthorized access and data breaches, especially in systems handling sensitive information.

The continuous evolution of real-time AI hinges on advances in hardware acceleration, algorithm optimization, and distributed computing frameworks. Specialized hardware, such as Graphics Processing Units (GPUs), Tensor Processing Units (TPUs), and Field Programmable Gate Arrays (FPGAs), significantly boost processing efficiency and performance, enabling more complex models to run in real-time.

To leverage the full potential of real-time AI, organizations must foster interdisciplinary collaboration, combining domain expertise with technical acumen in data engineering, AI algorithm design, and system architecture. Practical implementations involve iterative development, empirical testing, and refinement to align performance with domain-specific needs.

As real-time AI continues to expand its footprint, it promises to redefine how systems and users interact with digital environments, offering unprecedented opportunities for innovation and enhancement across industries. By advancing real-time capabilities, AI systems are poised to deliver smarter, more intuitive, and responsive solutions that cater to an increasingly data-driven and instantaneous world.

5.7 Case Studies

Exploring case studies of vector database integration with AI systems offers valuable insights into practical applications and their transformative impacts across various industries. These case studies illustrate the real-world implementation of vector databases in diverse domains, showcasing how such integrations enable the efficient handling of high-dimensional data and empower AI systems to deliver enhanced accuracy and speed.

- **Case Study 1: Enhancing Image Recognition Systems in E-Commerce**

  In the competitive realm of e-commerce, visual search capabilities have become a critical differentiator, allowing users to find products through images rather than text descriptions. A lead-

143

ing e-commerce platform integrated vector databases to bolster its image recognition system, significantly improving search accuracy and reducing latency.

The platform utilized deep learning models, specifically Convolutional Neural Networks (CNNs), to convert product images into high-dimensional vector embeddings that capture detailed visual features. These embeddings were stored in a vector database optimized for similarity search, allowing the system to quickly identify and recommend similar products based on a user's uploaded image.

Key to this implementation was the use of an Approximate Nearest Neighbor (ANN) search algorithm within the vector database, which provided efficient retrieval without sacrificing too much accuracy. The shift from traditional database solutions to a vector-based approach reduced search response times from several seconds to milliseconds, enhancing user experience and engagement.

The following example describes how the vector embeddings might be generated using a deep learning framework like TensorFlow:

```
import tensorflow as tf
from tensorflow.keras.applications import ResNet50
from tensorflow.keras.preprocessing import image
from tensorflow.keras.applications.resnet50 import preprocess_input

# Load ResNet50 model
model = ResNet50(weights='imagenet', include_top=False, pooling='avg')

# Function to preprocess and extract image embeddings
def extract_embedding(img_path):
    img = image.load_img(img_path, target_size=(224, 224))
    img_data = image.img_to_array(img)
    img_data = np.expand_dims(img_data, axis=0)
    img_data = preprocess_input(img_data)
    embedding = model.predict(img_data)
    return embedding.flatten()

# Generate embedding for a sample product image
embedding_vector = extract_embedding('path/to/product_image.jpg')
```

- **Case Study 2: Semantic Search Optimization in Digital Libraries**

  A digital library aiming to enhance its search capabilities

144

employed vector databases to incorporate semantics into their search algorithms. Traditional keyword-based searches often failed to understand the context and intent behind queries, resulting in suboptimal user satisfaction.

By storing document embeddings generated through transformer-based language models like BERT, the library leveraged the semantic richness encapsulated in vectors. When users queried the library, the system parsed the query into embeddings and retrieved documents whose embeddings were closely aligned in vector space, thus recognizing synonyms and related concepts naturally.

Integration with vector databases not only enhanced search relevance but also improved the discovery of related documents and topics, providing a more insightful and intuitive user experience. Additionally, leveraging GPU-based acceleration cut down processing times, facilitating near-instantaneous retrieval.

This Python example demonstrates how document embeddings might be generated using Hugging Face's Transformers library for integration into a vector search engine:

```python
from transformers import BertTokenizer, BertModel
import torch

# Initialize BERT models
tokenizer = BertTokenizer.from_pretrained('bert-base-uncased')
model = BertModel.from_pretrained('bert-base-uncased')

def generate_document_embedding(text):
    inputs = tokenizer(text, return_tensors='pt', padding=True, truncation=
        True)
    outputs = model(**inputs)
    # Use the pooled output as the document embedding
    return outputs.last_hidden_state.mean(dim=1).squeeze().detach().numpy()

# Example document text
document_text = "Exploring the evolution of vector databases in AI
    applications."
embedding_vector = generate_document_embedding(document_text)
```

- **Case Study 3: Real-time Fraud Detection in Financial Services**

In the financial sector, detecting and preventing fraud is paramount. Financial institutions integrated vector databases

145

into their fraud detection systems to monitor transactions in real-time and identify suspicious activities promptly.

The system maintained a vectorized representation of legitimate transaction patterns, updating continuously as new transactions were processed. By applying anomaly detection algorithms, the AI system could discern deviations from established patterns, flagging transactions that differed significantly in vector space from the norm.

Vector databases enabled the high throughput and low-latency processing necessary for real-time monitoring. The integration allowed institutions to respond to potential fraudulent activities within milliseconds, drastically reducing financial loss and improving customer trust.

To address scalability and rapid data handling, the deployment made extensive use of cloud-native solutions and container orchestration to handle peak load scenarios without degraded performance.

- **Case Study 4: Personalized Learning in Education Technology**

An education technology startup aimed to personalize learning experiences for students through AI-driven recommendations. The system constructed student profiles as vector representations based on interaction with platform resources, quiz performances, and learning preferences.

By using a vector database, the platform compared student vectors with available course content and learning materials, generating personalized recommendations that matched each student's unique learning path. The efficiency of vector search enabled dynamic and adaptive learning experiences, adjusting resources in real-time as student progress was tracked.

Implementing embeddings that contextualize educational content alongside student profiles required model training on large educational datasets. This integration fostered an engaging learning platform, supporting both traditional students and lifelong learners in a personalized and responsive manner.

- **Case Study 5: Healthcare Diagnostics and Patient Monitoring**

  In healthcare, a hospital integrated vector databases to support AI-powered diagnostic tools and patient monitoring systems. The system employed vector embeddings to translate complex medical records, imaging data, and genomic sequences into comprehensive patient profiles.

  Vector databases supported intelligent retrieval systems that tracked patient health changes in real-time, generating alerts and recommendations for clinicians. This integration enabled predictive analytics, such as forecasting disease progression, through similarity comparisons with historical data from a wide patient population.

  By dynamically processing large-scale patient vectors, healthcare providers improved diagnosis accuracy, treatment plans, and patient outcomes. The adoption of explainable AI mechanisms provided transparency and interpretability of predictions, bolstering clinician trust and informed decision-making.

These case studies illustrate the profound impact of vector database integration across varied domains. Through enhanced efficiency, improved accuracy, and rapid data processing, vector databases empower AI systems to deliver smarter, richer, and more scalable solutions. As these technologies continue to evolve, their potential to drive innovation and enhance operational capabilities across industry sectors holds significant promise for the future.

Chapter 6

Performance Optimization and Scaling

Performance optimization and scaling are critical aspects of managing vector databases, ensuring they can handle increasing data volumes and query demands effectively. This chapter covers techniques for identifying performance bottlenecks, optimizing queries, and implementing scalable solutions. It discusses strategies for efficient load balancing, data partitioning, and caching mechanisms, all essential for enhancing system performance. Additionally, the chapter emphasizes the importance of continuous monitoring and tuning, offering insights into maintaining high-performance levels while accommodating growth in data and user queries.

6.1 Understanding Performance Bottlenecks

In any database system, particularly vector databases, performance bottlenecks can significantly affect throughput and latency. Understanding these bottlenecks is crucial for improving system efficiency and reliability. Vector databases, which deal extensively with high-dimensional data and complex similarity searches, often encounter unique challenges that traditional databases may not face. This section focuses on identifying common performance bottlenecks in vector databases and their underlying causes, offering insights into addressing these challenges.

A performance bottleneck occurs when the capacity of an application or a component of the database cannot meet the demand, leading to increased response times and reduced efficiency. In vector databases, such bottlenecks may stem from a variety of sources including hardware limitations, data complexity, inefficient query mechanisms, and network constraints.

1. Hardware Limitations:

Vector databases require substantial computational resources to perform operations like vector similarity searches, which involve computing distances between high-dimensional vectors. CPUs, GPUs, memory bandwidth, and disk I/O are critical hardware components that can become bottlenecks.

To diagnose hardware-related issues, monitoring tools like perf, top, or iostat can be utilized. These tools aid in assessing CPU load, memory usage, and disk activity. You can visualize the CPU usage over time with the following script:

```
#!/bin/bash
# Script to monitor CPU usage
while true; do
  top -b -n1 | grep "Cpu(s)" | \
  awk '{print $2 + $4}'
  sleep 1
done
```

Often, sufficient hardware is not dedicated to the vector database system, leading to operational delays. Upgrading processors or integrating GPUs for tasks like nearest neighbor searches can mitigate these limitations.

2. Data Complexity:

The complexity and dimensionality of the data itself can result in performance bottlenecks. Vector databases often manage large-scale datasets with high-dimensional vectors, which can be computationally expensive to handle.

To address these issues, dimensionality reduction techniques such as Principal Component Analysis (PCA) and t-Distributed Stochastic Neighbor Embedding (t-SNE) can be employed. These methods reduce the number of dimensions while preserving the essential characteristics of the data, facilitating faster computation.

3. Inefficient Query Mechanisms:

Query performance significantly affects database efficiency. The choice of similarity measurement techniques and indexing strategies can lead to substantial differences in execution speed.

Vector similarity is commonly determined by metrics such as Euclidean distance, cosine similarity, or Manhattan distance. Choosing the appropriate metric based on the dataset characteristics can reduce query time. Additionally, indexing methods like Approximate Nearest Neighbors (ANN) algorithms, such as locality-sensitive hashing (LSH) or KD-trees, offer performance improvements over brute-force search.

Consider the following Python code snippet for a brute-force search in a vector database:

```
import numpy as np

def euclidean_distance(vec1, vec2):
    return np.sqrt(np.sum((vec1 - vec2)**2))

def brute_force_search(query, data_vectors):
    closest_distance = float('inf')
    closest_vector = None
    for vector in data_vectors:
        distance = euclidean_distance(query, vector)
        if distance < closest_distance:
            closest_distance = distance
            closest_vector = vector
    return closest_vector

# Example usage:
query_vec = np.array([1.0, 2.0, 3.0])
```

```
data = [np.random.rand(3) for _ in range(1000)] # A list of 1000 random vectors
result = brute_force_search(query_vec, data)
print("Closest vector:", result)
```

This approach can become a bottleneck as datasets grow. Hence, transitioning to ANN methods and implementing efficient data partitioning strategies to limit search space become crucial for optimization.

4. Network Constraints:

Network latency and bandwidth limitations can also be significant bottlenecks, especially in a distributed system or cloud-based environment where data and computation are spread across multiple nodes.

To alleviate network-induced bottlenecks, optimizing data movement by compressing data transmission and leveraging direct data paths between nodes is critical. Additionally, employing caching strategies to minimize the need for frequent data access over the network can provide performance benefits.

Conclusion on Diagnosing and Resolving Bottlenecks:

A systematic approach is necessary for diagnosing and addressing performance bottlenecks. Begin by monitoring and measuring system performance to identify potential constraints, categorizing them into hardware, data, query mechanics, or network-related issues. Solutions like hardware upgrades, algorithm optimization, dimensionality reduction, and improved network configurations can address these constraints.

Appropriate monitoring and diagnosing tools must be in place to gather detailed usage statistics and application metrics. An iterative process of profiling, identifying bottlenecks, and deploying targeted optimizations ensures continuous performance enhancement of the vector database.

Understanding the intricacies of these performance bottlenecks and applying the right strategies can lead to substantial enhancement in the efficiency and reliability of vector databases, making them more equipped to handle increasingly complex workloads and data volumes.

6.2 Techniques for Query Optimization

Query optimization is vital for reducing retrieval time and improving the performance of vector databases, especially as data complexity and volume increase. This section explores various techniques and strategies designed to optimize queries in vector databases, where the focus is on speeding up similarity searches and enhancing access to high-dimensional data.

The primary goal of query optimization is to execute queries in the shortest time while utilizing the least amount of resources, ensuring that the database remains responsive and efficient even under substantial loads. This involves a set of techniques that can be categorized into three main areas: index optimization, query rewriting, and execution plan efficiency.

1. Index Optimization:

Indexes are essential for efficient query processing, especially for complex similarity search operations common in vector databases. Various indexing techniques are applicable based on the data structure and use case, such as tree-based, hash-based, and graph-based indexing.

Tree-Based Indexing: Structures like KD-trees and Ball trees facilitate nearest neighbor searches by organizing data into a tree form, allowing rapid traversals and pruned search spaces. Tree-based structures are effective for lower-dimensional data but often require adaptations for high-dimensional spaces due to performance degradation.

Hash-Based Indexing: Techniques such as Locality-Sensitive Hashing (LSH) transform the data into hash codes that preserve proximity. This approach excels in approximating nearest neighbors in high-dimensional spaces.

Consider a basic implementation of LSH for query optimization:

```
import numpy as np

class LSH:
    def __init__(self, num_hashes, dimensions):
        self.hash_tables = [{} for _ in range(num_hashes)]
        self.hash_functions = [np.random.randn(dimensions) for _ in range(
            num_hashes)]

    def _hash(self, vector, random_vector):
```

```
        return np.dot(vector, random_vector) >= 0

    def add(self, vector):
        for table, func in zip(self.hash_tables, self.hash_functions):
            hash_code = tuple(self._hash(vector, func))
            if hash_code not in table:
                table[hash_code] = []
            table[hash_code].append(vector)

    def query(self, vector):
        candidates = set()
        for table, func in zip(self.hash_tables, self.hash_functions):
            hash_code = tuple(self._hash(vector, func))
            candidates.update(table.get(hash_code, []))
        return candidates

# Initialize LSH with 10 hash tables for 128-dimensional vectors
lsh = LSH(num_hashes=10, dimensions=128)
data = [np.random.randn(128) for _ in range(1000)]
for vec in data:
    lsh.add(vec)

# Query a random vector
query_vec = np.random.randn(128)
nearest_candidates = lsh.query(query_vec)
print("Number of candidates found:", len(nearest_candidates))
```

Graph-Based Indexing: Graph approaches like Hierarchical Navigable Small World (HNSW) graphs offer superior performance by constructing a multi-layered graph that efficiently narrows down potential
nearest neighbors.

2. Query Rewriting:

Rewriting queries is a technique that improves efficiency by transforming a query into a form that can be executed more rapidly or produce
the same results with less computational cost. This often involves decomposing complex queries into simpler parts or leveraging statistical
insights to guide the rewrite process.

In vector databases, query rewriting can mean pre-calculating transformations or embeddings to minimize on-the-fly computations. For
example, if a system frequently performs similarity queries using cosine distance:

$$\text{cosine\_similarity}(A, B) = \frac{A \cdot B}{\|A\| \|B\|}$$

You could pre-calculate and store the norms of vectors alongside the

154

vectors themselves to reduce redundant computation during query execution.

By applying query rewriting, the database management system (DBMS) becomes smarter in deciding the optimal execution sequence or redefining the scope of required searches, consequently saving valuable resources and time.

3. Execution Plan Efficiency:

Execution plan optimization involves selecting the most efficient way to execute a query from multiple possibilities. This step includes selecting the right combination of algorithms and data access paths, which minimizes I/O and computation overhead.

Analyzers integrated within database systems play a crucial role. They inspect queries and utilize cost-based optimization models to select the most efficient path based on statistics and resources. This might mean choosing to scan subsets of data or leveraging existing indices and cache effectively.

The example below illustrates a pseudo-process of analyzing and optimizing query execution plans:

```
def cost_based_optimization(query, data_store):
    execution_plans = generate_possible_plans(query, data_store)

    def evaluate_cost(plan):
        # Cost evaluation logic based on I/O, CPU time, etc.
        num_io = estimate_io(plan, data_store)
        cpu_cost = estimate_cpu(plan)
        return num_io + cpu_cost

    best_plan = min(execution_plans, key=evaluate_cost)
    return best_plan

# Example usage:
current_query = "SELECT * FROM vectors WHERE similarity > 0.8"
optimal_plan = cost_based_optimization(current_query, database)
execute_query_plan(optimal_plan)
```

Effective query execution optimization also means utilizing parallel processing capabilities. Modern vector databases often deploy multithreading or distributed processing frameworks to accelerate query execution, enabling simultaneous processing of multiple query components.

By employing indexing optimizations, rewriting queries, and refining

155

execution plans, vector databases become more adept at handling intricate similarity searches with lower latencies. Continual performance advancements come from profiling the query behaviour, adjusting algorithms, and involving machine learning models that predict the optimal query paths based on historical data.

Query optimization in vector databases, thus, ensures that systems remain performant, scalable, and reliable under varying loads, leveraging both algorithmic improvements and architectural enhancements. These optimizations sustainably manage the growing demands and complexities of modern data environments.

6.3   Scaling Vector Databases

Scaling vector databases is a critical capability that ensures they can handle increasing data volumes, heightened query demands, and more complex operations effectively. As applications grow, the underlying database must accommodate these changes without suffering a loss in performance or becoming unreliable. This section discusses methods and best practices for scaling vector databases, focusing on architectural strategies, data distribution techniques, and computational optimizations.

Scaling can be approached along two principal axes: horizontal scaling (scaling out) and vertical scaling (scaling up). Each has its own advantages and application contexts, and they are often used in combination to meet specific performance and capacity goals.

1. Horizontal Scaling:

Horizontal scaling involves adding more nodes to the database architecture, effectively distributing the load across multiple machines. This approach is beneficial for achieving high availability and redundancy, as it ensures a failure in one node does not compromise the entire system.

Sharding: One prevalent technique in horizontal scaling is sharding, a strategy that divides data into smaller, manageable pieces called shards, each residing on a different node. By partitioning the dataset, each node only processes a subset of data during query execution, thus improving overall throughput.

Consider the following pseudo-code example demonstrating how sharding might be implemented:

```
class VectorDatabase:
    def __init__(self, num_shards):
        self.shards = [{} for _ in range(num_shards)]

    def add_vector(self, vector_id, vector):
        shard_index = hash(vector_id) % len(self.shards)
        self.shards[shard_index][vector_id] = vector

    def query_vector(self, vector_id):
        shard_index = hash(vector_id) % len(self.shards)
        return self.shards[shard_index].get(vector_id)

# Creating a vector database with 5 shards
vec_db = VectorDatabase(num_shards=5)
vec_db.add_vector('vec1', [0.5, 0.5, 0.5])
result = vec_db.query_vector('vec1')
print("Queried Vector:", result)
```

Replication: Another key consideration in horizontal scaling is replication. Replication involves maintaining copies of the same data on multiple nodes to ensure consistency and fault tolerance. While replication can increase storage overhead, it enhances data availability and reliability.

The challenge with sharding and replication lies in maintaining data consistency and synchronization across distributed nodes. Techniques such as eventual consistency and read-repair can be employed to ensure that the system remains consistent over time.

2. Vertical Scaling:

Vertical scaling, or scaling up, involves enhancing the capacity of a single node by adding more powerful CPUs, increasing memory, or improving I/O capabilities. This approach is often easier to implement than horizontal scaling but can reach a limit once the maximum physical capabilities of a machine are exhausted.

In high-performance vector databases, vertical scaling may support the intensive computational requirements for tasks like vector similarity computations, dimensionality reduction, and data indexing. By investing in more powerful hardware or utilizing specialized hardware such as GPUs and FPGAs, databases can achieve higher performance for certain operations.

In-Memory Databases: Scaling vertically with in-memory databases can offer significant performance boosts. These databases use RAM for data storage to achieve lower latency than disk-based storage systems. In-memory databases can be particularly beneficial for applications requiring rapid access to high-dimensional vector data.

3. Computational Optimizations:

Parallel Processing: To scale computationally intensive tasks, vector databases can utilize parallel processing. This involves dividing a larger computation into smaller, independent tasks that can be executed concurrently across multiple compute resources, such as CPU cores or distributed nodes.

For example, processing nearest neighbor searches or vector algebra operations can be parallelized:

```python
import numpy as np
from concurrent.futures import ThreadPoolExecutor

def vector_operation(vector):
    # Simulation of a computationally intensive operation
    return np.dot(vector, vector)

# Generate a list of random vectors
vectors = [np.random.rand(1000) for _ in range(10000)]

# Use ThreadPoolExecutor for parallel processing
with ThreadPoolExecutor() as executor:
    results = list(executor.map(vector_operation, vectors))

print("Processed vectors:", len(results))
```

Batch Processing: Implementing batch processing is another computational scaling method. Instead of processing individual queries or updates one at a time, the database processes multiple simultaneous operations in batches, reducing overhead and improving throughput.

4. Cloud-Based Scaling Solutions:

With the advent of cloud computing, vector databases have new avenues for scaling. Cloud platforms provide flexible resources, enabling dynamic scaling based on current demand.

Auto-Scaling: Cloud services offer auto-scaling capabilities, automatically adjusting resources such as compute instances or storage volumes in response to workload fluctuations. Auto-scaling ensures that vector databases maintain performance and cost-efficiency even during spikes or dips in usage.

Serverless Architectures: Serverless computing abstracts infrastructure management, allowing developers to focus solely on application logic. For vector databases, this means leveraging managed services that autonomously handle scaling and resource allocation.

5. Monitoring and Optimization:

Regardless of the scaling strategy chosen, continuous monitoring and optimization are necessary to maintain optimal performance. Tools for monitoring system health, resource usage, and database performance provide insights that guide scaling decisions. Regular assessments can identify bottlenecks or inefficiencies, leading to informed scaling and tuning decisions.

Scaling vector databases requires careful planning and implementation, aligning technical efforts with organizational needs. By selecting appropriate scaling strategies, whether horizontal, vertical, or cloud-based, combined with tactical optimizations, vector databases can efficiently address evolving data needs and query loads.

6.4 Load Balancing Approaches

Load balancing is a critical aspect of maintaining efficient performance and ensuring the reliability of vector databases, particularly as they scale to handle larger datasets and increased query loads. The main objective of load balancing is to distribute queries and data across multiple resources so that no single node becomes a performance bottleneck. This section delves into various load balancing techniques, architectural considerations, and innovative methods to enhance the effective distribution of workload in vector databases.

Load balancing can be implemented at several levels, including network, data, and computational load balancing. Each level addresses different aspects of system demands and resource utilization.

- **Architectural Considerations in Load Balancing:**

  Implementing an effective load balancing strategy begins with understanding the architecture of the vector database system.

Key considerations include the type of databases, whether it is centralized or distributed, and whether the deployment is on-premises or cloud-based.

- *Centralized vs. Distributed Systems:* Centralized databases, with a single point of access, often require a network load balancer to manage incoming traffic. In contrast, distributed databases benefit from both network and data-level load balancing to ensure evenly distributed processing and storage across nodes.

- *Cloud vs. On-Premises Deployment:* Cloud services offer built-in load balancing capabilities that can dynamically adjust to varying loads, taking advantage of cloud elasticity. On-premises setups, however, may require custom solutions and hardware to achieve similar flexibility.

- **Network Load Balancing:**

  At the core level, network load balancing ensures efficient management of incoming traffic by distributing requests among servers. It is crucial for avoiding network congestion and ensuring high throughput and low latency.

- *Round Robin:* A basic approach for network load balancing is the round robin method, where each incoming query is forwarded to the next server in line sequentially. This method works well for homogenous workloads but may not perform optimally for varied or complex data distributions.

- *Least Connections:* This strategy directs queries to the server with the fewest active connections, thus balancing load based on current utilization rather than a static schedule. It is effective for managing real-time fluctuations in server loads.

The following configuration represents a conceptual model of a round robin load balancer in Python:

```python
from itertools import cycle

class RoundRobinBalancer:
    def __init__(self, servers):
        self.servers = cycle(servers)
```

```
    def get_next_server(self):
        return next(self.servers)

servers = ["server1", "server2", "server3"]
balancer = RoundRobinBalancer(servers)

# Simulate incoming requests
for _ in range(10):
    server = balancer.get_next_server()
    print(f"Redirecting request to: {server}")
```

- **Data-Level Load Balancing:**

  Data load balancing involves effectively distributing data across nodes in a vector database. By dividing the dataset into evenly sized partitions, this method ensures more balanced query processing.

  - *Partitioning:* Effective data partitioning strategies such as horizontal partitioning (sharding) and vertical partitioning are vital. In horizontal partitioning, data is divided into rows distributed across nodes, while vertical partitioning involves distributing columns. Clever partitioning based on data access patterns greatly enhances load balancing.

  - *Replication:* Maintaining multiple copies of data across different nodes (data replication) supports load balancing by allowing the database to handle queries on any replica, thus sharing the load across several nodes.

Consider a pseudo-code example where two different data partitioning strategies are applied:

```
class DataPartitioner:
    def __init__(self, data, partition_strategy):
        self.data = data
        self.partition_strategy = partition_strategy

    def partition_data(self):
        if self.partition_strategy == 'horizontal':
            return self._horizontal_partition()
        elif self.partition_strategy == 'vertical':
            return self._vertical_partition()

    def _horizontal_partition(self):
        return [{"shard_1": self.data[:len(self.data)//2]},
                {"shard_2": self.data[len(self.data)//2:]}]
```

161

```
def _vertical_partition(self):
    # Assuming data as list of dictionaries (columns as keys)
    columns = list(self.data[0].keys())
    midpoint = len(columns) // 2
    return [{"partition_1": [{k: row[k] for k in columns[:midpoint]} for row in self.
        data]},
            {"partition_2": [{k: row[k] for k in columns[midpoint:]} for row in self.
                data]}]

data = [{"id": 1, "value_a": 100, "value_b": 200},
        {"id": 2, "value_a": 110, "value_b": 210}]
partitioner = DataPartitioner(data, 'horizontal')
shards = partitioner.partition_data()
print(shards)
```

- **Computational Load Balancing:**

  This aspect focuses on distributing the computational effort required for query execution across available processors, cores, or even different systems, which is critical for handling complex vector operations efficiently.

  - *Task Queuing:* A queue-based task distribution mechanism can help map incoming queries to available computational resources, ensuring that no processor is overburdened while others are idle. Dynamic scheduling techniques can adaptively assign high-priority or time-sensitive queries to underutilized nodes.

  - *MapReduce Model:* Some vector database operations can be transformed into a MapReduce model, which splits a query into smaller computations (Map), processes them in parallel, and integrates the results (Reduce).

Below is a simplified implementation of a task queuing system for handling vector calculations:

```
from queue import Queue
from threading import Thread

def worker(task_queue, results):
    while not task_queue.empty():
        vector, operation = task_queue.get()
        result = operation(vector)
        results.append(result)
        task_queue.task_done()

# Simulate vector operations
```

```
def compute_magnitude(vector):
    return sum(x ** 2 for x in vector) ** 0.5

task_queue = Queue()
results = []

# Insert tasks into queue
vectors = [[1, 2, 3], [4, 5, 6], [7, 8, 9]]
for vec in vectors:
    task_queue.put((vec, compute_magnitude))

# Start threads
num_worker_threads = 3
threads = []

for _ in range(num_worker_threads):
    thread = Thread(target=worker, args=(task_queue, results))
    thread.start()
    threads.append(thread)

for thread in threads:
    thread.join()

print("Computed Results:", results)
```

- **Strategies for Load Balancing:**

- *Dynamic Load Balancing:* In complex environments, workload distributions can vary significantly. Dynamic load balancing systems adjust workloads in real-time by monitoring system performance metrics, ensuring an equitable distribution of resources.

- *Feedback Loops:* Implementing feedback loops where nodes report their load status back to the load balancer allows for continual adjustment and optimal distribution.

- *Predictive Load Balancing:* Leveraging machine learning techniques to predict workload spikes and redistributing resources proactively can enhance the efficiency of load balancing systems, reducing latency and improving throughput.

Load balancing is an essential practice for maintaining the robustness and responsiveness of vector databases, especially as they scale. By employing a combination of strategies aimed at network, data, and computation, along with using modern dynamic and predictive models, vector databases can achieve optimal performance under diverse and challenging conditions. These methodologies ensure that resources

163

are used effectively, minimizing downtimes and maximizing the capabilities of the system infrastructure.

6.5 Data Partitioning Strategies

Data partitioning is a fundamental approach to managing performance and scalability in vector databases. By dividing a large dataset into smaller, more manageable pieces, partitioning allows for efficient data access, reduced query response times, and optimized storage utilization. In vector databases, where managing high-dimensional data is routine, effective partitioning strategies play a critical role in system performance and manageability. This section explores various data partitioning strategies, their applications, and implementation considerations, providing insights into optimizing vector databases.

1. Introduction to Data Partitioning:

Partitioning is the process of distributing data across multiple storage segments to enhance database efficiency. The primary aim is to facilitate faster query processing by narrowing the search space, reducing the volume of data any given query needs to sift through.

The key benefits of effective data partitioning include:

- Improved query performance by enabling parallel processing.

- Enhanced scalability by seamlessly adding more segments as data grows.

- Better resource utilization through balanced load distribution.

- Simplified management and maintenance of large datasets.

2. Horizontal Partitioning (Sharding):

Horizontal partitioning, or sharding, involves splitting the dataset into rows that are distributed across different partitions or shards. Each shard typically contains a subset of rows from the table but with all the same attributes.

164

Sharding is particularly beneficial for distributing data of high volume and achieving parallel query execution. It enables horizontal scaling by adding more machines to host additional shards.

Range-Based Sharding: In this approach, data is divided into shards based on a range of values for a specific column, often a timestamp or an identifier. This method can lead to hotspot issues if most queries are concentrated around a particular shard.

Hash-Based Sharding: Data is partitioned based on a hash function applied to a key attribute (e.g., a user ID). This approach helps distribute data evenly but can lead to complexity in managing shard keys and rebalancing shards.

Below is a basic example illustrating hash-based sharding in a vector database context:

```
class HashPartitioner:
    def __init__(self, num_shards):
        self.shards = [{} for _ in range(num_shards)]

    def get_shard(self, key):
        return hash(key) % len(self.shards)

    def add_data(self, key, data):
        shard_index = self.get_shard(key)
        self.shards[shard_index][key] = data

    def get_data(self, key):
        shard_index = self.get_shard(key)
        return self.shards[shard_index].get(key)

# Example usage
partitioner = HashPartitioner(num_shards=3)
partitioner.add_data('user1', [1.0, 0.5, 0.3])
print(partitioner.get_data('user1'))
```

3. Vertical Partitioning:

Vertical partitioning involves dividing data into subsets of columns rather than rows. This strategy is effective when different columns are accessed independently or have different storage requirements.

Columnar Storage: By storing data in columns rather than rows, databases can optimize query performance for analytical applications where operations commonly access entire columns.

Benefits: Vertical partitioning enhances I/O performance for read-heavy operations and reduces data redundancy. However, it may increase the complexity of handling join operations where access to the original table structure is required.

4. Hybrid Partitioning:

Hybrid partitioning combines elements of both horizontal and vertical partitioning to optimize performance across a wider variety of queries. For example, a database might employ hash-based sharding to distribute rows across nodes while also storing each shard's data in a columnar format.

5. Partitioning Strategies and Performance:

Selecting the appropriate partitioning strategy is crucial and depends heavily on the use case and query workload. The following factors should guide the choice of partitioning method:

- *Query Patterns:* Analyze query patterns to determine how data is accessed in typical scenarios. If queries often require access to all columns but only specific rows, horizontal partitioning is more appropriate.

- *Data Growth and Workload Scalability:* If data is expected to grow rapidly or there's a significant increase in query load, more dynamic partitioning strategies such as range-based or hash-based sharding might be required.

- *Data Access and Update Frequency:* For databases with frequent read operations against entire columns or data that does not change often, vertical partitioning may offer performance benefits.

6. Implementing Partitioning: Considerations:

- *Rebalancing Data Across Partitions:* Over time, the distribution of data might become uneven, requiring rebalancing. Automated tools or custom solutions must be in place to redistribute the data efficiently without impacting performance.

- *Data Locality and Caching:* Ensure that partitioning strategies maintain data locality for queries that may need to access closely related data points. Similarly, caching mechanisms should align with partitioning strategy to enhance performance.

- *Consistency Management:* In distributed systems, especially those applying horizontal partitioning, maintaining data consistency across partitions is a challenge. Techniques such as consensus protocols or distributed transactions can be utilized to ensure consistency.

- *Indexing Considerations:* Indexing strategies should be aligned with the partitioning scheme to avoid redundant indices that could deter performance benefits.

7. Advanced Partitioning Techniques:

For complex systems and diverse data distributions, more advanced techniques may be applicable:

Dynamic Partitioning: Adjusts partitions dynamically based on current system load and data access patterns. This approach can prevent overloading any single partition and adapt gracefully to variable workloads.

Machine Learning for Partitioning: Leveraging machine learning algorithms can forecast access patterns and data growth trends, informing intelligent partitioning decisions. Predictive models help anticipate which partitions will require sharding or replication to maintain balanced performance metrics.

Effective data partitioning strategies are integral to the optimization of vector databases, enabling them to scale efficiently while maintaining high performance. By understanding the underlying data access patterns and system requirements, database administrators can choose and implement appropriate partitioning techniques, ensuring the database continues to operate smoothly and sustainably as workloads and datasets grow. These strategies not only facilitate efficient storage and retrieval of information but also play a vital role in achieving a balanced, responsive, and scalable data architecture in modern applications.

6.6 Caching Mechanisms

Caching mechanisms are pivotal in enhancing data retrieval speed and overall system performance in vector databases. By temporarily storing frequently accessed data, caching allows databases to reduce retrieval times, lower network latency, and lighten the load on backend systems. This section explores various caching strategies, their implementation, usage scenarios, and how they integrate with vector databases to optimize performance.

Effective caching strategies require an understanding of access patterns, cache storage configurations, and timely invalidation policies. Different caching levels and techniques can be applied depending on the specific requirements of the database system, such as memory availability and network constraints.

1. Fundamentals of Caching:

Caching refers to the process of storing data in a temporary storage area, or cache, so that future requests can be served faster. This is achieved by eliminating the need for repeated and expensive data retrieval operations from slower backend databases.

Key benefits of caching include:

- Faster data retrieval times for frequently used queries or operations.

- Reduced load on the primary database, as fewer queries are needed against the main data store.

- Enhanced user experience due to lower latency in data access.

The efficiency of a caching mechanism depends significantly on the choice of cache strategy that aligns with access patterns and application needs.

2. Caching Strategies:

Several caching strategies can be implemented in vector databases to boost their performance:

Read-Through Cache: A read-through cache loads data into the cache on a cache miss, meaning when data requested by a query is not found in the cache, it is retrieved from the database and then stored in the cache before being returned to the client. This strategy is simple to implement and ensures up-to-date data in the cache.

Write-Through Cache: When data is written or updated, it is immediately added to both the cache and the backend database. This ensures data integrity but may lead to increased I/O and latency due to synchronous updates.

Write-Behind Cache: Updates are performed against the cache rather than directly to the database. The data is periodically synchronized with the database asynchronously. This approach can reduce write latencies but may increase the risk of data inconsistency.

Cache Aside (Lazy Loading): The application checks the cache first before querying the primary database. If the data is not present (cache miss), it retrieves the data from the database, stores it in the cache, and then returns it to the client. This strategy is useful in scenarios where data can be computed or fetched on demand without immediate need for freshness.

The following code snippet illustrates a simple implementation of cache aside technique using Python:

```python
class Cache:
    def __init__(self):
        self.storage = {}

    def get(self, key):
        return self.storage.get(key)

    def set(self, key, value):
        self.storage[key] = value

class Database:
    def fetch_from_db(self, key):
        # Simulation of database querying
        print("Fetching data from database...")
        return f"Value for {key}"

cache = Cache()
database = Database()

def get_data(key):
    # Check if data is in cache
    value = cache.get(key)
    if value is None:
        # Cache miss: fetch from database and cache the result
        value = database.fetch_from_db(key)
        cache.set(key, value)
    else:
```

```
        print("Cache hit!")
    return value

# Example usage
print(get_data("key1")) # Cache miss and fetch from DB
print(get_data("key1")) # Cache hit
```

3. Cache Invalidation Policies:

Maintaining cache coherence with the underlying data is crucial to ensure the cached data remains relevant. Various cache invalidation policies are employed to manage this:

Time-Based Expiry: Data is considered stale after a predetermined time-to-live (TTL) period, after which it is automatically invalidated.

Event-Based Invalidation: External triggers or events dictate when cached data should be invalidated, typically following an update to the database records.

Least Recently Used (LRU): This policy evicts the least recently accessed entries in favor of more frequently accessed data, optimizing for cache hits.

Random Replacement: An entry from the cache is randomly chosen and replaced. While simpler than LRU, it may lead to suboptimal caching of frequently accessed items.

4. Levels of Caching:

Caching can be applied at multiple levels to enhance efficiency and performance:

Client-Side Caching: Caches are implemented at the client level to reduce server load and latency, as the client can serve repeated data accesses locally without involving the network.

Edge Caching: By caching data closer to the network edge, often through Content Delivery Networks (CDN), systems can improve response times for geographically distributed users by reducing backhaul traffic to data centers.

Server-Side Caching: Server-side caches, which might involve distributed caching systems like Redis or Memcached, improve access speeds to frequently used data across multiple server instances.

5. Caching in Distributed Systems:

In distributed environments, special considerations are required to ensure cache consistency and coherence across nodes:

Distributed Cache System: A distributed cache like Redis Cluster or Memcached is shared across multiple nodes, enabling horizontal scaling of the cache layer to accommodate larger datasets or higher access frequencies.

Data Serialization: When dealing with complex vector data, serialization techniques should be optimized to minimize cache latency and improve access efficiency.

Consistency Models: Implementing consistency models like strong or eventual consistency helps maintain data coherence across distributed caches, balancing the trade-offs between immediacy and consistency.

6. Implementation Considerations:

Implementing an effective cache strategy involves careful planning and tuning:

- *Size and Capacity Planning:* Caches should be sized appropriately to maximize hit rates without consuming excessive memory.

- *Monitoring and Metrics:* Monitoring tools should be employed to analyze cache hit/miss ratios, throughput, and latency, to fine-tune cache parameters and policies for optimal performance.

- *Security and Data Sensitivity:* Ensure that sensitive data is not cached unless adequately encrypted and access-controlled, particularly in distributed or client-side caches.

- *Testing and Validation:* Rigorous testing is essential to ensure cache strategies align with application behavior under varying loads and conditions.

Caching mechanisms are instrumental in optimizing the performance of vector databases, offering significant improvements in data access times and reducing backend workloads. By carefully selecting and implementing the appropriate caching strategies and policies, databases can achieve a balance between performance, data consistency, and resource utilization, ultimately enhancing user experience and operational efficiency.

6.7 Monitoring and Performance Tuning

Monitoring and performance tuning are integral components in the maintenance of vector databases, ensuring that they operate at optimal levels while accommodating increases in data size and query complexity. An effective strategy combines thorough monitoring practices with performance tuning techniques to identify bottlenecks and enhance system capabilities. This section investigates tools and techniques for monitoring system performance, as well as methodologies for implementing tuning practices to maintain high-functioning vector databases.

1. Importance of Monitoring:

Monitoring serves as the eyes and ears of a database management system. It provides critical insights into operational health, resource utilization, and potential issues before they escalate into major problems.

The benefits of systematic monitoring include:

- Early detection of performance bottlenecks and anomalies.

- Comprehensive understanding of database usage patterns.

- Enhanced capacity planning and resource allocation.

- Improved reliability and availability of the database system.

2. Key Metrics for Vector Databases:

Monitoring efforts should focus on collecting key performance metrics that accurately reflect the state of the database:

Resource Utilization: Monitoring CPU, memory, disk, and network usage helps ascertain if hardware resources are adequately provisioned or if there are areas of congestion.

Query Performance: Metrics such as query throughput, response time, and latency provide insights into the efficiency of query processing and potential areas for optimization.

Data Volume and Growth: Keeping track of data size and growth trends supports informed decisions about scaling and partitioning strategies.

Error Rates and Failures: Monitoring error logs and failure rates is crucial for identifying problematic queries, indexing issues, or hardware faults.

3. Monitoring Tools and Technologies:

Several tools and technologies are available to facilitate detailed monitoring of vector databases:

Prometheus and Grafana: This powerful combination offers extensive metrics collection, storage, and visualization capabilities, allowing users to create detailed dashboards and alerts that track database performance in real-time.

ELK Stack (Elasticsearch, Logstash, and Kibana): ELK is used for log aggregation, real-time data analysis, and visualization, providing valuable insights into application and database activities.

Custom Monitoring Scripts: Tailored scripts can be developed to cater to specific monitoring requirements, offering flexibility in data collection and analysis. For example, a simple Python script can gather CPU and memory usage statistics:

```python
import psutil
import time

def monitor_system():
    while True:
        cpu_usage = psutil.cpu_percent(interval=1)
        memory_usage = psutil.virtual_memory().percent
        print(f"CPU Usage: {cpu_usage}% | Memory Usage: {memory_usage}%")
        time.sleep(5) # Gather stats every 5 seconds

monitor_system()
```

4. Performance Tuning Techniques:

Performance tuning is the process of modifying a system to operate more efficiently by optimizing various components. This involves a careful balance between enhancing performance and maintaining resource efficiency:

Query Optimization: Analyzing query plans and rewriting queries to minimize execution time is crucial for performance improvements. Applying indexing strategies and ensuring query predicates can access indexed columns effectively reduces search space, resulting in faster execution.

173

Index Tuning: Maintaining optimal index structures is important for improving data access times. This may involve creating new indices for frequently queried fields or periodically updating and rebuilding existing indices to reduce fragmentation.

Memory Tuning: Configuring memory allocation settings, such as buffer pool sizes, can significantly impact database performance by reducing the need for disk I/O operations. Memory optimization tools can help identify ideal settings for memory-bound operations.

Concurrency Control: Fine-tuning concurrency controls, such as lock granularity and transaction isolation levels, can balance between concurrent access and data consistency while minimizing overheads related to locking and serialization.

5. Advanced Tuning Practices:

Data Partitioning Re-evaluation: Revisiting and optimizing data partitioning methods can alleviate bottlenecks associated with uneven data distribution by ensuring balanced workload across shards or columns.

Load Balancing Enhancements: Implementing adaptive load balancing strategies based on monitored metrics can dynamically distribute loads more effectively, preventing hotspots and uneven resource utilization.

Profiling and Bottleneck Identification: Profiling tools help identify specific areas in the system that contribute to performance degradation. By isolating and addressing these bottlenecks, substantial performance gains can be achieved.

Below is an example of a simple profiler script that measures execution time for functions:

```
import time

def profile(func):
    def wrapper(*args, **kwargs):
        start_time = time.time()
        result = func(*args, **kwargs)
        end_time = time.time()
        print(f"Execution time for {func.___name___}: {end_time - start_time:.4f}
            seconds")
        return result
    return wrapper

@profile
```

```
def sample_query():
    # Simulate a database operation
    time.sleep(2)
    return "Query Result"

# Example usage
sample_query()
```

6. Continuous Improvement Cycle:

Performance tuning should be an iterative and continuous process, where monitoring informs tuning decisions, and tuning efforts are validated by monitoring outcomes. This cycle involves:

- *Detecting and Analyzing Issues:* Regularly reviewing monitoring data to identify emerging trends or problem areas.

- *Implementing Optimization Strategies:* Deploying tuning techniques based on identified issues and expected improvements.

- *Validating Changes:* Using monitoring data to assess the effectiveness of implemented strategies, refining approaches as needed.

- *Feedback Loop:* Consistently feeding back observations into the tuning process, allowing for adaptive changes that align with evolving data and workload requirements.

Monitoring and performance tuning in vector databases constitute a strategic approach to achieving and maintaining peak operational efficiency. With the right tools, metrics, and methodologies, system administrators can ensure that their databases deliver fast, reliable, and scalable service, ready to meet the demands of modern data-centric applications.

Chapter 7

Applications of Vector Databases

Vector databases are pivotal in a wide range of modern applications, leveraging their ability to handle and analyze complex, high-dimensional data. This chapter explores various use cases where vector databases excel, such as recommendation systems, image and video retrieval, and natural language processing tasks. It also examines their role in biometric data analysis, fraud detection, and powering semantic search engines. By presenting industry-specific case studies, the chapter highlights the practical implementation and benefits of vector databases in enhancing the effectiveness and efficiency of diverse applications across different sectors.

7.1   Recommendation Systems

The application of vector databases in recommendation systems takes a pivotal role in shaping the user experience across digital platforms. These databases enhance the performance of recommendation systems by leveraging vector similarities, permitting the handling of complex, high-dimensional data essential for personalizing services effectively.

177

Their capacity to analyze and process vast amounts of data quickly makes vector databases an indispensable tool in this domain.

Recommendation systems are integral in guiding users toward products or content they may find interesting, based on past behaviors, preferences, and other contextual data. Traditionally, recommendation algorithms have depended heavily on collaborative filtering and content-based filtering techniques. However, the advent and integration of vector databases have significantly advanced these methods by enhancing data similarity computations and reducing computational overheads.

In a typical recommendation system, users and items can be represented as vectors in a high-dimensional space. The central task is to identify those items similar to a given user's preferences. Here, vector databases come into play by efficiently storing these high-dimensional vectors and facilitating quick similarity searches through advanced indexing techniques.

```
import numpy as np

# Example vectors representing user preferences and items
user_vector = np.array([0.82, 0.15, 0.03]) # User data
item_vectors = np.array([
    [0.60, 0.20, 0.20], # Item 1
    [0.90, 0.05, 0.05], # Item 2
    [0.30, 0.40, 0.30], # Item 3
])

# Computing cosine similarities
cosine_similarities = np.dot(item_vectors, user_vector) / (
    np.linalg.norm(item_vectors, axis=1) * np.linalg.norm(user_vector))
```

In this example, user and item vectors are defined in a three-dimensional space with computing their cosine similarities to assess the relevance of each item to the user. Vector databases adeptly manage such operations at scale by supporting efficient nearest neighbor searches.

Vector similarity operations, such as cosine similarity used in the example above, are foundational in assessing the closeness of different vectors. The computational complexity of these operations challenges traditional databases, particularly when expanding to millions of user and item interactions. However, vector databases employ highly optimized search algorithms like locality-sensitive hashing (LSH) and partition-based methods, which dramatically reduce the time required to return relevant results.

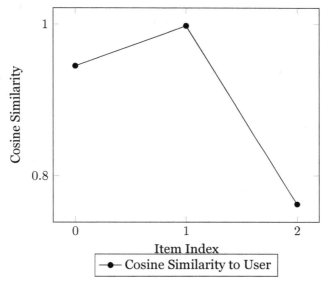

Figure 7.1: Cosine Similarities between User Vector and Item Vectors

Figure 7.1 illustrates the computed cosine similarities for the sample data. The similarity scores are crucial for the ranking of items, determining which items should be recommended.

Beyond computation optimizations, vector databases also support hybrid recommendation strategies that combine multiple types of data and dimensions. For instance, they can integrate contextual information like time of day, location, or current events, enriching the user profile vectors and improving recommendation accuracy.

One of the challenges in recommendation systems is dealing with the "cold start" problem, where new users or items are introduced without sufficient historical data to make effective recommendations. Vector databases address this issue by leveraging content-based filtering methodologies that use attributes and features of items to build vectors. This approach allows for synthesizing recommendations until sufficient user interaction data is available.

```
from sklearn.feature_extraction.text import TfidfVectorizer

# Sample item descriptions
descriptions = [
    "Action-packed adventure with thrilling battles",
    "A romantic story set in the 19th century",
    "Science fiction exploration of parallel universes"
]

# TF-IDF feature extraction
vectorizer = TfidfVectorizer()
item_tfidf_matrix = vectorizer.fit_transform(descriptions)

# New user prefers action and adventure
new_user_profile = vectorizer.transform(["Adventure action thrilled"])
cosine_similarities = np.dot(item_tfidf_matrix, new_user_profile.T).toarray()
```

The example demonstrates using TF-IDF (Term Frequency-Inverse Document Frequency) vectors for generating recommendations for "cold start" users, focusing on the content attributes of the items.

Further intricacies of recommendation systems involve concepts like diversity and fairness. In an effort to personalize experiences, the diversity of recommendations ensures users are not confined to monotone or repetitive suggestions. Similarly, fairness addresses bias that might arise, for instance, from disproportionately promoting items from certain categories or sources. Vector databases mitigate these issues by implementing multi-objective optimization strategies, ensuring they can balance relevance with diversity and fairness.

Utilizing sophisticated machine learning models further augments vector-based recommendation systems. Deep learning models, particularly neural network architectures like Siamese networks and autoencoders, transform user and item representations into dense, latent vectors that capture more intricate relationships and interactions. Vector databases then store and manage these complex embeddings, ensuring efficient retrieval and application within recommendation systems.

```
from tensorflow.keras.models import Model
from tensorflow.keras.layers import Input, LSTM, RepeatVector, TimeDistributed,
    Dense

# Sequence Input
timesteps = 10
input_dim = 3

inputs = Input(shape=(timesteps, input_dim))
encoded = LSTM(128, activation='relu')(inputs)
decoded = RepeatVector(timesteps)(encoded)
```

```
decoded = LSTM(128, activation='relu', return_sequences=True)(decoded)
outputs = TimeDistributed(Dense(input_dim))(decoded)

autoencoder = Model(inputs, outputs)
autoencoder.compile(optimizer='adam', loss='mse')

# Autoencoders to compress user-item interaction sequences into latent vectors
```

The Python snippet illustrates constructing an LSTM-based autoencoder designed to compress and reconstruct user-interaction sequences, generating latent vectors embodying user patterns effectively.

Recommendation system pipelines are facilitated in vector databases by parallel processing capabilities and distributed architectures, facilitating high-throughput and real-time recommendations among extensive datasets. The scalability of these systems affords adaptability in accommodating varying data scales and enables the conclusion of extensive similarity calculations that would typically impede performance.

Furthermore, integrating feedback loops within vector databases nurtures the continuous improvement of recommendations. By capturing user interactions and updating vectors dynamically, the database supports the fine-tuning and adaptation of recommendations, responding rapidly to evolving user preferences and behaviors.

The application of vector databases significantly reduces the entropy and computational complexity inherent in generating recommendations, bringing precise, scalable, and efficient solutions. Consequently, vector databases are transformative in developing sophisticated recommendation systems that transcend traditional limitations, substantially enhancing personalization and user satisfaction.

7.2 Image and Video Retrieval

The utilization of vector databases in image and video retrieval tasks represents a significant advancement in the field of multimedia information retrieval. Vector databases enhance these processes by efficiently handling and processing high-dimensional data, such as feature vectors extracted from images and videos, enabling rapid and precise content retrieval. With the exponential growth of multimedia content, effective retrieval methods become crucial, benefiting from the capacity of vector databases to manage and exploit vector similarities.

Image and video retrieval systems rely heavily on feature extraction algorithms, which transform visual content into vector representations. These vectors typically encapsulate various visual characteristics such as color, texture, and shape for images, and extend to capturing temporal dynamics for videos. Vector databases store these high-dimensional feature vectors, providing the foundational infrastructure for executing similarity searches and facilitating the retrieval process.

```
import cv2

# Load an image
image = cv2.imread('example_image.jpg', cv2.IMREAD_GRAYSCALE)

# Initialize the SIFT feature detector
sift = cv2.SIFT_create()

# Detect SIFT features and compute descriptors
keypoints, descriptors = sift.detectAndCompute(image, None)

# Descriptors serve as feature vectors for image retrieval
print(descriptors.shape) # Outputs: (Number of keypoints, 128)
```

Using the Scale-Invariant Feature Transform (SIFT), key features from images are extracted yielding vectors stored within a vector database, enabling similarity-based searches for retrieval.

Once the images and videos are converted into their corresponding feature vectors, the retrieval systems employ these vectors to match against a query vector derived from a user's input image or video. This task predominantly involves conducting nearest neighbor searches where vector databases excel by using efficient indexing structures such as KD-trees or enhanced methods like Approximate Nearest Neighbor (ANN) techniques.

Vector databases harness these methodologies to not only retrieve visually similar content based on user queries but also support query-by-example functionality, where retrieved content closely resembles a given example image or video clip. A user seeking to find a similar video or image within a large repository can furnish a sample, and the system subsequently computes the vector similarity across the database to return the most relevant matches.

>>> Searching for images similar to the provided example...

182

```
>>> Retrieving top 5 most similar images...
>>> Completed in 0.002 seconds.
```

The retrieval output is expressed in ranked similarity scores, easily interpretable by user interfaces facilitating rapid content identification. As shown above, efficiency in retrieval can even support real-time applications, a fundamental requirement in modern online systems.

Beyond the efficiency in retrieving simple image data, vector databases handle the complexities inherent in videos by managing sequential frames as temporal vectors. Each frame can be decomposed into feature vectors, typically employing convolutional neural networks (CNNs), which capture nuanced spatial and temporal transitions inherent to video files. These intricate vectorizations are stored and managed within vector databases, allowing precise and comprehensive video retrieval capabilities.

For video data, vector representation extends into using specialized models like Long Short-Term Memory (LSTM) networks or more advanced methods that capture temporal dependencies uniquely present in video sequences. By embedding these layers of representation, vector databases offer enhanced fetching functionality where retrieval can be executed based on temporal patterns recognized from the user-defined query.

```python
import torch
from torchvision import models, transforms
from PIL import Image

# Pretrained model
model = models.resnet50(pretrained=True)
model.eval()

# Image preprocessing
preprocess = transforms.Compose([
    transforms.Resize(256),
    transforms.CenterCrop(224),
    transforms.ToTensor(),
    transforms.Normalize(mean=[0.485, 0.456, 0.406], std=[0.229, 0.224, 0.225]),
])

# Frame extraction and preprocessing
frame = Image.open('frame_from_video.jpg')
input_tensor = preprocess(frame)
input_batch = input_tensor.unsqueeze(0)

# Feature extraction
with torch.no_grad():
    features = model(input_batch)
```

The code showcases utilizing a ResNet model to extract high-dimensional features representing a video frame, underlying the transformation of video content into vector forms suitable for storage and retrieval tasks.

With increasing attention towards multimodal retrieval avenues, vector databases play a heavyweight role in realizing integrated image, video, and text-based querying systems.   These systems cross-represent content such that text descriptions and tags accompanying multimedia content are also expressible in vector form, allowing extensive and versatile querying paradigms. Whether the query originates from textual input, an image, or video, the database effectively correlates vectors of all modalities, and retrieval is unbounded by the input form, brokering more natural and user-responsive interaction.

Addressing scale challenges, vector databases solve large-scale multimedia retrieval requirements by capitalizing on distributed systems architectures that decompose workloads across servers, each specializing in localized datasets. This setup guarantees scalability enabling vast volumes of data to be processed without appreciable latency compromises.

Support for online inserts and updates enables real-time systems to assimilate new data, important for continuously expanding datasets within domains like social media, where fresh content influxes are persistent. This asynchronous handling ensures vector databases remain up-to-date and optimally perform concurrent retrieval tasks while buffering concurrent user queries seamlessly.

In highly dynamic arenas such as live video streaming, retrieval becomes closely intertwined with real-time analytics, where vector databases shuttle dynamically computed features for instantaneously derived insights. Here, the automated handling of stream-based data feeds coupled with vector representation fosters adaptive retrieval functionalities that respond to emergent trends in datasets.

Overall, vector databases markedly enrich image and video retrieval systems with distinct merits in scalability, retrieval accuracy, and computational efficiency. By employing sophisticated feature extraction techniques, and coupling these with robust vector processing algorithms, an ecosystem is established that superbly meets the demands of contemporary multimedia data retrieval requirements. These foundations set the stage for future advancements within multimedia search technologies, driven by the nonparametric and flexible nature of vector databases.

7.3 Natural Language Processing Enhancements

Vector databases significantly enhance various facets of Natural Language Processing (NLP) by providing a robust framework for managing and processing vectorized text data. NLP encompasses a broad range of computational techniques aimed at enabling the interaction between computers and humans through natural language. The introduction of vector databases into NLP workflows innovates how text is understood, processed, and retrieved, thereby contributing to more sophisticated and efficient language models and text analysis applications.

At the heart of NLP improvements is the ability to represent words, sentences, and documents as vectors. This representation captures semantic similarities and contextual relationships, which are crucial for comprehending language nuances. Various algorithms, notably word embeddings such as Word2Vec, GloVe, and FastText, have become foundational in creating these vector spaces. These embeddings generate dense vector representations where proximity in the vector space reflects semantic similarity, enabling enhanced text processing capabilities.

The advent of vector databases allows for the efficient storage and retrieval of these embeddings, facilitating real-time operations within NLP systems. A typical use case is in assessing sentence similarity, where vector databases provide the infrastructure for quickly evaluating the closeness of different sentence embeddings. This capability underpins various NLP applications, including semantic search, sentiment analysis, and language translation.

```
from sentence_transformers import SentenceTransformer

# Load pre-trained model
model = SentenceTransformer('distilbert-base-nli-mean-tokens')
```

```
# Sample sentences
sentences = [
    "Vector databases empower NLP technologies.",
    "Efficient retrieval of embeddings enhances applications."
]

# Generate sentence embeddings
sentence_embeddings = model.encode(sentences)

# Display the shape of generated embeddings
print(sentence_embeddings.shape) # Outputs: (2, 768)
```

In this example, using the Sentence Transformers library, sentences are converted into 768-dimensional embeddings. The embeddings encapsulate semantic information that is stored within vector databases for subsequent similarity-based operations.

One of the profound enhancements brought by vector databases to NLP is semantic search. Traditional keyword-based search mechanisms often fall short when it comes to understanding context or synonyms involved in user queries. Semantic search, by contrast, leverages vector embeddings to retrieve documents that are semantically aligned with the user's query, even if there are no direct keyword matches. This semantic matching significantly improves search accuracy and user satisfaction by delivering more relevant results.

Visualizing such a search setup involves a query being transformed into a vector using the same model as the indexed documents. The vector database performs efficient similarity searches to retrieve documents with the highest cosine similarity scores relative to the query vector.

```
>>> Input Query: "Understanding NLP with vector databases."
>>> Similarity Search Results:
    1. "Vector databases empower NLP technologies."
    2. "Efficient retrieval of embeddings enhances applications."
```

Semantic search exemplifies the practical benefits of adopting vector databases, making information retrieval more intuitive and aligned with user intent.

Moreover, vector databases facilitate advancement in multilingual NLP by supporting language-agnostic embeddings. These embeddings are instrumental in applications requiring language translation or those desiring cross-linguistic semantic equivalence. By employing models like LASER or multilingual BERT (mBERT), sentences from

186

different languages can be represented in a shared embedding space, enabling cross-linguistic retrieval and comparative analyses directly within the vector space.

Word sense disambiguation (WSD) presents another intricacy of NLP wherein vector databases deliver enhancements. WSD seeks to determine the intended meaning of a word that has multiple definitions, based on its context within a sentence. By utilizing contextually rich embeddings, NLP applications can discern these subtleties more accurately, further contributing to nuanced text comprehension.

Integrating learning models into vector databases, such as transformers, generates embeddings capable of associative learning. Transformers like BERT and GPT exploit large corpora to pre-train and fine-tune models, which output embeddings capturing complex linguistic patterns. These embeddings, once stored in vector databases, enable applications to deploy sophisticated analytical processes over text corpuses, unraveling insights within otherwise opaque language structures.

```
from transformers import BertTokenizer, BertModel
import torch

# Load pre-trained model and tokenizer
tokenizer = BertTokenizer.from_pretrained('bert-base-uncased')
model = BertModel.from_pretrained('bert-base-uncased')

# Example sentence
text = "Vector space models transform text into embeddings."

# Tokenize input text
input_ids = tokenizer.encode(text, add_special_tokens=True)
input_tensor = torch.tensor([input_ids])

# Obtain the hidden states from the model
with torch.no_grad():
    outputs = model(input_tensor)
    hidden_states = outputs.last_hidden_state

# Contextual embeddings for each token in the sentence
```

The code demonstrates how a transformer model derives contextual embeddings, which embed intricate linguistic nuances into vector formats. These are stored and utilized by vector databases for downstream NLP tasks.

Furthermore, by enabling rapid similarity search and comparison tasks, vector databases augment sentiment analysis workflows. They facilitate the detection and categorization of sentiments expressed across massive datasets, transforming how businesses engage in sentiment-driven decision-making processes. The prompt retrieval and analysis offered by vector databases allow organizations to monitor sentiment fluctuations in real time and respond swiftly to emerging trends.

Vector databases have also permeated other advanced NLP endeavors, such as reading comprehension systems, by underpinning question-answering frameworks. By using embeddings to match questions with the pertinent sections of text, these databases enable systems to parse and understand complex questions, connecting users directly with the information they seek.

As vector databases continue to evolve, they renounce traditional limitations of text storage and processing, leading to vast performance improvements in NLP pipelines. Engineered to accommodate complex models and large datasets, these databases form a critical backbone for developing adaptive, intelligent applications capable of understanding and leveraging human language effectively.

Overall, the convergence of vector databases and NLP encompasses meaningful advancements across various strata of text analysis, contributing fundamentally to the modern capabilities of language processing technologies.

7.4 Biometric Data Analysis

Biometric data analysis significantly benefits from the integration of vector databases, which offer a robust framework for handling, storing, and querying high-dimensional data patterns intrinsic to biometric information. Biometric systems are tasked with identifying or verifying individuals based on unique biological characteristics, such as fingerprints, facial recognition, voice, and iris patterns. Efficient management of these complex datasets is crucial for ensuring quick and accurate biometrics-based identification and authentication processes.

Biometric systems commence by capturing raw data through sensors or imaging devices, translating these physical traits into digital formats. An essential step involves extracting and representing these traits as numerical vectors, often forming feature vectors using advanced algorithms specifically tailored for each biometric modality. For instance, in fingerprint recognition, minutiae points—characteristic points on the fingerprint patterns—are transformed into vectors encapsulating the spatial relationships among these points.

Vector databases play a critical role in managing these representations by providing efficient storage, retrieval, and similarity comparison capabilities. At a fundamental level, similarity searches within vector databases aid in matching a probe (birth sample) to one among many stored templates, relying on metric distance calculations such as Euclidean or cosine distance.

For a streamlined demonstration of feature extraction and vectorization in biometrics, consider facial recognition—a prevalent application augmented by the use of deep learning models like Convolutional Neural Networks (CNNs) to derive informative feature vectors.

```
import face_recognition

# Load a sample image
image = face_recognition.load_image_file('sample_face.jpg')

# Detect facial features and compute encodings
face_encodings = face_recognition.face_encodings(image)

# Output the length of the encoding vector
print(len(face_encodings)) # Prints the number of faces detected
if face_encodings:
    print(face_encodings[0].shape) # Outputs: (128,), typical for face recognition
        feature vectors
```

This Python code uses the face_recognition library to extract a 128-dimensional facial encoding from an image, illustrating the transformation of biometric data into vector form for storage and comparison within a vector database.

Once biometric vectors are stored in a vector database, the system supports varied tasks. In a verification scenario, the objective is to match a submitted biometric sample against the claimed identity, essentially a one-to-one match. Conversely, identification tasks involve comparing the sample against all available stored templates to determine a match, functioning in a one-to-many mode. Both tasks critically lean on the rapid retrieval and comparison affordances unique to vector database systems.

Consider the importance of biometric data in security-critical environments, such as airports or secure facilities, where efficiency and accuracy directly impact operational effectiveness. Precise real-time identification or verification capabilities are paramount, motivating the need for vector databases that excel in high-speed processing and rapid querying of vast datasets with low latency.

Advanced indexing techniques implemented in vector databases, including Locality Sensitive Hashing (LSH) and various tree-based strategies, notably KD-trees and Vantage-Point trees, facilitate this by optimizing the retrieval processes. For large repositories encompassing millions of biometric profiles, these methods enable vector databases to quickly narrow down search spaces and expedite similarity searches.

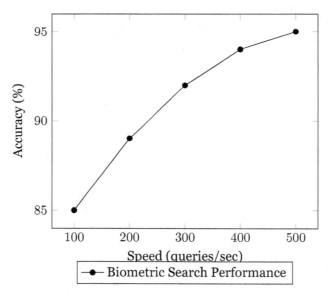

Figure 7.2: Trade-off between Speed and Accuracy in Biometric Vector Databases

Figure 7.2 presents a typical relationship between query speed and accuracy in biometric vector databases, emphasizing the balance maintained through advanced vector indexing strategies.

Security concerns regarding biometric data storage demand stringent practices, such as encrypting vectorized biometric data or implementing multi-factor authentication processes to protect sensitive information. Vector databases often integrate seamlessly with these security protocols, adding layers of protection without sacrificing retrieval speed or accuracy. Furthermore, by supporting distributed architectures, vector databases ensure redundancy and failover capability, important for high-availability systems.

The deployment of biometric systems utilizing vector databases spans numerous industry domains. Healthcare systems employ biometrics for patient identification, ensuring seamless linkage to medical records while safeguarding sensitive personal information. Similarly, financial institutions leverage biometrics to authenticate transactions securely, enhancing both user convenience and fraud resilience.

Advancements in deep learning further support biometric systems by enhancing feature extraction methodologies, resulting in more discriminative and resilient embeddings. Techniques such as Deep CNNs, Siamese Networks for one-shot learning, and adversarial methods for increased robustness against spoofing attempts are increasingly integral to biometric vector systems.

```
import librosa
import numpy as np
from sklearn.preprocessing import StandardScaler

# Load an audio file (voice sample)
voice_sample, sr = librosa.load('voice_sample.wav', sr=None)

# Extract MFCC features
mfcc = librosa.feature.mfcc(y=voice_sample, sr=sr, n_mfcc=13)

# Standardize MFCC features
scaler = StandardScaler()
mfcc_scaled = scaler.fit_transform(mfcc)

# Use a trained model to extract voice embeddings
voice_embeddings = np.mean(mfcc_scaled, axis=1) # Simplified representation
```

The extraction of voice features demonstrated involves computing Mel-frequency cepstral coefficients (MFCCs), resulting in a reduced-dimension vector that can be analyzed using neural networks, reinforcing the capacity to handle biometric voice data authentically and efficiently.

Vector databases provision for analytical capabilities that support on-going system adjustments and tuning—vital for maintaining the dynamic requirements innate to biometric systems. System managers can employ in-depth analytics to monitor system usage patterns, enrolment updates, and verification accuracy, utilizing these insights to refine algorithms and update database schemas dynamically.

The integration of vector databases with biometric systems signifies a transformative approach, optimizing the processing of high-dimensional biometric data for identification and verification tasks. By facilitating rapid similarity search, integrating advanced security measures, and accommodating ongoing technological enhancements, vector databases ensure the continued efficacy and reliability of biometric data analysis within increasingly complex operational landscapes. Through these technological synergies, biometrics become not only more secure and efficient but also scalable and adaptable for future innovations and growing demands across various sectors.

7.5   Fraud Detection Systems

Fraud detection systems have become increasingly sophisticated, leveraging vector databases to improve the accuracy and efficiency of spotting fraudulent activities. With digital transactions burgeoning and fraud strategies growing concurrently in complexity, it is vital for these systems to be agile, scalable, and capable of processing vast amounts of real-time data. Vector databases enable these capabilities by facilitating rapid pattern recognition through advanced vector-based data storage and retrieval methods.

Fraud detection aims to identify abnormal behaviors or anomalies within transactions that deviate from established patterns. These deviations can signal potential fraud, warranting further scrutiny. Vector databases aid in this critical task by managing high-dimensional feature vectors that represent transaction data, user behavior profiles, and other relevant entities. By employing similarity searches and clustering techniques, these systems can effectively discern patterns indicative of fraud among seemingly benign activities.

Developing and tuning feature vectors play a central role in enhancing fraud detection systems. These vectors capture transaction attributes, including amount, frequency, geographic data, user identifiers, and other context-specific details. Moreover, by incorporating historical data, machine learning models can refine these vectors, producing representations that encapsulate both temporal and behavioral nuances.

```python
import numpy as np
import datetime

# Example transaction details
transaction_data = {
    'amount': 250.50,
    'timestamp': datetime.datetime.now(),
    'location': 'New York',
    'merchant': 'Electronics Hub',
    'user_id': 67894021
}

# Function to encode transaction data into a vector
def encode_transaction(data):
    # Simple vectorization logic for illustration
    vector = np.array([
        data['amount'] / 1000, # Normalized amount
        data['timestamp'].timestamp(), # Convert date to a numeric format
        hash(data['location']) % 1000, # Simple hash of location
        hash(data['merchant']) % 1000, # Simple hash of merchant
        data['user_id'] % 1000 # User identifier
    ])
    return vector

transaction_vector = encode_transaction(transaction_data)
print(transaction_vector)
```

The code transforms transactional data into a feature vector, capturing essential transaction attributes. Vector databases store these vectors, enabling them to participate in similarity comparisons and anomaly detection processes.

Fraud detection systems are intrinsically reliant on anomaly detection algorithms, which benefit substantially from vector database capabilities. These algorithms assess vector distance metrics to identify transactions that fall beyond norm-like manifestations within specified confidence intervals, flagging transactions that could potentially indicate fraud.

Machine learning, particularly unsupervised techniques such as clustering and autoencoders, is commonly employed to define these norms. These models classify data into clusters representing typical transactions, while those outside these clusters are considered anomalies. Vector databases optimize the storage and rapid retrieval of clustered data points, ensuring efficient anomaly identification in real-time contexts.

```
from sklearn.cluster import KMeans
import numpy as np

# Example dataset with transaction vectors
transaction_vectors = np.random.rand(1000, 5)

# Define and train the K-Means model
kmeans = KMeans(n_clusters=10, random_state=0).fit(transaction_vectors)

# Predict the cluster for a new transaction and identify outliers
new_transaction_vector = np.array([[0.45, 1593622158, 475, 536, 541]])
cluster_label = kmeans.predict(new_transaction_vector)

# Calculate distance to cluster centroid
distances = np.linalg.norm(kmeans.cluster_centers_ - new_transaction_vector, axis
    =1)
threshold = np.max(distances) * 1.5 # Define the anomaly threshold
is_anomaly = np.any(distances > threshold)

print(f"Is the transaction anomalous? {'Yes' if is_anomaly else 'No'}")
```

By leveraging clustering algorithms such as K-Means, transaction vectors are grouped into clusters, revealing potential anomalies flagged as suspicious outside predefined cluster bounds. Vector databases enable real-time processing of these calculations, crucial for immediate fraud detection.

Beyond unsupervised methods, vector databases bolster supervised learning approaches in fraud detection by allowing easy integration of labeled datasets. Here, classifiers such as random forests, gradient boosting, or deep learning models discern fraud patterns using historical labels. These classifiers predict the likelihood of a transaction being fraudulent and adjust to evolving fraud strategies through continuous learning processes.

Another advancement vector databases bring to fraud detection systems is enhancing multi-modal approaches. These systems synthesize multiple data modalities—transaction vectors, device fingerprints, geolocation data, and even user interactions—into unified models that improve detection accuracy. Through efficient multi-modal vector storage and retrieval, vector databases provide holistic views of transaction behaviors, facilitating nuanced analysis and robust fraud detections.

194

Visualizing and monitoring fraud detection processes also become streamlined with vector databases. By integrating with visualization tools and dashboards, stakeholders gain real-time insights into system performance, detection rates, and evolving fraud patterns. These insights are crucial for continually optimizing detection algorithms, adjusting thresholds, and implementing personalized fraud prevention strategies.

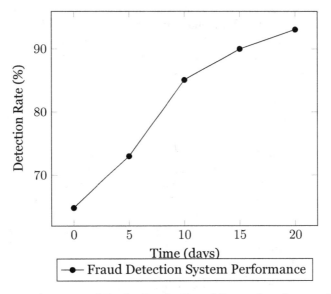

Figure 7.3: Time-Based Evolution in Fraud Detection System Performance

Figure 7.3 reflects the system's detection rate improvements over time, underscoring the adaptive nature of machine learning methodologies supported by vector databases.

Vector databases are indispensable in modern fraud detection systems. By providing scalable, high-speed processing and secure vector storage, they significantly enhance the ability to detect fraudulent patterns and anomalous behaviors. This integration supports the continuous evolution and customization necessary to combat the ever-changing landscape of digital fraud. As fraud strategies perpetually evolve, vector databases ensure systems remain efficient, effective, and resilient, safeguarding financial systems and user information with reliable precision.

7.6 Semantic Search Engines

Semantic search engines represent an evolution beyond traditional keyword-based search mechanisms by utilizing the advancements afforded by vector databases. These search engines aim to understand the intent behind a user's query, delivering results that are semantically related, even if they do not contain the exact keywords present in the query. Vector databases support this transformation by managing the high-dimensional vector embeddings that encode semantic meanings of text, ultimately enhancing retrieval precision and user experience.

The cornerstone of semantic search engines is the vectorization of text data, which translates words, phrases, and documents into dense numerical vectors. These embeddings represent semantic proximity in the vector space, allowing search engines to determine relevance through vector similarities rather than simple keyword matches. Techniques like Word2Vec, GloVe, and more recently, transformer-based models like BERT (Bidirectional Encoder Representations from Transformers) and Sentence-BERT have revolutionized the encoding of text into meaningful vectors.

Vector databases serve as the backbone of semantic search engines by storing these embeddings and enabling rapid similarity searches, often mediated through algorithms like cosine similarity or Euclidean distance. This capability facilitates the swift matching of user queries to relevant document embeddings stored in the database, producing more accurate and contextually aligned search results.

```
from sentence_transformers import SentenceTransformer

# Load the Sentence-BERT model
model = SentenceTransformer('stsb-roberta-base')

# Sample corpus and query
corpus = [
    "Vector databases enhance search with semantic understanding.",
    "Traditional search methods rely heavily on keywords.",
    "Machine learning models transform text into contextual embeddings."
]
```

```
query = "How do vector databases improve search capabilities?"

# Encode the corpus and query
corpus_embeddings = model.encode(corpus)
query_embedding = model.encode([query])

# Output the embedding shapes
print(corpus_embeddings.shape) # Outputs: (3, 768)
print(query_embedding.shape) # Outputs: (1, 768)
```

Using the Sentence-BERT model, both the corpus and user query are transformed into embeddings. These numerical representations encapsulate the semantic content crucial for a coherent search experience.

The capability to compute the semantic similarity between query embeddings and corpus embeddings lies at the heart of semantic search engines. By leveraging similarity measures, semantic search supports producing results aligned with the underlying meaning of the query, not just lexical matching. This capability becomes particularly powerful when dealing with synonymous terms or contextually similar phrases, where keyword-based systems falter.

```
from sklearn.metrics.pairwise import cosine_similarity
import numpy as np

# Compute cosine similarities between the query and the corpus
similarity_scores = cosine_similarity(query_embedding, corpus_embeddings)

# Output sorted results based on similarity
sorted_indices = np.argsort(similarity_scores[0])[::-1]
sorted_corpus = [corpus[idx] for idx in sorted_indices]

print("Ranked Retrieval Results:", sorted_corpus)
```

The snippet above calculates cosine similarity scores to rank the corpus based on semantic relevance to the query, yielding a semantically effective search result order.

Vector databases enhance these operations by providing optimization strategies, such as employing Approximate Nearest Neighbors (ANN) techniques or leveraging hierarchical navigable small world graphs, to scale efficiently with increasing dataset sizes. This approach ensures that search engines can manage extensive document repositories without a significant loss of speed or accuracy.

Another notable benefit of implementing semantic search engines is the retrieval of conceptually related results, which enriches user exploration and discovering associated information. This utility is part of why semantic search is adaptable across various domains, ranging from generic web search engines to specialized search within scientific databases and e-commerce product discovery.

Further extending the prowess of semantic search, vector databases support multilingual search capabilities. Models like LASER, which provide language-agnostic embeddings, enable cross-linguistic searches where a query in one language can effectively retrieve relevant documents in another. This ability breaks down language barriers, providing seamless access to information regardless of the language of the query and corpus.

Moreover, semantic search engines enriched by vector databases wield the adaptability required for personalized search experiences. By integrating user behavior data and preferences into user profile vectors, search engines can offer personalized results that align with individual user interests and past interactions, thus elevating engagement and satisfaction.

Support for context-aware search elaborates on semantic sophistication. By including situational factors, such as time, location, and user intent, into the vector representations, these systems adeptly provide contextually accurate results. For instance, a search for "Java" could yield programming-related results for a software developer while providing travel information about Java Island for a leisure traveler, depending on contextual vectors.

Visualizing semantic search processes and query performance through dashboards and analytics tools allows for continuous refinement and optimization. By analyzing query trends, search success rates, and user feedback, developers can iteratively enhance semantic representations, vector database performance, and overall retrieval quality.

Figure 7.4 illustrates the positive impact of continuous refinement cycles on the accuracy and relevance of search results in a semantic search engine.

Semantic search engines harnessing vector databases offer profound enhancements over traditional search methods, delivering enriched, contextually relevant, and personalized search experiences. By capital-

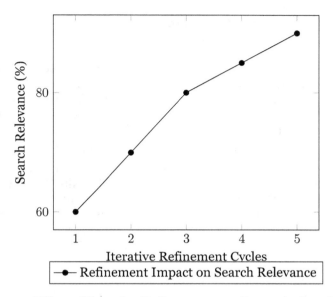

Figure 7.4: Effect of Iterative Refinements on Semantic Search Relevance

izing on vector spaces and relational embeddings, they empower users to engage with information in ways that truly respect the complexities of natural language and intent. As semantic search continues its trajectory fueled by vector databases, future endeavors promise even more innovative approaches to understanding and navigating the vast landscapes of digital content.

7.7 Industry Case Studies

The implementation of vector databases across various industry verticals showcases their capacity to revolutionize data management and processing paradigms. Through detailed case studies, this section explores how vector databases have been successfully applied to solve complex industry-specific challenges, enhancing efficiency, scalability, and the capacity to derive actionable insights from data.

- ## E-commerce: Personalized Recommendations

In the e-commerce sector, personalized recommendation systems are pivotal for enhancing user experience and driving sales. Vector databases have become instrumental in this domain, enabling the storage and rapid retrieval of user and product embeddings that inform personalized suggestions.

Consider a leading online retailer aiming to enhance its recommendation system. By leveraging deep learning models, the retailer generates embeddings that capture user preferences and product features. These embeddings are then indexed in a vector database, providing the infrastructure for real-time similarity searches that identify recommended products based on user behavior and interaction history.

```
from sentence_transformers import SentenceTransformer
import numpy as np

# Load model for generating embeddings
model = SentenceTransformer('distilbert-base-nli-stsb-mean-tokens')

# Sample product descriptions
products = [
    "Wireless noise-cancelling over-ear headphones",
    "Smartphone with 64MP camera and 6.5-inch screen",
    "Stainless steel watch with leather strap",
    "Compact digital camera with 4K video recording"
]

# Generate embeddings
product_embeddings = model.encode(products)

# User purchase history to generate user preferences embedding
user_history = ["Over-ear active noise-cancelling headphones"]
user_embedding = model.encode(user_history)

# Compute cosine similarities to find most similar products
from sklearn.metrics.pairwise import cosine_similarity
similarity_scores = cosine_similarity([user_embedding], product_embeddings)
recommended_indices = np.argsort(similarity_scores[0])[::-1]

# Display recommendations
recommended_products = [products[idx] for idx in recommended_indices[:3]]
print("Recommended Products:", recommended_products)
```

In this example, product descriptions and a user's purchase history are transformed into embeddings. The system computes similarity scores to recommend products aligned with user preferences, stored and processed efficiently within a vector database.

Such implementations not only enhance user engagement by delivering relevant recommendations but also drive upselling and cross-selling strategies by exposing users to complementary and trending products. The scalability and real-time processing capabilities of vector databases allow e-commerce platforms to personalize user experiences dynamically, adapting to changing preferences and market trends.

- **Healthcare: Precision Medicine**

Healthcare is another sector benefitting significantly from vector databases, particularly within the precision medicine domain. Precision medicine involves tailoring medical treatments to individual patient characteristics, leveraging genomic data, medical histories, and other personal health information.

A healthcare provider seeking to implement precision medicine practices utilizes vector databases to manage and analyze vast genetic datasets. By representing patient genomic sequences as vectors, clinicians can efficiently query and compare genetic profiles, identifying genetic markers and links to specific medical conditions.

```
from Bio import SeqIO
import numpy as np
from sklearn.preprocessing import OneHotEncoder

# Function to one-hot encode a DNA sequence
def encode_sequence(sequence):
    mapping = {'A': 0, 'C': 1, 'G': 2, 'T': 3}
    integer_encoded = [mapping[base] for base in sequence]
    one_hot_encoded = OneHotEncoder(sparse=False, categories='auto').
        fit_transform(np.array(integer_encoded).reshape(-1,1))
    flattened = one_hot_encoded.flatten()
    return flattened

# Example genomic sequence
genomic_seq = "ACGTACGT"
vectorized_seq = encode_sequence(genomic_seq)
print("Vectorized Genomic Sequence:", vectorized_seq)
```

This example demonstrates encoding genomic sequences into vectors, which subsequently enter a vector database, making it possible to swiftly perform similarity queries and comparison analyses across genetic datasets.

Vector databases enable healthcare providers to engage in comprehensive genomic analyses and derive insights critical for developing personalized treatment strategies. The speed and scale of vector searching are crucial in identifying patient-specific solutions, ultimately improving patient outcomes and advancing the practice of precision medicine.

- **Finance: Fraud Detection**

In the finance industry, fraud detection systems are paramount in safeguarding against illicit financial activities. Vector databases play a vital role by facilitating advanced pattern recognition to identify anomalous transactions indicative of fraud. Financial institutions deploy machine learning models to generate feature vectors representing transaction characteristics—amount, frequency, location, and more—which vector databases process to identify deviations from expected patterns.

Consider a bank using a vector database to enhance its fraud detection system. By storing transaction vectors, the bank quickly computes similarities and uncovers anomalies based on pre-defined models of typical customer behavior.

```
import numpy as np
from sklearn.ensemble import IsolationForest

# Mock transaction vectors dataset
transaction_vectors = np.random.rand(1000, 10)

# Train an IsolationForest model for anomaly detection
clf = IsolationForest(contamination=0.01)
clf.fit(transaction_vectors)

# New transaction vector
new_transaction = np.random.rand(1, 10)

# Predict whether the new transaction is an anomaly
is_anomalous = clf.predict(new_transaction) == -1

print("Anomaly Detected:", bool(is_anomalous))
```

The code uses an IsolationForest model to identify anomalies within transaction vectors. Transactions flagged as anomalies are investigated for potential fraud, with vector databases ensuring efficient storage and comparison.

By leveraging vector databases, financial institutions enhance their ability to detect and respond to fraudulent activities promptly, reducing potential losses and maintaining customer trust. The advanced analytics enabled by these databases steer organizations toward proactive fraud prevention strategies, fortifying overall financial security.

- ## Telecommunications: Network Optimization

Telecommunication companies utilize vector databases for network optimization, managing the complexities involved in monitoring and improving network performance. As the demand for high-quality, uninterrupted connectivity grows, providers require sophisticated systems to analyze network metrics and optimize service delivery.

In this context, vector databases manage telemetry data from a multitude of network nodes—signal strength, bandwidth usage, latency, and more—transforming it into vectors for consistent analysis. Companies implement real-time monitoring systems coupled with predictive algorithms that anticipate network congestion or failures.

```
import numpy as np
from sklearn.svm import SVR

# Mock network performance data
network_data = np.random.rand(100, 5) # Example metrics: Signal, Bandwidth,
    Latency, etc.

# Train a Support Vector Regression model for predictive analysis
svr_model = SVR()
svr_model.fit(network_data[:, :-1], network_data[:, -1])

# Predict future performance using the trained model
future_metrics = np.random.rand(1, 4)
predicted_performance = svr_model.predict(future_metrics)

print("Predicted Network Performance:", predicted_performance)
```

This code trains a Support Vector Regression model to analyze network data, stored efficiently within a vector database, enabling predictive insights for optimizing network performance.

Vector databases allow telecommunication providers to continuously monitor and adjust network parameters, ensuring optimal resource allocation and improved service quality. By leveraging real-time analytics, these companies preempt potential disruptions and maintain competitive service standards.

Vector databases are instrumental across a diverse array of industries, revolutionizing data processing and analysis methodologies. Through the detailed case studies presented, it is evident that the application of vector databases brings about significant enhancements in personalization, precision, security, and optimization. As industries continue to face evolving challenges, vector databases will undeniably remain key players in fostering innovative solutions and driving operational excellence forward.

Chapter 8

Future Trends in Vector Databases

In exploring future trends, this chapter identifies key directions in the evolution of vector databases, driven by technological advancements and emerging industry needs. It covers anticipated improvements in scalability, efficiency, and integration with AI and cloud services. Furthermore, it discusses privacy and security enhancements, the expansion of real-time processing capabilities, and contributions from the open-source community. By examining these trends, the chapter provides insights into how vector databases will continue to evolve, addressing both current challenges and future opportunities in data management and retrieval.

8.1 Emerging Technologies

Exploring new technologies and innovations driving the future of vector databases requires an understanding of both contemporary enhancements and potential breakthroughs. Vector databases, pivotal in managing multidimensional data points, are significantly influenced by emerging technologies. This section delves into three prominent

205

areas: quantum computing, blockchain integration, and advanced indexing methods within vector databases, elucidating their potential impact and practical applications.

Quantum computing represents a paradigm shift in computational capabilities, leveraging quantum bits or qubits to perform calculations exponentially faster than traditional computers. For vector databases, quantum algorithms offer promising avenues for executing faster similarity searches and optimizing data retrieval processes. Shor's and Grover's algorithms, quintessential in quantum computing, may significantly impact vector operations, particularly in executing rapid search and encryption tasks.

```
from qiskit import QuantumCircuit, Aer, execute
import numpy as np

# Define quantum circuit parameters
num_qubits = 4
circuit = QuantumCircuit(num_qubits, num_qubits)

# Initialize quantum circuit with Hadamard gate
circuit.h(range(num_qubits))

# Apply phase oracle for vector database search
oracle_matrix = np.identity(2**num_qubits)
oracle_matrix[-1, -1] = -1 # Example oracle modification
circuit.unitary(oracle_matrix, range(num_qubits), label='Oracle')

# Implement Grover's algorithm steps for amplitude amplification
circuit.h(range(num_qubits))
circuit.x(range(num_qubits))
circuit.h(num_qubits - 1)
circuit.mcrz(np.pi, list(range(num_qubits - 1)), num_qubits - 1)
circuit.h(num_qubits - 1)
circuit.x(range(num_qubits))
circuit.h(range(num_qubits))

# Measure results
circuit.measure(range(num_qubits), range(num_qubits))

# Execute the quantum algorithm simulation
backend = Aer.get_backend('qasm_simulator')
result = execute(circuit, backend, shots=1024).result()

# Display results
counts = result.get_counts()
print(counts)
```

This pseudocode illustrates the foundation of applying quantum algorithms within a vector database, showcasing rapid search capabilities that transcend classical limits. Transitioning these principles from simulation to practical use remains an ongoing challenge, but advancements in quantum hardware are steadily bridging this gap. As quantum computing matures, its inclusion in vector databases can revolutionize fields requiring massive data processing and high-dimensional vector spaces.

Blockchain technology, initially designed for secure financial transactions, presents novel benefits when integrated with vector databases. The decentralized, immutable ledger system of blockchains enhances transparency and traceability in vector data management. Integrating blockchain infrastructures allows vector databases to record every change securely, mitigating unauthorized tampering while ensuring data consistency across distributed systems.

Consider the impact of blockchain in a collaborative scientific research environment where vector databases store metadata of published experiments:

```
from hashlib import sha256
import json
from datetime import datetime # Missing import for datetime

class Block:
    def __init__(self, index, previous_hash, transactions, proof):
        self.index = index
        self.previous_hash = previous_hash
        self.timestamp = str(datetime.now())
        self.transactions = transactions
        self.proof = proof
        self.hash = self.calculate_hash()

    def calculate_hash(self):
        block_data = json.dumps(self.__dict__, sort_keys=True)
        return sha256(block_data.encode()).hexdigest()

class Blockchain:
    def __init__(self):
        self.chain = [self.create_genesis_block()]
        self.transaction_pool = []

    def create_genesis_block(self):
        return Block(0, '0', [], 100)

    def add_new_block(self, proof):
        previous_hash = self.chain[-1].hash
        new_block = Block(len(self.chain), previous_hash, self.transaction_pool, proof)
        self.chain.append(new_block)
        self.transaction_pool = []

    def create_transaction(self, vector_metadata):
        self.transaction_pool.append(vector_metadata)
```

207

```
blockchain = Blockchain()
blockchain.create_transaction({'vector_id': '12345', 'author': 'Dr. Smith', 'field': '
    quantum physics'})
blockchain.add_new_block(proof=200)
```

The code above outlines the basic structure of a blockchain mechanism recording metadata transactions within a vector database setting. This integration facilitates automated audit trails, driving a transparent evolution of data, ensuring integrity across multiple research endeavors.

Furthermore, advancements in indexing methods such as Hierarchical Navigable Small World (HNSW) graphs and product quantization (PQ) have become pivotal in refining vector database performance. Traditional indexing approaches struggle with scalability issues as data dimensionality burgeons. HNSW addresses these by offering a robust solution through its navigable graph structure, empowering faster and more accurate nearest neighbor searches in high-dimensional spaces.

```
import hnswlib
import numpy as np

# Define data characteristics
num_elements = 10000
dim = 128 # Dimensions of vectors

# Initialize HNSW index parameters
p = hnswlib.Index(space='l2', dim=dim)
p.init_index(max_elements=num_elements, ef_construction=200, M=16)

# Generate random data for the vector database
data = np.float32(np.random.random((num_elements, dim)))

# Add data to the HNSW index
p.add_items(data)

# Perform a similarity search
query_vector = np.float32(data[0])
labels, distances = p.knn_query(query_vector, k=5)

# Results
print("Nearest neighbors:", labels)
print("Distances:", distances)
```

The HNSW algorithm significantly enhances vector database capabilities by reducing search time complexity, thus accommodating burgeoning data quantities while maintaining computational efficiency. Moreover, product quantization further compresses data while preserving accuracy, contributing to both advanced storage solutions and faster vector comparisons.

208

These methods, executed either independently or synergistically, reflect the transformative power endowed by emerging technologies on the landscape of vector database management. As these technologies mature, their cumulative contributions are poised to yield unparalleled advancements and efficiencies.

The evolving matrix of emerging technologies in vector databases is rich with promise and complexity. Quantum computing's unparalleled processing capabilities, blockchain's inherent security mechanisms, and the sophisticated indexing methods are emblematic of a future where data management transcends contemporary limitations. This confluence of advancements predicates a trajectory marked by enhanced precision, efficiency, and reliability in the field, opening avenues for both innovative applications and fundamental reforms in data science frameworks.

8.2 AI and Machine Learning Advancements

As artificial intelligence (AI) and machine learning (ML) continue to evolve, their integration within vector databases has become a focal point of technological innovation and development. Vector databases, designed for storing and querying complex vectors such as those found in neural network models, benefit greatly from AI and ML techniques to enhance data retrieval efficiency and accuracy. This section explores the significant advances in AI and ML that are shaping the future of vector databases, focusing on neural network models for vector augmentation, automated feature extraction, and refined similarity searches.

Neural network models have become instrumental in creating more sophisticated and dynamic vector databases. Convolutional neural networks (CNNs) and recurrent neural networks (RNNs) are employed to extract high-level features from raw data, offering direct utility in vector database architecture. By transforming raw inputs into meaningful vector representations, these neural networks facilitate efficient storage and querying processes in high-dimensional spaces.

```
from keras.models import Sequential
from keras.layers import Conv2D, MaxPooling2D, Flatten, Dense
```

```
# Initialize the CNN model
model = Sequential()

# Add convolutional and pooling layers for feature extraction
model.add(Conv2D(32, (3, 3), activation='relu', input_shape=(64, 64, 3)))
model.add(MaxPooling2D(pool_size=(2, 2)))

model.add(Conv2D(64, (3, 3), activation='relu'))
model.add(MaxPooling2D(pool_size=(2, 2)))

model.add(Flatten())

# Add dense layer to convert features into vector space
model.add(Dense(units=128, activation='relu'))

# Model compilation
model.compile(optimizer='adam', loss='binary_crossentropy', metrics=['accuracy'])

# Assuming 'training_data' and 'labels' are preloaded datasets
# model.fit(training_data, labels, epochs=10, batch_size=32)

# Vector extraction for the database
# feature_vectors = model.predict(input_images) # Feature vectors for retrieval
```

This neural network effectively processes image data to extract distinguishing features, converting them into vectors that can be stored in a vector database for rapid retrieval. By employing such models, vector databases can perform complex querying on multimedia data, facilitating applications in image recognition and classification.

Automated feature extraction facilitated by AI algorithms replaces traditional labor-intensive manual tagging with sophisticated, self-learning systems. Natural Language Processing (NLP) techniques are prevalent in this domain for text vectorization, utilizing pre-trained models such as BERT (Bidirectional Encoder Representations from Transformers) to generate meaningful vector representations of textual data.

```
from transformers import BertTokenizer, BertModel
import torch

# Load pre-trained BERT model and tokenizer
tokenizer = BertTokenizer.from_pretrained('bert-base-uncased')
model = BertModel.from_pretrained('bert-base-uncased')

# Sample sentence to transform into a vector
sentence = "Exploring advancements in AI for vector databases."

# Tokenize and encode the sentence
inputs = tokenizer(sentence, return_tensors='pt')
```

```
# Extract vector representation of the sentence
outputs = model(**inputs)
sentence_vector = outputs.last_hidden_state.mean(dim=1) # Mean pooling for the
    sentence vector

print(sentence_vector)
```

In this example, BERT facilitates the transformation of text data into vectors for integration into vector databases. The ability to efficiently represent linguistic subtleties as vectors enables robust semantic searches and enhanced retrieval accuracy, pivotal in applications like sentiment analysis, information retrieval, and document classification.

Refined similarity searches, enabled by AI-driven optimizations, are instrumental in managing large-scale vector databases. AI models optimize search algorithms to reduce latency and improve the accuracy of nearest neighbor searches. Approximate Nearest Neighbor (ANN) methods are often used in conjunction with AI models to efficiently handle large datasets without compromising precision.

```
import faiss
import numpy as np

# Number of vectors and their dimension
num_vectors = 100000
dimension = 128

# Creating random vector data
vectors = np.float32(np.random.random((num_vectors, dimension)))

# Building an index for the vectors using FAISS
index = faiss.IndexFlatL2(dimension) # L2 distance
index.add(vectors)

# Vector querying example
query_vector = np.float32(np.random.random((1, dimension)))
k = 5 # Find 5 nearest neighbors
distances, indices = index.search(query_vector, k)

# Outputting search results
print("Nearest neighbors indexes:", indices)
print("Distances to neighbors:", distances)
```

The FAISS library, developed by Facebook AI Research, exemplifies how AI-driven tools optimize the performance of vector databases through efficient execution of ANN searches. By reducing the computational cost associated with high-dimensional data operations, FAISS supports large-scale, real-time applications, pushing the boundaries of

211

what vector databases can achieve.

Moreover, AI and ML models can dynamically adapt vector databases in response to evolving data patterns, cultivating adaptive systems capable of self-optimizing based on historical performance. Reinforcement learning algorithms, in particular, offer promising avenues for enhancing the autonomous management of vector database indexing and querying strategies.

The integration of AI and ML within vector databases is a continually advancing frontier, offering increased precision, scalability, and adaptability. By leveraging the capabilities of neural networks, automated feature extraction, and optimized search algorithms, vector databases are not only poised to efficiently manage vast and varied datasets but are also set to unlock new possibilities in AI-driven insights and applications. This convergence of technologies signifies a profound transformation in the future of data management, underscoring the pivotal role of AI and ML in the evolution of vector databases.

8.3 Scalability and Efficiency Improvements

The ever-increasing volume and complexity of data necessitate continuous improvements in the scalability and efficiency of vector databases. These essential enhancements ensure that vector databases can handle large-scale datasets and real-time operations. This section examines pivotal strategies for improving scalability and efficiency through distributed systems, parallel processing, indexing techniques, and resource optimization.

Distributed database architectures have emerged as a cornerstone for achieving scalability in modern vector databases. By distributing data across multiple nodes, distributed systems allow for concurrent data access and processing, enhancing both throughput and fault tolerance. The implementation of distributed architectures like Apache Cassandra or Google Bigtable is an exemplar of how horizontal scaling can be leveraged to accommodate colossal datasets within vector databases.

```
from cassandra.cluster import Cluster
from cassandra.query import SimpleStatement
```

```
# Cluster connection to Apache Cassandra
cluster = Cluster(['127.0.0.1'])
session = cluster.connect()

# Create a keyspace and table for storing vectors
session.execute("""
CREATE KEYSPACE IF NOT EXISTS vector_db
WITH replication = {'class': 'SimpleStrategy', 'replication_factor': '3'};
""")

session.set_keyspace('vector_db')

session.execute("""
CREATE TABLE IF NOT EXISTS vectors (
    vector_id UUID PRIMARY KEY,
    vector_values list<float>,
    metadata text
);
""")

# Inserting vector data into the database
insert_vector = SimpleStatement("""
INSERT INTO vectors (vector_id, vector_values, metadata)
VALUES (uuid(), ?, ?);
""")

session.execute(insert_vector, ([0.1, 0.2, 0.3, 0.4], 'sample metadata'))

# Querying vector data
select_vectors = "SELECT * FROM vectors;"
results = session.execute(select_vectors)
for row in results:
    print(row)
```

Apache Cassandra's design exemplifies a NoSQL approach that emphasizes decentralization and scalability without the need for complex transaction management peculiar to traditional relational databases. The ability to scale horizontally by adding nodes is intrinsic to its architecture, facilitating seamless management of large-scale vector datasets.

Parallel processing, an indispensable strategy in enhancing efficiency, enables the concurrent execution of multiple operations, decreasing processing time and increasing throughput. By employing parallel processing frameworks such as Apache Spark or Dask, vector databases can efficiently process and analyze massive data volumes while distributing workload across a cluster of machines.

```
from pyspark.sql import SparkSession
from pyspark.sql.functions import udf
from pyspark.sql.types import ArrayType, FloatType
```

```
# Initialize Spark session
spark = SparkSession.builder.appName("Vector Processing").getOrCreate()

# Sample data
data = [
    (1, [0.1, 0.2, 0.3], "data1"),
    (2, [0.2, 0.3, 0.4], "data2"),
    (3, [0.3, 0.4, 0.5], "data3")
]

# Create DataFrame
df = spark.createDataFrame(data, ["id", "vector", "metadata"])

# Define a UDF to scale vector values
@udf(returnType=ArrayType(FloatType()))
def scale_vector(vector, scale_factor=2.0):
    return [x * scale_factor for x in vector]

# Apply UDF in parallel
df = df.withColumn("scaled_vector", scale_vector(df.vector))
df.show()
```

This use of Apache Spark demonstrates the parallelization of vector operations, capable of handling wide-ranging data transformations and aggregations efficiently. The scalability of Spark, combined with its ability to operate on distributed data, provides a significant boost in processing capabilities.

Furthermore, the refinement of indexing techniques, such as Locality-Sensitive Hashing (LSH) and Inverted File Indexes (IVF), has considerably elevated vector database efficiency. LSH offers an efficient method for nearest neighbor searches by projecting high-dimensional data into a lower-dimensional space, thus reducing computational overhead.

```
from datasketch import MinHash, MinHashLSH
import numpy as np

# Create an LSH index with a threshold for similarity
lsh = MinHashLSH(threshold=0.8, num_perm=128)

# Generate MinHash objects for sample vectors
vectors = [np.random.random(128) for _ in range(1000)]
min_hashes = [MinHash(num_perm=128) for _ in vectors]

# Adding vectors to the LSH index
for idx, vector in enumerate(vectors):
    for dimension_value in vector:
        min_hashes[idx].update(dimension_value.to_bytes(8, byteorder='big'))
    lsh.insert(str(idx), min_hashes[idx])
```

214

```
# Query a similar vector
similar_vector = vectors[0]
query_minhash = MinHash(num_perm=128)

for dimension_value in similar_vector:
    query_minhash.update(dimension_value.to_bytes(8, byteorder='big'))

# Retrieve matches using LSH
result = lsh.query(query_minhash)
print("Similar vectors:", result)
```

This example illustrates how LSH reduces the dimensionality of data space, enabling it to perform quick, approximate similarity queries. Such innovative indexing techniques permit vector databases to efficiently handle significant increases in data volume while maintaining accurate retrieval times.

Lastly, resource optimization through fine-tuning configurations, efficient use of computational resources, and leveraging cloud-native solutions have become increasingly vital. Cloud platforms offer scalable infrastructures where resources can be easily allocated based on workload demands, promoting cost-effectiveness and agility.

The scalability and efficiency of vector databases are continuously enhanced through distributed architectures, parallel processing, advanced indexing techniques, and comprehensive resource optimizations. These improvements are not only vital for managing the rapidly growing scale of data but also for ensuring high-performance and reliability in data retrieval processes. As technological environments become increasingly data-driven, these strategies will continue to be indispensable for the advancement of vector database systems.

8.4   Integration with Cloud Services

The integration of vector databases with cloud services has become a critical component in the modern technological landscape, driven by the need for scalable, flexible, and cost-effective solutions. This section examines the capabilities, benefits, and implementation strategies associated with cloud-enabled vector databases, highlighting their importance in fostering innovation and operational efficiency. Key areas of focus include the infrastructure-as-a-service (IaaS) and platform-as-a-service (PaaS) offerings, serverless architecture, and hybrid cloud models, each providing unique advantages in enhancing the performance and scalability of vector databases.

Cloud services, particularly IaaS and PaaS, offer foundational building blocks for creating scalable and resilient vector databases. IaaS solutions allow organizations to rent server and storage capacity, providing the raw infrastructural resources necessary to deploy and manage vector databases. Amazon Web Services (AWS), Microsoft Azure, and Google Cloud Platform (GCP) offer such services with robust capabilities for configuring virtual machines and storage systems optimized for vector data operations.

```
import boto3

# Initialize a session using Amazon EC2
ec2 = boto3.resource('ec2')

# Launch a new EC2 instance for the vector database
instances = ec2.create_instances(
    ImageId='ami-0abcdef1234567890', # Example AMI ID
    MinCount=1,
    MaxCount=1,
    InstanceType='t2.micro',
    KeyName='MyKeyPair'
)

# Output instance ID
instance = instances[0]
print(f'Launched EC2 instance for vector database with ID: {instance.id}')
```

This code showcases how AWS's IaaS offerings empower users to swiftly deploy essential infrastructure tailored for vector database operations. Virtual machines can be configured with the necessary hardware prerequisites, ensuring they are adaptively scalable to handle varying data workloads.

PaaS elevates this by abstracting further the infrastructure layer, enabling developers to focus predominantly on application logic. Services like AWS's Relational Database Service (RDS), Azure SQL Database, and Google Cloud SQL offer managed database services that streamline operations and support rapid deployment of vector databases. Through PaaS, users can reap the benefits of automated scaling, backups, and simplified management, which collectively reduce overhead.

Another transformative trend is the adoption of serverless architecture,

216

such as AWS Lambda, Azure Functions, and Google Cloud Functions. Serverless computing offers a paradigm where function execution is triggered automatically in response to events, without the need to provision or manage servers explicitly. This architecture aligns well with vector databases in scenarios demanding dynamic, event-driven processing, thereby facilitating highly responsive and cost-efficient workflows.

```python
import json

def lambda_handler(event, context):
    # Process incoming vector data
    vectors = event.get('vectors', [])

    # Example processing logic: scaling vector values
    scaled_vectors = [[x * 2 for x in vector] for vector in vectors]

    return {
        'statusCode': 200,
        'body': json.dumps({'scaled_vectors': scaled_vectors})
    }
```

In this example, AWS Lambda is leveraged to perform real-time vector transformations without explicit server management. The flexibility and efficiency of serverless architecture make it an optimal solution for sporadic or unpredictable vector database workloads, fundamentally altering how resources are consumed and billed.

Hybrid cloud models represent another compelling approach, combining on-premises, private cloud, and public cloud resources to create a unified, flexible computing environment. This model is preferable in scenarios where organizations seek to maintain certain datasets on-site due to regulatory or latency considerations while leveraging public cloud resources for elasticity and innovation. A hybrid approach facilitates seamless data movement and operation continuity between on-premises infrastructures and cloud environments.

```python
from google.cloud import storage

# Initialize a Google Cloud Storage client
client = storage.Client()

# Specify bucket for storing vector data
bucket_name = 'vector_data_bucket'
bucket = client.bucket(bucket_name)

# Upload on-premises vector data to the cloud bucket
local_file_path = '/path/to/local/vector_data.json'
blob = bucket.blob('vector_data.json')
```

```
with open(local_file_path, 'rb') as vector_data_file:
    blob.upload_from_file(vector_data_file)

print(f'Uploaded {local_file_path} to {bucket_name} in Google Cloud Storage.')
```

This code example illustrates the integration of vector databases across a hybrid cloud infrastructure using Google Cloud services. Seamless storage and retrieval of vector data between on-premises and cloud platforms exploit the strengths of both approaches, maximizing operational efficiency without compromising resource governance or compliance.

The integration of cloud services with vector databases fosters an environment ripe for innovation, reducing the barriers to entry for scaling and deploying advanced data management solutions. These integrations provide users the flexibility to choose architectures best suited to their needs, adaptively adjust resources, and enable the innovative use of data through enhanced accessibility and reliability. As cloud services advance, the synergistic potential with vector databases will undeniably expand, providing a potent combination that addresses contemporary data processing and analysis requirements.

8.5   Privacy and Security Enhancements

With the proliferation of vector databases and their integration into critical data ecosystems, ensuring privacy and security has become a paramount concern. As these databases store sensitive and structured high-dimensional data, enforcing privacy measures and robust security protocols is essential. This section delves into privacy-preserving techniques and security enhancements, focusing on encryption methods, access control mechanisms, secure multi-party computation, and regulatory compliance for data protection.

Encryption is a fundamental cornerstone in safeguarding data within vector databases. Advanced encryption techniques, such as homomorphic encryption and asymmetric key encryption, provide robust frameworks for protecting vector data, ensuring that it remains confidential even in the event of unauthorized access.

Homomorphic encryption enables computations on encrypted data without revealing the data itself. This technique is particularly valuable for vector databases as it allows for the execution of complex queries on encrypted vectors without decrypting them, preserving data privacy throughout the process.

```python
from seal import SEALContext, EncryptionParameters, scheme_type, KeyGenerator
from seal import Encryptor, Decryptor, Evaluator, Ciphertext, IntegerEncoder
import numpy as np

# Setup encryption scheme
parms = EncryptionParameters(scheme_type.BFV)
parms.set_poly_modulus_degree(4096)
parms.set_coeff_modulus(CoeffModulus.BFVDefault(4096))
parms.set_plain_modulus(1032193)
context = SEALContext(parms)

keygen = KeyGenerator(context)
public_key = keygen.public_key()
secret_key = keygen.secret_key()
encryptor = Encryptor(context, public_key)
decryptor = Decryptor(context, secret_key)
evaluator = Evaluator(context)
encoder = IntegerEncoder(context)

# Example vector data
vector = np.random.randint(0, 10, size=10)

# Encrypt vector
encrypted_vector = [Ciphertext() for _ in vector]
for i, value in enumerate(vector):
    encrypted_vector[i] = encryptor.encrypt(encoder.encode(value))

# Perform encrypted computations (e.g., addition)
encrypted_sum = Ciphertext()
for encrypted_value in encrypted_vector:
    evaluator.add_inplace(encrypted_sum, encrypted_value)

# Decrypt result
result = decryptor.decrypt(encrypted_sum)
decoded_result = encoder.decode_int32(result)
print(f"Decoded sum of encrypted vector: {decoded_result}")
```

In this example, homomorphic encryption is applied to a vector dataset, allowing operations like summation to occur on encrypted data. Such capabilities are instrumental in scenarios where data privacy is non-negotiable but computational processes on the data remain necessary.

Access control mechanisms are integral to maintaining selective data access within vector databases. Role-Based Access Control (RBAC) and Attribute-Based Access Control (ABAC) paradigms enforce strict

219

control over who can access, modify, or delete data, based on user roles or specific attributes. Implementing these controls ensures that sensitive vector data is accessible only to authorized parties, preventing accidental or malicious data compromise.

```
class VectorDatabaseRBAC:
    def __init__(self):
        # Define roles and permissions
        self.roles = {
            'admin': {'read', 'write', 'delete'},
            'data_scientist': {'read', 'write'},
            'analyst': {'read'}
        }
        self.user_roles = {}

    def assign_role(self, user, role):
        if role in self.roles:
            self.user_roles[user] = role

    def check_permission(self, user, permission):
        role = self.user_roles.get(user)
        if role and permission in self.roles[role]:
            return True
        return False

# Usage
rbac = VectorDatabaseRBAC()
rbac.assign_role('alice', 'data_scientist')

if rbac.check_permission('alice', 'write'):
    print("Alice can write to the vector database.")
else:
    print("Permission denied.")
```

This RBAC system demonstrates how roles and permissions can be managed, ensuring that data manipulation capabilities are aligned with predefined organizational responsibilities and requirements.

Secure Multi-Party Computation (SMPC) is an advanced technique that enhances privacy by distributing vector database computations across multiple parties. This enables collaborative analysis without exposing individual data contributions, preserving both privacy and cooperative potential. It is particularly beneficial in environments where data needs to remain siloed while still offering aggregated insights.

```
import torch as th
import syft as sy

# Setup virtual workers
alice = sy.VirtualWorker(id="alice", hook=sy.TorchHook(th))
bob = sy.VirtualWorker(id="bob", hook=sy.TorchHook(th))
```

```
# Sample vector data to be shared
data_alice = th.tensor([1.0, 2.0, 3.0]).send(alice)
data_bob = th.tensor([0.5, 1.5, 2.5]).send(bob)

# Perform computation without revealing raw data
result = (data_alice + data_bob).get()

print(f"Securely computed result: {result}")
```

By using SMPC, this solution facilitates secure data computations without requiring any entities to reveal their data inputs, thereby reinforcing collaboration in data-sensitive projects.

Compliance with data protection regulations, such as the General Data Protection Regulation (GDPR) and California Consumer Privacy Act (CCPA), remains an imperative aspect of privacy and security strategies for vector databases. These regulations impose stringent requirements on data management practices, necessitating mechanisms for data consent, access transparency, and right-to-erasure. Fulfilling these obligations requires diligent oversight and adherence to best practices in data anonymization and auditability.

The need for robust privacy and security enhancements in vector databases cannot be overstated, given their growing role in sensitive applications requiring meticulous data handling. Encryption, access control, secure computation, and compliance are critical elements that collectively build a secure framework for data management within vector databases, ensuring data confidentiality, integrity, and availability. As data privacy regulations become more stringent and the exploits of cyber threats more sophisticated, these enhancements will continue to be pivotal in securing the integrity of vector database environments.

8.6 Real-time Data Processing

Real-time data processing has emerged as a pivotal capability for vector databases, driven by the exponential growth of data and the increasing demand for instantaneous data analysis and decision-making. Vector databases, optimized for managing high-dimensional data, are particularly well-suited for real-time applications. This section explores the methodologies, technologies, and implementations involved in achieving real-time data processing in vector databases, focusing on data stream processing, real-time querying, and the integration of event-driven architectures.

Data stream processing is a fundamental aspect of real-time data systems. Unlike traditional batch processing, real-time stream processing involves continuous data ingestion and processing as data flows into the system. This approach is crucial for applications that require immediate insights or actions based on incoming data. Technologies such as Apache Kafka, Apache Flink, and Apache Storm have become staples for building robust data streaming pipelines.

Apache Kafka, with its distributed publish-subscribe messaging system, enables high-throughput and fault-tolerant data streaming. It acts as a real-time data pipeline that ingests and publishes data streams to and from vector databases, maintaining order and durability.

```python
from kafka import KafkaProducer, KafkaConsumer
import json

# Configure Kafka producer
producer = KafkaProducer(
    bootstrap_servers=['localhost:9092'],
    value_serializer=lambda v: json.dumps(v).encode('utf-8')
)

# Sample data stream - vector data
data_stream = [
    {'vector_id': 1, 'vector': [0.1, 0.2, 0.3]},
    {'vector_id': 2, 'vector': [0.4, 0.5, 0.6]},
    {'vector_id': 3, 'vector': [0.7, 0.8, 0.9]}
]

# Stream data to Kafka topic
for data in data_stream:
    producer.send('vector_topic', data)

# Configure Kafka consumer
consumer = KafkaConsumer(
    'vector_topic',
    bootstrap_servers=['localhost:9092'],
    value_deserializer=lambda m: json.loads(m.decode('utf-8'))
)

# Process data from stream
for message in consumer:
    processed_vector = message.value
    print(f"Processing vector: {processed_vector}")
```

Python's Kafka client, confluent-kafka, is a robust choice for managing real-time data flows between producers and consumers. Here, data representing vectors is streamed into Kafka, mimicking live data ingestion into a vector database, with consumers prepared to handle and process the data as needed.

Event-driven architectures play a vital role in real-time data processing, allowing vector databases to react promptly to changes or triggers. By utilizing events and triggers, systems can automatically execute specified actions or processes upon certain conditions or incoming data.

The advent of serverless computing has further complemented this paradigm. Platforms like AWS Lambda support event-driven computing that automatically scales, responding in milliseconds to incoming requests or changes in a data stream.

```
import json

def lambda_handler(event, context):
    # Process records from the S3 event
    for record in event['Records']:
        s3_object_key = record['s3']['object']['key']

        # Simulate vector processing logic
        print(f"Triggered by the addition of object: {s3_object_key}")

    return {
        'statusCode': 200,
        'body': json.dumps('Vector data processed successfully.')
    }
```

By leveraging event-driven, serverless architectures, vector databases ensure seamless scalability and responsiveness, which is crucial for applications requiring instantaneous processing, such as real-time analytics, anomaly detection, and automated decision systems.

Real-time querying provides the capabilities for instant data retrieval and manipulation within vector databases, empowering applications that demand rapid access and updates without delays. In-memory databases, such as Redis and Memcached, excel in this domain by offering low-latency data access, which is especially useful for retrieving vector data in real-time.

```
import redis
import numpy as np

# Connect to Redis
redis_client = redis.StrictRedis(host='localhost', port=6379, db=0)

# Example data - vectors stored in Redis
vector_id = 'vector_1'
```

```
vector__data = np.random.random(10).tolist() # Simulating 10-dimensional vector
redis__client.set(vector__id, vector__data)

# Real-time vector data retrieval
retrieved__vector = redis__client.get(vector__id)
print(f"Retrieved vector: {retrieved__vector}")
```

Through Redis, real-time querying and fast data retrieval from vector databases is demonstrated. This approach, characterized by high speeds and low latency, is instrumental in applications that require real-time feedback and processing.

Graph databases, integrated with vector data processing functionalities, offer another layer of real-time querying capabilities. They efficiently manage interconnected vector data, enabling complex queries and analysis on interrelated datasets.

Ultimately, achieving real-time processing in vector databases involves the confluence of advanced data stream processing systems, event-driven architectures, and rapid querying capabilities. The use of these technologies allows for the continuous ingestion, processing, and analysis of data, driving responsive and adaptive systems. As the need for real-time insights becomes ubiquitous across industries, the seamless integration of these methods within vector databases will play an increasingly critical role, facilitating data-driven decisions and operations that are timely, efficient, and effective.

8.7   Open Source Contributions

Open source contributions have significantly influenced the landscape of vector databases, propelling innovation, diversity, and rapid progression within the field. The collaborative nature of open source projects fosters a dynamic environment where developers and organizations can contribute, share, and improve technologies collectively. This section explores the impact of open-source projects on vector databases, identifies leading open-source initiatives, and delves into community contributions, development practices, and future directions.

The open-source model has catalyzed the development and dissemination of vector databases by enabling a community-driven approach.

By providing access to source code, open-source projects encourage a shared responsibility for improvements, bug fixes, and feature enhancements. This collective intelligence fosters a robust ecosystem, resulting in enhanced quality, security, and performance of vector databases.

Several key open-source projects have emerged as leaders in the vector database domain. Milvus, Faiss, and Annoy are noteworthy contributors that have become integral tools for managing high-dimensional vector data efficiently.

Milvus, spearheaded by Zilliz, is an industrial-grade open-source vector database engineered for scalable similarity search. Its architecture supports various index types, such as IVF, HNSW, and ANNOY, providing flexibility to tailor searches based on accuracy and speed requirements.

```
from pymilvus import connections, FieldSchema, CollectionSchema, DataType,
    Collection

# Connect to Milvus
connections.connect(host='localhost', port='19530')

# Define collection schema for vectors
fields = [
    FieldSchema(name="vector_id", dtype=DataType.INT64, is_primary=True),
    FieldSchema(name="vector", dtype=DataType.FLOAT_VECTOR, dim=128)
]
schema = CollectionSchema(fields, description="Vector database collection")

# Create the collection
collection = Collection(name="vector_col", schema=schema)

# Insert vectors into the collection
vectors = [[0.1 * i for i in range(128)] for _ in range(1000)]
ids = list(range(1000))
collection.insert([ids, vectors])

# Query the collection for similar vectors
collection.load()
search_params = {"metric_type": "L2", "params": {"nprobe": 10}}
results = collection.search(vectors[:1], "vector", search_params, limit=5)

# Display results
for result in results:
    print(f"Retrieved vectors IDs: {[hit.id for hit in result]}")
```

In this example, Milvus manages vector data as a dedicated database solution, highlighting its capacity for handling extensive high-dimensional datasets with efficiency and precision.

225

Faiss, an open-source library created by Facebook AI Research, specializes in efficient similarity search and clustering of dense vectors. Faiss is widely renowned for its speed and versatility, optimizing searches with GPU support for both small and large-scale datasets.

```
import faiss
import numpy as np

# Create a set of random vectors
d = 128 # Dimension of vectors
nb = 10000 # Number of database vectors
vectors = np.random.random((nb, d)).astype('float32')

# Build IndexFlatL2 index and add vectors
index = faiss.IndexFlatL2(d)
index.add(vectors)

# Query with random vector
vq = np.random.random((1, d)).astype('float32')
D, I = index.search(vq, k=5) # Search for top-5 similar vectors

# Display results
print("Distances of retrieved vectors:", D)
print("Indices of retrieved vectors:", I)
```

Through Faiss, users can execute rapid similarity searches on vector datasets, taking advantage of its advanced indexing techniques that prioritize efficiency and accuracy.

Annoy, developed by Spotify, is another exemplary tool optimized for memory usage and speed in nearest neighbor searches. Its applications are particularly suited for recommendation engines and data mining tasks involving massive datasets.

```
from annoy import AnnoyIndex
import numpy as np

# Create and build Annoy index
d = 128 # Dimension of vectors
annoy_index = AnnoyIndex(d, 'angular')
num_nodes_to_build = 10

# Add vectors to Annoy index
for i in range(num_nodes_to_build):
    vector = np.random.random(d).tolist()
    annoy_index.add_item(i, vector)

annoy_index.build(10) # Number of trees
annoy_index.save('annoy_index.ann')

# Query similar vectors
index_query = np.random.random(d).tolist()
similar_vectors = annoy_index.get_nns_by_vector(index_query, 5, include_distances
```

```
    =True)

# Display results
print("Indices of retrieved vectors:", similar_vectors[0])
print("Distances of retrieved vectors:", similar_vectors[1])
```

This showcases Annoy's lightweight and efficient approach to indexing that is well-suited for memory-constrained environments and real-time applications.

Open-source contributions are not limited to code; community engagement often drives innovation through forums, discussion groups, and collaborative platforms like GitHub. Users contribute to the evolution of vector databases by reporting bugs, suggesting features, and verifying fixes through peer reviews. Such cooperative development practices ensure rapid iterations and integrations of cutting-edge developments.

Fundamentally, open-source initiatives democratize technology development by lowering barriers to entry, facilitating learning environments, and enhancing diversity in problem-solving approaches. The symbiotic relationship between users and developers fosters a culture of knowledge sharing that yields highly adaptable and resilient systems.

The future of open-source vector databases holds exciting potential for advancements driven by artificial intelligence, machine learning, and cloud integration. As open-source communities continue to thrive and grow, they will undoubtedly propel vector databases to new heights, addressing challenges and exploring opportunities that lie ahead in the ever-evolving field of data management and analysis.

Chapter 9

Security and Privacy in Vector Databases

Security and privacy are paramount in the realm of vector databases, necessitating robust measures to protect sensitive data. This chapter investigates the unique security challenges faced by vector databases, including unauthorized access and data breaches. It explores access control mechanisms, encryption techniques, and privacy-preserving data retrieval strategies. An emphasis is placed on anomaly detection and intrusion prevention to maintain database integrity. Additionally, the chapter considers compliance with regulatory standards, offering best practices for implementing secure and private database solutions in an ever-evolving digital landscape.

9.1 Security Challenges in Vector Databases

The pervasive use of vector databases introduces a complex set of security challenges that are distinct from those faced by traditional relational database systems. These challenges stem from the intricate structure and semantics of high-dimensional data encoded in vectors, necessitating tailored security strategies. The potential vulnerabilities can lead to unauthorized access, data breaches, and compromise of sensitive information. This section delves into the primary security concerns intrinsic to vector databases and examines the mechanisms to preemptively address these vulnerabilities.

- **1. Complexity and Dimensionality**

  Vector databases are designed to store and manipulate high-dimensional data, commonly used in applications such as machine learning, natural language processing, and computer vision. The complexity inherent in handling such data poses unique security challenges. High-dimensional vectors can become susceptible to adversarial attacks where noise added to the inputs can mislead the system to generate incorrect outputs. An adversary with knowledge of the vector encoding scheme can execute such attacks, thus compromising the integrity and reliability of the database.

  The dimensionality of the data also implicates the database's storage and retrieval security. The intricate relationships between vectors, when exposed to unauthorized parties, can disclose sensitive information. It becomes imperative to encrypt and obfuscate these relationships to mitigate potential information leakage. Moreover, high computational complexity involved in vector calculations demands robust security mechanisms that can operate efficiently without degrading performance.

- **2. Authentication and Access Control Vulnerabilities**

  A significant challenge in securing vector databases lies in the effective authentication and authorization of users. Improper implementation of access control mechanisms may allow unauthorized entities to query high-dimensional data, potentially misusing the results. Furthermore, fine-grained access control is essential as users may require access to specific data dimensions rather than entire vector datasets.

  To illustrate, consider a vector database implemented for a facial recognition system. Users might need access to different attributes of the facial vector representation. Implementing role-based access control (RBAC) can provide differentiated access rights. The consistent management of access lists and role definitions is crucial for robust security.

```
{
  "roles": {
    "admin": {
      "permissions": ["read", "write", "modify"],
      "data_scope": "all"
    },
    "user": {
      "permissions": ["read"],
      "data_scope": "personal"
    },
    "analyst": {
      "permissions": ["read", "analyze"],
      "data_scope": "aggregate"
    }
  }
}
```

In this example, the RBAC policy delineates permission levels and associated data scopes, allowing for a modular and scalable access control configuration.

- **3. Inference Attacks**

  Inference attacks represent another formidable challenge to vector databases, where attackers use legitimate queries to infer sensitive information. Such attacks exploit statistical correlations within the data to construct meaningful insights that should otherwise remain confidential.

  Consider a scenario where an attacker repeatedly queries the database with slight modifications, exploiting the responses to discern patterns. These patterns, in turn, can unravel sensitive attributes of the data. To thwart such attacks, implementing differential privacy mechanisms can provide a statistical noise addition that masks individual records, thereby preserving privacy even against sophisticated inference strategies.

```
import numpy as np

def add_differential_privacy(vector, epsilon=0.1):
    noise = np.random.laplace(0, 1/epsilon, size=len(vector))
    priv_vector = vector + noise
    return priv_vector

sensitive_vector = np.array([1.0, 2.0, 3.0, 4.0])
```

231

```
priv_vector = add_differential_privacy(sensitive_vector)
```

The function add_differential_privacy imbues the original vector with Laplace noise to achieve differential privacy, balancing utility and privacy protection.

- **4. Data Breaches and Unauthorized Access**

Vector databases face traditional data breach threats but with enhanced repercussions due to the inherently sensitive nature of vectors, often employed in confidential domains such as healthcare diagnostics and biometric identification. Breaches can expose training datasets or vector representations that may correspond to proprietary or personal information.

To mitigate these risks, rigorous authentication processes and encryption strategies are essential. Encryption at rest and in transit ensures that data remains inaccessible without appropriate cryptographic keys. Implementing Transport Layer Security (TLS) for data transmission and database encryption with Advanced Encryption Standard (AES) can reinforce security measures.

```
# Generate a private key
openssl genpkey -algorithm RSA -out server-key.pem -aes256

# Generate a CSR (Certificate Signing Request)
openssl req -new -key server-key.pem -out server-req.pem

# Self-sign the CSR to obtain a certificate
openssl x509 -req -in server-req.pem -signkey server-key.pem -out server-cert.
    pem -days 365
```

These commands illustrate generating a self-signed certificate for securing data transmission between client applications and the vector database server using TLS.

- **5. Adversarial Machine Learning**

Vector databases are often employed in training machine learning models. Adversarial attacks, specifically targeting these models, represent an imminent threat. Such attacks can involve manipulating input vectors to induce model misbehavior or compromising the training data integrity itself, leading to faulty model predictions and decisions.

232

Implementing robust security practices in the machine learning pipeline, such as model validation, adversarial training, and monitoring, is critical to mitigating these threats. Adversarial training involves augmenting training data with adversarial examples to enhance model robustness against potential attacks.

- **6. Scalability Concerns**

  As data volume and complexity grow, scalability presents a concurrent challenge to securing vector databases. Security measures must adapt to accommodate expansive datasets without impeding performance. Integration of distributed ledger technology, such as blockchain, can offer promising security solutions by maintaining immutable records of data transactions. However, the high dimensionality of vectors presents new considerations for such integration, requiring tailored approaches for efficient management.

  Vector databases need to be architected considering future scaling needs while ensuring that security controls scale correspondingly. This often involves leveraging cloud-based infrastructure with inherent security features such as identity and access management (IAM), data logging, and threat detection services, ensuring a seamless security posture even with increased data loads.

Addressing the security challenges in vector databases necessitates a holistic view encompassing authentication, data encryption, inference attack mitigation, and scalability planning. Vector databases demand vigilant security practices, tailored to the unique nature of high-dimensional data and the sensitive use cases they accommodate. Understanding and implementing robust security measures are paramount to safeguarding these complex systems against the multifaceted landscape of cyber threats.

9.2 Access Control Mechanisms

Implementing effective access control mechanisms is essential to maintain the security and integrity of vector databases. Access control is a fundamental security component that ensures only authorized entities can access or modify data, safeguarding it against unauthorized use or malicious exploitation. This section provides an in-depth analysis of access control methodologies pertinent to vector databases. It explores various models and techniques, highlighting their efficacy and applicability to the unique demands posed by high-dimensional data environments.

1. Role-Based Access Control (RBAC)

Role-Based Access Control (RBAC) is a widely adopted and implemented model for managing user permissions efficiently across complex database environments. This model revolves around the concept of assigning permissions to roles rather than individual users, simplifying the administration of access rights.

In vector databases, RBAC serves well due to its ability to segregate permissions across different roles within an organization. For instance, a machine learning engineer might require read and writing permissions to a subset of vector spaces, while a data analyst might only need read access.

```
{
  "roles": {
    "ml_engineer": {
      "permissions": ["read", "write", "train"],
      "data_scope": ["feature_vectors", "parameter_settings"]
    },
    "data_analyst": {
      "permissions": ["read", "aggregate"],
      "data_scope": ["aggregate_data"]
    },
    "admin": {
      "permissions": ["read", "write", "manage"],
      "data_scope": "all"
    }
  },
  "users": {
    "alice": {
      "roles": ["ml_engineer"]
    },
    "bob": {
      "roles": ["data_analyst"]
    }
  }
}
```

The above listing illustrates a role-based policy, delineating specific access rights for different user roles within a vector database. Each role's

234

operational scope is clearly defined, providing a structured approach to user management.

2. Attribute-Based Access Control (ABAC)

Attribute-Based Access Control (ABAC) is renowned for its flexibility, utilizing user attributes, resource attributes, and environmental conditions to define access capabilities. In vector databases, ABAC can accommodate complex access scenarios by applying finer granularity and contextual awareness. The access control decision derives from a set of dynamic rules evaluating multiple attributes at runtime.

ABAC is particularly effective in environments where access decisions must consider diverse criteria beyond mere user roles. For instance, in a healthcare application, a clinician's access to certain patient vectors might depend on their specialization and the patient's treatment stage.

```python
def abac_decision(user_attributes, resource_attributes, environment):
    if user_attributes['role'] == 'clinician' and environment['time'] >= 9:
        if 'patient_data' in resource_attributes:
            if user_attributes['specialization'] == resource_attributes['
                patient_condition']:
                return True
    return False

user_attrs = {'role': 'clinician', 'specialization': 'cardiology'}
resource_attrs = {'data_type': 'vector', 'patient_condition': 'cardiology'}
environment = {'time': 10}

access_granted = abac_decision(user_attrs, resource_attrs, environment)
```

In this Python function, access is granted based on a clinician's specialization, time of day, and patient condition, exemplifying ABAC's flexibility in handling nuanced access decisions in vector databases.

3. Discretionary Access Control (DAC)

Discretionary Access Control (DAC) is another common access model that grants individuals the ability to assign access rights at their discretion. DAC configurations are more suited to environments where data ownership and collaborative access are dynamic and user-driven.

In vector databases, DAC allows data creators or owners to specify who can read or modify their vector datasets, fostering a more decentralized access control methodology.

```json
{
  "data_owners": {
```

```
    "charlie": {
      "datasets": {
        "project_alpha_vectors": ["alice", "bob"]
      }
    }
  },
  "dataset_permissions": {
    "project_alpha_vectors": {
      "alice": ["read", "modify"],
      "bob": ["read"]
    }
  }
}
```

DAC provides targeted control over access permissions, as depicted in this JSON example where specific users obtain designated access levels on datasets owned by another user.

4. Mandatory Access Control (MAC)

Mandatory Access Control (MAC) is a more rigid and hierarchical model where the system enforces rules that define permissions, typically seen in environments requiring high security and compliance. MAC restricts user capabilities based on predefined security policies.

Its applicability in vector databases is prevalent in sectors that demand strict adherence to security regulations, such as military databases or government-operated systems. Users must operate according to higher-level classifications that control data manipulation rights.

In implementing MAC, labeling data vectors with security levels is crucial, ensuring data confidentiality through enforced access constraints. Despite its regimented structure, MAC remains effective where compliance and data sensitivity are prioritized over flexibility.

5. Access Control List (ACL) Implementation

Access Control Lists (ACLs) provide another approach to access management by maintaining specific entries for each user's permissible actions on data objects. ACLs afford precise control in vector databases by allowing detailed permissions at the object level.

For example, individual vectors or collections can have distinct access lists that dictate user access and alteration permissions. This level of granularity is beneficial when certain vector data requires protection or exposure based on explicit user requirements.

```
{
```

```
"vectors": {
  "vector_1023": {
    "acl": [
      {"user": "alice", "permissions": ["read", "update"]},
      {"user": "bob", "permissions": ["read"]}
    ]
  },
  "vector_2047": {
    "acl": [
      {"user": "charlie", "permissions": ["read", "delete"]},
      {"user": "dave", "permissions": ["read", "write", "update"]}
    ]
  }
}
}
```

Through this JavaScript example, specific vectors within a database are equipped with ACLs, assigning unique permission sets to respective users.

6. Challenges and Considerations in Access Control Implementation

Implementing comprehensive access control in vector databases is not without challenges. The unique nature of vector data—often used in high-stakes applications across various industries—requires meticulous planning and execution of access control measures. Several considerations arise during implementation:

- *Scalability*: As vector databases grow, scalable access control mechanisms are imperative. The chosen access control model must seamlessly integrate with the database's expansion.

- *Performance*: Access control mechanisms should not impede performance, especially in high-dimensional vector operations where computational efficiency is crucial.

- *Audit and Compliance*: Maintaining comprehensive logs and audits of access events ensures compliance with regulatory requirements and fortifies security transparency.

- *Contextual Awareness*: Incorporating contextual elements into access decisions can enhance security effectiveness, especially in dynamic environments utilizing ABAC.

- *Policy Management*: Effective policy management tools are required to maintain and update access control policies, ensuring they remain aligned with organizational needs and security requirements.

237

The synergy of these considerations, alongside an understanding of the prescribed access control methodologies, facilitates the construction of robust security frameworks. Access control in vector databases is pivotal, knitting together principles of security, user experience, and operational efficiency. These mechanisms must evolve continually, paralleling the advancements in database capabilities and the growing sophistication of security threats.

9.3   Data Encryption Techniques

Securing data in vector databases requires robust encryption strategies tailored to the unique characteristics of high-dimensional data. Encryption acts as a critical safeguard, barring unauthorized access and ensuring data integrity and confidentiality throughout its lifecycle. This section explores various encryption techniques applicable to vector databases, delving into their methodologies, advantages, and potential implementation strategies. Understanding these techniques equips database administrators and security professionals with the tools necessary to fortify vector databases against a spectrum of cyber threats.

1. Symmetric Encryption

Symmetric encryption, a cornerstone of data protection, employs a single, shared key for both encryption and decryption processes. This method is prized for its computational efficiency, making it viable in environments where performance is paramount.

In symmetric encryption, Advanced Encryption Standard (AES) stands out due to its robust security and widespread adoption. AES ciphers the data using block sizes of 128 bits, with key sizes of 128, 192, or 256 bits. The choice of key size is pivotal, influencing both the encryption strength and performance metrics.

```
from Crypto.Cipher import AES
from Crypto.Random import get_random_bytes
import base64

def encrypt_vector(vector_data, key):
    cipher = AES.new(key, AES.MODE_EAX)
    ciphertext, tag = cipher.encrypt_and_digest(vector_data)
    return base64.b64encode(cipher.nonce + tag + ciphertext)
```

```
key = get_random_bytes(16)
vector_data = b"Sample vector data for encryption"
ciphertext = encrypt_vector(vector_data, key)
```

The above Python script utilizes the PyCryptodome library to encrypt a sample vector using AES in EAX mode, providing both confidentiality and integrity assurances.

2. Asymmetric Encryption

Unlike symmetric methods, asymmetric encryption utilizes a pair of cryptographic keys: a public key for encryption and a private key for decryption. This separation between encryption and decryption keys introduces versatility, facilitating secure key exchanges and ensuring robust data protection.

Asymmetric encryption is instrumental in scenarios where secure key distribution is imperative, notably for transmitting keys or encrypting small data volumes.

```
from Crypto.PublicKey import RSA
from Crypto.Cipher import PKCS1_OAEP

def rsa_encrypt_data(data):
    key = RSA.generate(2048)
    public_key = key.publickey()
    cipher = PKCS1_OAEP.new(public_key)
    encrypted_data = cipher.encrypt(data)
    return encrypted_data, key

data = b"Secure data transfer"
encrypted_data, key = rsa_encrypt_data(data)
```

The script generates an RSA key pair and employs the public key to encrypt sample data, highlighting the asymmetric encryption process's intricacies.

3. Homomorphic Encryption

Homomorphic Encryption is a transformative approach enabling computations on encrypted data, outputting encrypted results that correspond to the operations performed on plaintext. This method is invaluable in vector databases for preserving privacy while allowing meaningful data analysis without decryption.

Homomorphic encryption can be either partially homomorphic (supporting additive or multiplicative operations) or fully homomorphic

239

(supporting arbitrary computations). The latter, though more complex and computationally intensive, is crucial for comprehensive data manipulation in encrypted states.

```
from phe import paillier

def homomorphic_encryption_operation(data1, data2):
    public_key, private_key = paillier.generate_paillier_keypair()
    encrypted_data1 = public_key.encrypt(data1)
    encrypted_data2 = public_key.encrypt(data2)

    encrypted_sum = encrypted_data1 + encrypted_data2
    return encrypted_sum, private_key

data1, data2 = 5, 7
encrypted_sum, private_key = homomorphic_encryption_operation(data1, data2)
decrypted_sum = private_key.decrypt(encrypted_sum)
```

Through this example, we simulate homomorphic addition operations using the Python Paillier library, underscoring the potential for secure data computation in encrypted domains.

4. Format-Preserving Encryption (FPE)

Format-Preserving Encryption maintains the format of the plaintext in the ciphertext, permitting encrypted data to uphold structural requirements, such as data type or field size. FPE is particularly relevant to vector databases where stringent format constraints exist.

Applications of FPE ensure data integrity across heterogeneous systems, enabling seamless integration and compatibility even when data is encrypted, thereby maintaining system functionality and regulatory compliance.

```
from Crypto.Cipher import AES
import pyffx

def fpe_encrypt_numeric(data, key):
    ffx = pyffx.Numeric(key, length=len(data))
    encrypted_data = ffx.encrypt(data)
    return encrypted_data

data = "1234567890"
key = get_random_bytes(16)
encrypted_data = fpe_encrypt_numeric(data, key)
```

This implementation leverages an external library to encrypt numeric data without altering its format, illustrating FPE's adaptability.

5. Key Management

Effective key management is vital to ensuring the security of encryption processes. Key lifecycle management—encompassing key generation, distribution, storage, rotation, and destruction—forms the backbone of a secure encryption framework, especially in environments dealing with high-dimensional data like vector databases.

Integration with professional key management solutions, such as AWS Key Management Service (KMS) or HashiCorp Vault, is recommended for optimal security and management of cryptographic keys.

```
# Create a key in AWS KMS
aws kms create-key --description "Key for vector database encryption"

# Describe the newly created key
aws kms describe-key --key-id <key-id>

# Encrypt data using the KMS key
aws kms encrypt --key-id <key-id> --plaintext "vector_data" --output text --query
    CiphertextBlob
```

These commands highlight fundamental operations performed with AWS KMS to manage encryption keys securely within cloud environments.

6. Considerations and Challenges

The adoption of encryption techniques suited for vector databases must reconcile the performance-security dichotomy, ensuring robust protection mechanisms do not detrimentally impact system efficiency.

- *Computational Overhead*: Encryption, especially involving complex techniques like homomorphic encryption, introduces performance overheads. Balancing computational demands with encryption strength is necessary for system efficiency.

- *Compliance and Standards*: Adherence to regulatory standards, such as GDPR or HIPAA, is crucial. These standards necessitate stringent data encryption to protect sensitive information.

- *Scalability*: As databases scale, encryption techniques must scale correspondingly to maintain security without sacrificing performance. Solutions should accommodate the expansion in vector data volume and variety.

- *Key Longevity and Security*: Regular key rotation and secure storage are fundamental to preventing key compromise. Key

Management solutions maintain encryption integrity, especially in dynamically scaling environments.

Addressing these challenges with appropriate strategies ensures encryption remains a reliable cornerstone in the data protection arsenal of vector databases. As encryption technologies evolve, database systems must adapt, embracing advancements to avert emerging threats and ensure the resilience of their security postures. By leveraging diverse encryption methodologies and diligent key management practices, organizations can protect their high-dimensional data, consolidating data integrity, confidentiality, and regulatory compliance.

9.4 Privacy-preserving Data Retrieval

Vector databases, integral to modern data-driven applications, present challenges of privacy preservation during data retrieval. As organizations increasingly rely on these databases to store sensitive, high-dimensional data, ensuring privacy becomes imperative. Privacy-preserving data retrieval techniques aim to allow legitimate data access without exposing sensitive aspects, thus guarding against unauthorized inference and data leakage. This section elucidates methodologies and practices crucial for achieving privacy-preserving data retrieval, focusing on their applicability in vector databases.

1. Private Information Retrieval (PIR)

Private Information Retrieval (PIR) emerges as a pivotal protocol, permitting users to retrieve records from a database without disclosing which records they are accessing. PIR protocols operate under zero-knowledge proofs or other cryptographic assumptions to maintain query confidentiality.

In vector databases, PIR secures sensitive queries, ensuring that neither the query patterns nor the data vectors reveal insights to potential adversaries who might eavesdrop on database interactions.

```
from math import log2
import random

def private_information_retrieval(database, index):
    n = len(database)
```

```
binary_index = bin(index)[2:].zfill(int(log2(n)))
random_mask = [random.getrandbits(1) for _ in range(len(binary_index))]
obfuscated_index = [(int(binary_index[i]) ^ random_mask[i]) for i in range(len(
    binary_index))]

retrieved_data = []
for i, x in enumerate(database):
    if (i & int(''.join(map(str, obfuscated_index)), 2)) == int(''.join(map(str,
        obfuscated_index)), 2):
        retrieved_data.append(x)
return retrieved_data

database = ['vector_1', 'vector_2', 'vector_3', 'vector_4']
retrieved_data = private_information_retrieval(database, 2)
```

This Python function provides an abstract exemplification of how PIR might function, using binary masking to retrieve data without revealing the exact query index.

2. Differential Privacy

Differential Privacy offers a mathematically robust framework for conducting data retrieval while safeguarding individual record privacy. By injecting carefully calibrated noise into query responses, differential privacy ensures that the output remains statistically similar regardless of whether any single individual's data exists in the dataset.

When applied to high-dimensional vectors, differential privacy can maintain the analytical utility of datasets while obfuscating sensitive data patterns.

```
import numpy as np

def apply_differential_privacy(vec, epsilon=1.0):
    noise = np.random.laplace(0, 1/epsilon, len(vec))
    private_vec = vec + noise
    return private_vec

vector_data = np.array([1.0, 2.0, 3.0, 4.0])
private_vector = apply_differential_privacy(vector_data)
```

The provided code snippet demonstrates the addition of Laplace noise to a vector dataset, illustrating differential privacy's application in obscuring identifiable data while permitting useful data retrieval.

3. Secure Multi-Party Computation (SMPC)

Secure Multi-Party Computation (SMPC) facilitates computations over distributed data sources without exposing sensitive data among the participants. It allows parties to collaboratively compute a function over their inputs while revealing nothing but the function's output.

For vector databases, SMPC can enable privacy-preserving computations over partitioned vector datasets, typically stored across different parties or regions, without leaking individual vector details.

```
def secret_share(number, total_shares=3):
    shares = [random.randint(0, number) for _ in range(total_shares-1)]
    shares.append(number - sum(shares))
    return shares

def reconstruct_secret(shares):
    return sum(shares)

number = 42
shares = secret_share(number)
reconstructed_number = reconstruct_secret(shares)
```

This example simulates secret sharing, a fundamental primitive of SMPC, by dividing a number into random shares and reconstructing it, illustrating the principles underlying SMPC operations in data retrieval.

4. Query Obfuscation

Query obfuscation enhances privacy-preserving data retrieval by disguising the query's purpose or content, making it difficult for adversaries to deduce sensitive information from query patterns.

Approaches such as query randomization, padding or injecting noise in query parameters obscure the true intent of the queries, adding a protective layer over the data retrieval processes in vector databases.

```
def obfuscate_query(original_query, noise_level=0.1):
    noise = np.random.normal(0, noise_level, original_query.shape)
    obfuscated_query = original_query + noise
    return obfuscated_query

query_vector = np.array([0.5, 1.5, 2.5])
obfuscated_query = obfuscate_query(query_vector)
```

The function adds Gaussian noise to a query vector, transforming it into an obfuscated form, thus camouflaging the original query parameters.

5. Secure Enclaves

Secure enclaves, a hardware-based solution, extend environments where computations on encrypted data can safely occur without exposing sensitive contents to the system or potential adversaries. Technologies such as Intel's Software Guard Extensions (SGX) facilitate computation within secure enclaves, providing a trusted execution environment.

In vector databases, secure enclaves ensure that sensitive data operations remain concealed, significantly mitigating risk when running queries that involve confidential data components.

```
# Prepare and initialize an Intel SGX enclave
sgx_create_enclave -path /path/to/enclave/file -output enclave_token

# Run application within the created enclave
sgx_execute_application -enclave enclave_token -app /path/to/application
```

The bash commands hint at the steps to initialize and execute applications within a secure enclave, offering a glimpse into the operational facet of secure enclaves in data processing.

6. Challenges and Futuristic Considerations in Privacy Preservation

Implementing privacy-preserving data retrieval mechanisms in vector databases is laden with challenges and demands continuous innovation to cope with evolving privacy threats.

- *Performance Strain*: Many privacy-preserving techniques, particularly homomorphic or SMPC-based methods, impose extensive computational overheads, thereby challenging database performance. Balancing privacy with performance remains a critical design consideration.

- *Balancing Accuracy*: Techniques like differential privacy may alter the dataset's statistical properties, potentially impacting the accuracy of data-driven insights generated from those vectors. Tuning privacy parameters is crucial to achieve a trade-off between data utility and privacy.

- *Exposure to New Threats*: Adversaries continuously refine attack methodologies targeting cryptographic assumptions and zero-knowledge protocols fundamental to privacy-preserving techniques.

- *Scalability of Solutions*: Extending privacy-preserving techniques across vector datasets of growing scale necessitates scalable implementations that can efficiently handle vast amounts of high-dimensional data.

The trajectory towards complete privacy-preserving data retrieval pivots on addressing these challenges while enhancing technology with state-of-the-art cryptographic innovations and interdisciplinary research in database management and data security. As vector databases evolve, privacy preservation techniques must parallel advancements to maintain a resilient defense framework, fostering trust and compliance across diverse disciplines reliant on this data paradigm.

9.5 Anomaly Detection and Intrusion Prevention

The significance of anomaly detection and intrusion prevention mechanisms in vector databases cannot be overstated, particularly given the sensitive nature of the data often handled by these systems. With cyber threats becoming increasingly sophisticated, these mechanisms play a pivotal role in maintaining the integrity, confidentiality, and availability of vector databases. This section explores the various strategies and frameworks utilized for anomaly detection and intrusion prevention, specifically in the context of vector databases, highlighting the intricacies involved in implementing and managing these security measures effectively.

1. Understanding Anomalies in Vector Databases

Anomalies in vector databases often manifest as deviations from typical data patterns or access behaviors that can indicate a potential security threat. These anomalies could arise from erroneous data, unauthorized data modifications, or unexpected querying patterns possibly indicating intrusion attempts.

Vector databases, due to their high-dimensional data space, present unique challenges in detecting anomalies. The complexity of data relationships requires advanced, multidimensional analysis tools capable

246

of discerning subtle, nonlinear patterns not apparent in traditional relational database systems.

2. Machine Learning Techniques for Anomaly Detection

Machine learning algorithms furnish powerful tools for anomaly detection, leveraging the capability to learn and adapt from data to identify outliers accurately. In vector databases, these algorithms process high-dimensional datasets to discover anomalous patterns suggesting potential intrusions or data breaches.

2.1. Supervised Learning Approaches

Supervised learning methods utilize labeled datasets to train models capable of recognizing anomalous behaviors. Techniques such as Support Vector Machines (SVM) and Neural Networks can be employed to classify vector data based on historical anomaly patterns.

```
from sklearn import svm
import numpy as np

# Generate sample data
X_train = np.array([[0, 0], [1, 1], [0-0.5, 0.5], [1.5, 1.5]])
y_train = [0, 0, 1, 1] # Binary labels where 1 indicates anomaly

# Initialize and fit SVM model
clf = svm.SVC(kernel='linear', C=1)
clf.fit(X_train, y_train)

# Predict anomalies
anomaly_vector = np.array([[0.5, 0.2]])
is_anomaly = clf.predict(anomaly_vector)
```

This SVM model classifies vectors, determining if they deviate significantly from normal data patterns, thereby serving as potential indicators of anomalies.

2.2. Unsupervised Learning Techniques

Unsupervised learning approaches, such as clustering and principal component analysis (PCA), identify anomalies without predefined labels by examining data distribution characteristics. These models, such as k-means clustering or DBSCAN, are adept at discovering novel anomalies, a necessity in vector spaces where unique, unseen threat vectors may arise.

```
from sklearn.cluster import KMeans

def detect_anomalies_with_kmeans(data, n_clusters=2):
```

247

```
kmeans = KMeans(n_clusters=n_clusters, random_state=0).fit(data)
labels = kmeans.labels_

# Identify points distant from cluster centroids as anomalies
distances = kmeans.transform(data)
max_distance = distances.max(axis=1)
anomalies = data[max_distance > np.percentile(max_distance, 95)]
return anomalies

data = np.random.rand(100, 3) # Generate random data points
anomalous_data = detect_anomalies_with_kmeans(data)
```

K-means clustering segments data into clusters, facilitating the detection of data points that are distanced significantly from cluster centroids, marking them as potential anomalies.

3. Intrusion Prevention Systems (IPS)

Intrusion Prevention Systems provide proactive defense by detecting potentially harmful activities and blocking them before they can cause damage. In the context of vector databases, IPS must manage large-scale, continuous streams of high-dimensional data, a task necessitating robust processing capabilities and intelligent pattern recognition.

3.1. Signature-Based IPS

Signature-based IPS refer to predefined sets of rules that identify known threats based on signatures, which are unique identifiers of different attack types. These systems compare incoming data against these signatures, blocking any matches.

While effective against previously encountered threats, signature-based systems may struggle with novel attacks or zero-day exploits, requiring frequent updates and refinements to stay relevant.

3.2. Anomaly-Based IPS

Anomaly-based IPS detect abnormal patterns by analyzing the baseline behavior of data operations in vector databases. Any deviation from this baseline is flagged and investigated, providing a vigilant approach against unknown attacks.

Through machine learning models that continuously evolve by learning from data interactions, anomaly-based IPS can identify sophisticated threats unnoticed by simple signature mechanisms.

```
from sklearn.ensemble import IsolationForest
```

```
# Generate training data
training_data = np.random.rand(100, 10)
isolation_forest = IsolationForest(contamination=0.1).fit(training_data)

# Predict whether a vector is an anomaly
test_vector = np.random.rand(1, 10)
is_intrusion = isolation_forest.predict(test_vector)
```

Isolation Forest models effectively identify anomalies by isolating outlier vectors in high-dimensional spaces, crucial for detecting irregular access or usage patterns in vector databases.

4. Integrating Anomaly Detection with Intrusion Prevention

Integration of anomaly detection mechanisms with intrusion prevention systems significantly enhances security postures, ensuring robust defense across different threat vectors. It requires coherent architectures that synthesize insights from anomaly detectors into actionable policies on intrusion prevention fronts.

A hybrid model encompassing rule-based alerts and machine-learning-driven insights facilitates comprehensive protection against both known and novel threats, balancing detection accuracy with system performance.

5. Challenges and Considerations

Deploying anomaly detection and intrusion prevention systems in vector databases encounters several challenges:

- *High Dimensionality*: Managing and analyzing high-dimensional data poses computational challenges. Dimensionality reduction techniques like PCA may be needed to streamline data for faster processing without compromising detection accuracy.

- *Real-Time Processing*: Intrusion prevention demands real-time data analysis to forestall attacks. Ensuring minimal latency in detection mechanisms while maintaining high throughput is crucial to guard against fast-moving threats.

- *Handling False Positives*: With the sensitive nature of anomaly detection systems, false positives can trigger unnecessary alarms, leading to potential system disruptions. Calibration and fine-

249

tuning of anomaly detection algorithms mitigate such occurrences.

- *Evolving Threat Landscape*: Security threats continue to evolve, mandating continuous updates and advancements in detection strategies to remain ahead of attackers.

- *Interoperability*: Solutions for vector databases should integrate seamlessly with existing IT ecosystems, ensuring coherent threat management across heterogeneous database environments.

The development and execution of anomaly detection and intrusion prevention strategies within vector databases constitute an evolving field requiring a balanced amalgam of cutting-edge technology and operational strategies. Visionary frameworks ensure these systems remain equipped to confront both present and forthcoming challenges, fortifying database integrity while facilitating secure data operations across diverse applications.

9.6 Compliance and Regulatory Considerations

Compliance and regulatory requirements play a pivotal role in the management and operation of vector databases, especially given their application across sectors sensitive to privacy and data protection laws. Ensuring conformity with these standards is not only a legal obligation but also a strategic measure to enhance trust and ensure data integrity within the organization. This section delves into the various compliance frameworks relevant to vector databases and examines how organizations can align their database management practices to meet these regulatory demands effectively.

1. Understanding Relevant Regulations

Vector databases often handle data that falls under the purview of various international and local regulations designed to protect privacy and ensure data security. Key regulations impacting vector databases include:

- *1.1. General Data Protection Regulation (GDPR)*: The GDPR is a comprehensive data protection law that applies to organizations within the European Union (EU) and those handling EU residents' data. Key principles of GDPR that affect vector databases include data minimization, purpose limitation, and ensuring data subject rights. Organizations must ensure that vector data is processed lawfully and transparently and are required to implement appropriate security measures to safeguard personal data.

- *1.2. Health Insurance Portability and Accountability Act (HIPAA)*: HIPAA sets forth laws governing the protection of healthcare data in the United States. Vector databases containing electronic protected health information (ePHI) must adhere to HIPAA's Privacy Rule and Security Rule, ensuring that data confidentiality, integrity, and availability are safeguarded. Implementing encryption and access controls is crucial for compliance.

- *1.3. California Consumer Privacy Act (CCPA)*: The CCPA grants California residents' rights concerning their personal data and imposes obligations on businesses handling such data. For vector databases, this entails providing transparency in data collection practices and ensuring that data access is restricted to authorized personnel only.

2. Implementing Privacy by Design

Privacy by Design (PbD) is a proactive approach that integrates privacy considerations into technological and business practices throughout the development lifecycle of database systems. For vector databases, PbD principles can be implemented by:

- Embedding privacy features such as data anonymization and pseudonymization into the database design.

- Regularly conducting privacy impact assessments to identify and mitigate potential privacy risks.

- Implementing access control mechanisms and encryption by default to minimize the risk of unauthorized data access.

The adherence to PbD contributes significantly to regulatory compliance and enhances overall data protection strategies.

3. Data Anonymization Techniques

Data anonymization is a key method for securing personal data in vector databases, altering the data in such a way that individuals cannot be identified from it. Techniques include data masking, generalization, and perturbation.

```
import numpy as np

def anonymize_vector_data(vector_data, epsilon=0.5):
    noise = np.random.laplace(0, 1/epsilon, vector_data.shape)
    anonymized_data = vector_data + noise
    return anonymized_data

vector_data = np.array([100, 200, 300, 400])
anonymized_data = anonymize_vector_data(vector_data)
```

The script demonstrates a simple anonymization technique by applying Laplace noise to vector data, thus limiting re-identification risks and aiding compliance with privacy regulations.

4. Audit Logging and Monitoring

Maintaining detailed audit logs is essential for compliance, often mandated by regulations like GDPR and HIPAA. Audit logs should capture all data access and manipulation events, enhancing transparency and traceability within vector databases.

```
import logging

# Configure logging
logging.basicConfig(filename='access_log.txt', level=logging.INFO,
                    format='%(asctime)s - %(message)s')

def log_access_event(user_id, operation, data_reference):
    logging.info('User: %s performed %s on %s', user_id, operation, data_reference)

log_access_event('user123', 'read', 'vector_001')
```

The example logs user access events, contributing to accountability and compliance by ensuring comprehensive activity records for review and auditing purposes.

5. Data Transfer and Cross-Border Compliance

With increasing globalization, vector databases often involve cross-border data transfers. Ensuring compliance with data transfer regulations is critical, especially under frameworks like GDPR that impose strict conditions on data transmission to countries outside the EU.

Encryption of data in transit, along with adhering to standard contractual clauses or binding corporate rules, aids in maintaining compliance with cross-border data regulations.

6. Encryption Standards and Key Management

Implementing strong encryption protocols is a common regulatory requirement for protecting data both at rest and in transit. The choice of encryption standards, such as AES-256, must align with industry best practices and regulatory expectations.

Effective key management is equally important, encompassing secure storage, rotation, and revocation of cryptographic keys. Utilizing managed key services, such as AWS KMS or Azure Key Vault, can streamline key management processes and bolster compliance readiness.

```
openssl rand -base64 32 > encryption_key.bin
openssl enc -aes-256-cbc -kfile encryption_key.bin -in vector_data.txt -out
    vector_data.enc
```

These commands demonstrate generating an encryption key and using it with the AES-256 standard to encrypt vector data, providing a clear guide to implementing secure encryption practices within regulatory constraints.

7. Training and Awareness Programs

Building a culture of compliance within organizations involves consistent training and awareness initiatives. Ensuring that employees understand data protection laws, organizational policies, and their roles in maintaining compliance enhances the overall security posture and reduces accidental breaches.

Conducting regular workshops and updating training materials to reflect new regulatory developments or internal policy changes helps maintain rigorous compliance practices and fortifies employees' understanding of their responsibilities.

Challenges and Strategic Frameworks for Compliance

Ensuring compliance in vector databases presents organizations with various challenges:

- *Complex Regulatory Landscape*: Navigating the myriad of international regulations requires a dynamic compliance strategy that can adapt to legal changes and industry-specific requirements.

- *Balancing Security with Utility*: Organizations must balance strong data protection measures with the need for data accessibility and utility, avoiding overly restrictive security controls that impede legitimate use.

- *Resource Allocation*: Compliance efforts can be resource-intensive, necessitating investment in technology, training, and legal expertise to align with regulatory demands efficiently.

To address these challenges, organizations should adopt a holistic compliance strategy, integrating regulatory knowledge across technical, operational, and legal domains. Regular audits, continuous monitoring, and leveraging technology solutions for compliance automation contribute to maintaining an up-to-date and effective compliance framework.

By embracing these practices, organizations can achieve regulatory compliance while safeguarding the privacy and security of data within their vector databases. This, in turn, enhances trust with clients, partners, and regulatory bodies, positioning the organization as a responsible steward of sensitive information in a rapidly evolving digital landscape.

9.7 Best Practices for Secure Implementation

Implementing robust security measures in vector databases is crucial to protecting sensitive information and ensuring the integrity, availability, and confidentiality of stored data. As vector databases are increasingly employed in critical applications, from machine learning to financial analytics, it is essential to follow best practices for secure implementation. This section outlines key strategies and methodologies that organizations can employ to harden their vector database environments against potential threats.

1. Secure Configuration and Hardening

The foundation of a secure vector database starts with its configuration and hardening against unauthorized access and vulnerabilities. This involves several key steps:

1.1. Access Control Mechanisms

Implement granular access control policies using Role-Based Access Control (RBAC) or Attribute-Based Access Control (ABAC) to ensure users have the minimum necessary access. Define roles clearly and audit permissions regularly to prevent privilege creep:

```
{
  "roles": {
    "admin": {
      "permissions": ["create", "delete", "update", "audit"],
      "data_scope": "all"
    },
    "data_scientist": {
      "permissions": ["read", "query", "analyze"],
      "data_scope": "project_datasets"
    },
    "guest": {
      "permissions": ["read"],
      "data_scope": "public_data"
    }
  }
}
```

1.2. Network Security

Utilize firewalls and network segmentation to isolate the vector database from external networks and high-risk zones. Employ Virtual Private Networks (VPNs) and secure tunneling for remote database administration, further reducing exposure to attacks.

1.3. Secure Endpoints

Implement Endpoint Detection and Response (EDR) solutions to monitor and mitigate threats originating from user endpoints that access the vector database. Regularly update software to patch vulnerabilities, and ensure endpoint devices meet security compliance standards.

2. Encryption of Data

Robust encryption practices are central to securing data at rest and in transit. Implement encryption strategies to safeguard sensitive data:

2.1. Data-at-Rest Encryption

Encrypt database files and backups using industry-standard encryption algorithms like AES-256. Ensure encrypted data storage complies with regulatory requirements.

```
# Generate an AES-256 encryption key
openssl rand -base64 32 > aes_key.bin

# Encrypt vector database files
openssl enc -aes-256-cbc -salt -in vectors.db -out vectors_enc.db -pass file:aes_key.bin
```

2.2. Data-in-Transit Encryption

Utilize TLS/SSL encryption for data transmitted between clients and the database server to protect against eavesdropping. Configure secure certificate management practices to facilitate reliable authentication and encryption.

3. Regular Vulnerability Assessments and Penetration Testing

Regularly conduct vulnerability assessments and penetration testing to identify weaknesses in the database infrastructure. These activities can proactively reveal potential vulnerabilities that an adversary might exploit.

Employ automated tools like Nessus or OpenVAS for vulnerability scanning, and engage with ethical hackers for comprehensive penetration testing, including scenario-based attack simulations mimicking real-world threats.

4. Logging, Monitoring, and Incident Response

Continuous logging and monitoring are fundamental to maintaining a secure vector database. Implement a centralized logging solution to aggregate logs from all relevant systems and enable real-time threat detection:

4.1. Security Information and Event Management (SIEM)

Deploy a SIEM solution to analyze logs and detect unusual activities indicative of potential breaches. Utilize it to correlate events across the network and respond to incidents promptly:

```
{
  "alert_rule": {
    "name": "Unauthorized Access Attempt",
    "condition": {
      "source_ip_blacklisted": true,
      "access_attempts": ">10 in 5 minutes"
    },
    "actions": ["send_alert", "block_ip"]
  }
}
```

4.2. Incident Response Framework

Establish an incident response framework detailing procedures for identifying, investigating, and mitigating security threats. Conduct regular drills to ensure that the response team is prepared to react efficiently to various incidents.

5. Backup and Disaster Recovery

Robust backup and disaster recovery strategies are vital to safeguarding against data loss and maintaining business continuity:

5.1. Regular Backups

Conduct regular and automated backups of vector database data, ensuring they are stored in secure, geographically separated locations. Encrypt backups to protect data integrity and confidentiality.

5.2. Disaster Recovery Plans

Develop and test comprehensive disaster recovery plans. Ensure backup data can be restored quickly and systems can resume operations with minimal downtime in the event of a catastrophic failure.

6. Compliance with Legal and Ethical Standards

Ensure that the implementation of vector databases complies with legal and regulatory standards such as GDPR, HIPAA, or CCPA. Integrating compliance checks into database development and maintenance reduces the risk of violations.

7. Training and Awareness

Promote a culture of cybersecurity within the organization through ongoing training and awareness programs. Facilitate sessions on the importance of security best practices, data protection policies, and emerging threats to maintain high awareness levels among employees.

Keep security teams up-to-date with the latest tools and techniques, ensuring they have the necessary skills to implement and manage advanced security controls for vector databases.

8. Continuous Improvement

Establish a continuous improvement protocol to ensure the ongoing enhancement of security measures. This involves regularly reviewing security performance, analyzing threat landscapes, and adjusting strategies accordingly to maintain a robust security posture.

By integrating these best practices into the architecture and operational processes of vector databases, organizations can significantly reduce their risk profile and enhance data security. Proactively addressing potential vulnerabilities through diligent hardening and ongoing monitoring ensures the secure and efficient functioning of vector databases, fostering trust and enabling the safe realization of strategic objectives.